Three More Plays by Aristophanes

This volume provides modern, uncensored translations of Aristophanes' *Acharnians*, *Knights*, and *Wasps*. These plays, originally a series, are the world's earliest political satires, and are made available here for the first time in one volume, augmented by full introductions and notes.

In these three works, Aristophanes launched satirical attacks on Cleon, the world's first demagogue, and explored the vulnerability of democracy to populist manipulation and disinformation. Henderson's fresh translations and exploration of the themes within them enable readers to explore the perils facing democracy in its first century which are still with us today. The Introduction offers the reader background on Aristophanes' life, Athenian democracy, classical drama, as well as on political comedy, while introductions to each individual play provide the reader with context. An appendix also collects selected fragments from Aristophanes' lost political plays.

Three More Plays by Aristophanes offers an invaluable collection of these works for students and faculty working on classical studies, theatre and theatre history, and drama. The clear translations and contextualizing introductions and notes also make these plays accessible to students of government, law, and political science, and to the general reader interested in any of these subjects.

Jeffrey Henderson is the William Goodwin Aurelio Professor of Greek at Boston University in the United States, author of *The Maculate Muse*; a commentary on Aristophanes' *Lysistrata*; the Loeb edition of Aristophanes; *Three Plays by Aristophanes: Staging Women*; and numerous works on Greek comedy, literature, and history.

Three More Plays by Aristophanes

Staging Politics

Jeffrey Henderson

Routledge
Taylor & Francis Group

LONDON AND NEW YORK

Cover image: The Metropolitan Museum of Art, Rogers Fund, 1951 51.11.2.

First published 2022
by Routledge
4 Park Square, Milton Park, Abingdon, Oxon OX14 4RN

and by Routledge
605 Third Avenue, New York, NY 10158

Routledge is an imprint of the Taylor & Francis Group, an informa business

British Library Cataloguing-in-Publication Data
A catalogue record for this book is available from the British Library

Library of Congress Cataloging-in-Publication Data
A catalog record for this book has been requested

ISBN: 978-0-367-74762-6 (hbk)
ISBN: 978-0-367-74759-6 (pbk)
ISBN: 978-1-003-15940-7 (ebk)

DOI: 10.4324/9781003159407

Typeset in Times New Roman
by Apex CoVantage, LLC

Contents

Preface

This book offers annotated translations of three politically engaged comedies by the comic poet Aristophanes: *Acharnians* (425 BCE[1]: the world's earliest extant comedy), *Knights* (424), and *Wasps* (422). They are the three surviving plays of a series of at least five comedies written between 426 and 422 by the young Aristophanes (he had made his theatrical debut in 427) that satirized and criticized the operations of the Athenian democracy generally and in particular sought to discredit Cleon, the leading politician of the time. The plays characterized him as a "demagogue": a political category new to the world. The word *demagogos*, "leader of the people (*demos*)," until then had been applicable to any leader in a democracy (*demokratia*, "the rule of the people"); it was Aristophanes in *Knights* who first endowed it with the meaning "leader of the mob" or (in modern parlance) "populist."

In Aristophanes' portrayal, populists claim to serve and defend the *demos* but instead have usurped the people's power for their own personal gain; they are thugs and thieves who rely on flattery and lies, inflame partisan divisions and social resentments, and use the people's own governmental, judicial, and military systems to neutralize or destroy political enemies while lining their own pockets. Nor does Aristophanes spare the *demos*: in order to maintain undeserved power, wealth, and privilege, the populists rely on the ignorance, complacency, gullibility, and prejudices of the masses, the *hoi polloi*.

Beyond attacking Cleon and his like, these plays systematically question the key institutions of democracy, if not the ideals of democracy itself, seeking to expose weaknesses in the system as well as to reveal the dangers posed by the dishonest operators who manipulate it. They ask: Was the Athenian democracy set up the right way? Do its key institutions – the military, the assembly, the lawcourts – operate sensibly, effectively, and justly for all? Do the people listen to the right leaders? In *Acharnians* the focus is on gratuitous warmongering and deceitful international relations; in *Knights* on manipulation of the Assembly (policy and legislation); and in *Wasps* on the corruption and partisan use of the judicial system. How could the techniques of populist politicians and other dishonest operators be so successful? What could save "the rule of the people" if the people themselves allow their rule to be hijacked, and the fruits of their toil stolen?

These three plays take us back to a time when such issues were new and their implications uncharted. Aristophanes is among our earliest witnesses to, and commentators on democratic government, then a recent experiment with many doubters both within and outside Athens, and an experiment by no means assured of success. The oldest members of his audience had established the democracy themselves, having taken a leading role in repelling invading forces from the east during the Persian Wars (492–479), and then having won a maritime empire that had made Athens unprecedentedly powerful and prosperous, and that enabled its great artistic flowering in the golden "Age of Pericles" as well as its efforts to spread democracy abroad. The recent challenges to democracy and the success of Cleon-style populism in the United States and other democracies pique fresh interest in the strengths and vulnerabilities of democracy and in the origins of the populist phenomenon, and perhaps inspire hope that Aristophanes can provide useful insights and even guidance.

These plays are also landmarks in the history of political dissent: among the core provisions of Athenian democracy was the civil right of *parrhesia*, freedom to speak the truth as one saw it, which not only allowed but encouraged political criticism and dissent. Politically engaged playwrights like Aristophanes took advantage of this right, as well as their traditional role as poets and thus wise advisors, and they had an unusually prominent soapbox: their plays were performed at national festivals before the largest and most inclusive audiences to assemble during the year, and they were competing for prizes awarded by judges representing the people. In his attacks on the hugely popular populist, Cleon, framed as constructive advice to the people and very successful in the theater, Aristophanes tested the limits of *parrhesia* and justly prided himself on his bravery in doing so, for Cleon at least twice retaliated by taking serious, though unsuccessful, legal action against him. As public voices the comic poets thus provide a unique perspective on the sort of problems and issues also addressed by private writers like Thucydides, Plato, and the "Old Oligarch."

These three plays, as the world's earliest critiques of democracy and its first portraits of populist demagogy, hold, and will hold for years to come, unusually topical interest in light of today's politics and the trajectory of democracy in our new age of digital media, which both empowers and threatens the *demos* and its capacity for self-governance. And along with their importance as documents, these plays are comic masterpieces in their own right, showcasing a great poet and playwright in the most bold and exuberant period of what would be a long and brilliant career. They have nevertheless tended to be much less frequently read in courses, and are much less familiar to general readers, than other plays by Aristophanes, mainly for want of approachable translations.

And so I offer this annotated translation in order to make them available to general readers and useful to all students of Greek literature and culture, within and outside the field of classical studies. For each play I supply an introduction and explanatory notes, and for the collection as a whole, a note on the translations and a general introduction covering Aristophanes' life and career, the comic theater and its traditions cultural, civic, and religious, and the society in and for which his plays were produced.

In the introductions and notes I have not tried to develop particular interpretations of the plays but rather supply the basic descriptive and historical information and bibliography that readers will need to interpret the plays for themselves and pursue further investigation. Since the volume is geared particularly to readers interested in politics and political history, the introductions and notes concentrate on those areas. Beyond that, for basic information and bibliography about any particular topic bearing on Greek comedy, a good starting point is the *Encyclopedia of Greek Comedy* (Sommerstein 2019). Holzberg 2008 provides a thorough bibliography to that date, as does the periodical *L'année philologique* on an ongoing basis.

Aristophanes' invention of "demagogue comedy" inspired imitators – though only against the lesser populists who emerged after Cleon's death in 422 – and we have some fragmentary knowledge of their plays. I have accordingly supplied, in an Appendix, translations of such fragmentary remains, including those of Aristophanes' own lost comedies that bear on his portrayal of populism.

I wish to take this opportunity to thank students, colleagues, and fellow fans of Aristophanes for their encouragement, advice, insights, and expertise over many years, and to express special gratitude to my editor, Amy Davis-Poynter, who first suggested this project and patiently bore with me as it developed.

Note

1 All dates are BCE unless otherwise indicated.

Notes on the Translation

Like all classical playwrights Aristophanes wrote his plays in verse: for spoken dialogue he used a standard iambic trimeter line roughly similar to English "blank verse"; for speeches and formal debates he used a longer line in iambic, trochaic or anapestic rhythm, probably accompanied by the pipe (*aulos*); and for songs accompanied by music (songs for the chorus, arias or duets for the actors) he used various lyric rhythms, typically those reflecting popular styles, except when he was parodying the more elaborate styles of tragedy or archaic lyric (Parker 1997). Choral singing was strophic, meaning that the songs were normally written in pairs of matching stanzas called "strophe" and "antistrophe" that are often separated by intervening speech; I have indicated such strophic pairs in the translation. I have rendered the plays into English lines matching the Greek lineation, so as to maintain a sense of the plays' scale and pace and for ease of reference, and I have tried for as readable (even performable) a style as possible while staying faithful to the original, since these plays are documents as well as dramas.

By "faithful" I mean English that serves as an accurate guide to the original while reading naturally and capturing as far as possible the style, flavor, and character of the original. A faithful translation, as distinct from a literal one, seeks to translate meaning rather than words: classical Greek and English often differ in their semantic range, so that aside from words with a very narrow semantic range (e.g. "oak tree") there is often no exact correspondence in a given context, so that a Greek word with a broad semantic range, such as *agathos*, cannot always be rendered by the same English word, any more than the similar English word "good" always has the same meaning and therefore a single equivalent in another language (e.g. good person, good friend, good dog, good luck, good riddance, good looks, good shot, good show, good breeding, good knife, goods, the goods, etc.). And for some Greek terms or expressions there are no English equivalents. *Knights*, for example, is the traditional title for Aristophanes' play in the anglophone world, but that English word does not quite correspond to the original *Hippeis* in its classical Athenian meaning: an official corps of one thousand citizen men whose means and background qualified them to serve in battle on their own horses. But neither do any other available English terms, e.g. "horsemen" or "cavalry" or "riders." And then there are wit and jokes, which often rely on the properties of their own language and thus are difficult and sometimes impossible to translate "literally." In such cases of untranslatability, the introductions and notes supply information about the Greek.

Aristophanes' basic linguistic register was urbane, colloquial Attic Greek, but the conventions of his genre allowed, and evidently encouraged, a strong admixture of other registers both higher (e.g. parody of tragedy and other serious poetry) and lower (e.g. imitation of vulgar or indecent speech) than the colloquial norm (Willi 2003). The former category I have rendered by using elevated or archaic styles of English. In the latter category we find in fifth-century comedy much rough and abusive language, including outright obscenity (Henderson 1991), that will strike some readers as shockingly crude, sexist, misogynistic, homophobic, xenophobic, or otherwise offensive or discriminatory. But we should bear in mind (1) that Aristophanes was writing not for us but for contemporaries living in a society at once very sophisticated and very different from our own, and (2) that outrageousness was a traditional ingredient of his genre and one fully in keeping with its tendency to expose, deflate, and provoke. Thus not everything that we hear or see in an Aristophanic comedy can be assumed to reflect the norms, attitudes, or behavior of the average, or indeed any, Athenian. In this translation I have therefore made no attempt to spare the modern reader from potentially disturbing material by censoring or translating around it; instead I have tried to render each of Aristophanes' linguistic registers faithfully, by using the nearest English equivalent.

A Greek comedy requires of its translators more by way of editorial decisions than would a modern play. The earliest texts of ancient Greek plays, since they were made not for readers but for those who would perform them at a festival, were scripts including only the words to be spoken or sung. There were no cast-lists, stage-directions, notes, or even assignments of lines to speakers. In tragedy, whose plots follow traditional myths and feature relatively few characters, actions and props, it is usually possible to assign speakers and devise stage-directions confidently. In comedy, by contrast, plots and characters are original and not always consistent, the action is more complex and less predictable or logical, and props and scene-changes are much more numerous, so that in the absence of explicit references in the script, it is sometimes hard to infer what was happening on stage, the location of the action, the speaker of a given line, even a character's name: the Slaves who open *Knights*, for example, one of whom has a major role in the play, are never given names in the text – not a problem for spectators in the theater, but an editor or translator must write something!

What is more, we possess no authorial texts of any ancient Greek literature: in Aristophanes' case, our earliest texts derive from lost intermediate copies of a scholarly edition made over a century after his death, and the earliest copies available to us were written after ca. 950 CE, over twelve centuries after that. Until the first printed editions (nine of the 11 extant plays in 1498 and the final two in 1516), the texts were transmitted through handwritten copies, each copy differing to some degree from every other copy, so that the editor or translator must choose from the available texts (manuscript or printed) the readings (s)he thinks most likely reproduce Aristophanes' own lost text, and when no transmitted readings seem satisfactory, choose among suggested emendations or devise new ones. In making these translations I have based myself eclectically on my own editions (Henderson 1998–2007) and in light of subsequent scholarship, especially Sommerstein (2001), Olson (2007), Wilson (2007), and Olson and Biles (2015).

1. General Introduction

In order to appreciate the nature and status of Aristophanes' politically engaged comedy, it is necessary to understand at least the basics of the theatrical culture of fifth-century Athens. Unlike modern theater and media like film and television, which for the most part are privately organized entertainments occupying their own cultural niches, Aristophanes' theater was a major communal experience fully integrated with and reflecting the social, civic, and religious life of the Athenian polis in the first century of its democracy.

I. Life of Aristophanes

The comedies of Aristophanes have been prized since antiquity for their iridescent wit and exuberant fantasy, their originality and sophistication, their rich poetic palette (everything from the lofty to the obscene), the purity and elegance of their language, and their active engagement with social, intellectual, and political life in an important era of Athenian and world history, not least its great experiment called democracy. For political life in that era, Aristophanes provides rich reportage, trenchant analysis, advice, and admonishment from a theatrical platform with broad popular appeal.

Aristophanes was judged in antiquity to be the foremost poet of what is traditionally classified as Old Attic (Athenian) comedy, an era beginning ca. 486, when comedy became an official part of the annual dramatic festival, and ending early in the following century, when comedy began to change into its so-called "Middle" and then "New" periods. Aristophanes was one of the last practitioners of Old Comedy, and his 11 surviving plays are our only complete examples of the approximately 650 that were produced in that era. But in the following centuries scholars could still read 365 of them, and thousands of fragments (quotations or other testimonial information) survive from Aristophanes' lost comedies and the comedies of rivals; these help to form an idea of the different types and styles of comedy current in this "Old Comic" era. A selection of such fragments, drawn from politically engaged plays, is presented in the Appendix to this volume.

Aside from his theatrical career, little is known about Aristophanes' life. He was born ca. 447/46, the son of one Philippus of the urban deme[1] Cydathenaeum, and he died probably in 386 or shortly thereafter. By his twenties, his hair had

DOI: 10.4324/9781003159407-1

thinned or receded enough that he could be called bald. He seems to have had landholdings on, or some other connection with, the island of Aegina. He was twice prosecuted by the popular leader Cleon for the political impropriety of two of his plays (*Babylonians* and *Knights*) and perhaps again for a third, but he was never convicted. Early in the fourth century he served as one of his deme's representatives on the Council of 500, a representative body that steered and supervised the agenda for the sovereign assembly. At least two of his sons, Araros and Philippus, had careers as comic poets in the mid-fourth century. In Plato's dialogue *Symposium*, probably written in the late 380s and after Aristophanes' death, he is portrayed as being at home among the social and intellectual elite of Athens. Although in some respects the historical veracity of Plato's portrayal is unverifiable, Aristophanes does align himself in his plays with contemporary upper-class, landowning conservatives: he thanks influential fellow demesmen for their assistance when he was still a novice playwright (*Clouds* 528); in *Acharnians* (6–8, 299–302), and in *Knights* he claims solidarity with the upper-class cavalry corps against their common enemy, Cleon, whom he presents sneeringly as a lower-class tradesman; and in *Frogs* (686–705) he advocates for the re-enfranchisement of those punished for their involvement in a coup in 411–410, when for about 12 months the democratic constitution was replaced by oligarchic regimes. He also generally champions conservative social, intellectual, artistic, and political views, insofar as these could be portrayed as serving the interests of the democratic populace at large: see further "Comic Politics" (section VI, below).

Aristophanes' career spanned 40 eventful years. He was one of a number of impressive young comic poets who began their careers after the outbreak of the Peloponnesian War in 431 and the death of Pericles in 429, including Eupolis, Phrynichus, and Plato Comicus, and he was the most successful: after his debut in 427 he won in the 420s alone at least four first prizes and three second prizes; and not more than one or two lower rankings are known during his subsequent career. After his victory with *Frogs* in 405, the people voted him an honorific crown of sacred olive for the political advice that he had given in that play, and decreed that the play should have the unique honor of being performed a second time. After the war, which ended in 404, Aristophanes' creativity seems undiminished, as he played a leading role in the transition from Old to Middle to New comedy.

Forty-four comedies ascribed to Aristophanes were known to the Alexandrian scholars of the third and second centuries, who first collected and edited his plays; four of these they thought spurious. From these Alexandrian editions, 11 complete comedies and some 1,000 brief fragments of his lost comedies survive.

Aristophanes' plays are as follows: extant plays are asterisked, with their dates (if approximate, < means before, > after) and, when known, the festival at which each was performed (see II, below):

427 L? *Banqueters* (2nd prize); produced by Callistratus.
426 D *Babylonians* (probably 1st prize); produced by Callistratus
425 L **Acharnians* (1st prize); produced by Callistratus
424 L **Knights* (1st prize); produced by Aristophanes

424 (D?)-422 *Farmers*

423? L *Merchant-Ships*

423 D *Clouds I* (3rd prize or lower); produced by Aristophanes. *Clouds II*, an incomplete and never-produced revision abandoned ca. 417

< 422 (D 425?) *Dramas or Centaur*

422 L *Proagon* (1st prize); produced by Philonides

422 L *Wasps* (2nd prize); produced by Aristophanes.

421 D *Peace I* (2nd prize); produced by Aristophanes.

421–12 *Seasons*

418? > *Women Claiming Tent-Sites*

417 > *Anagyrus*

ca. 415 > *Polyidus*

414 L *Amphiaraus*; produced by Philonides

414 D *BIRDS* (2nd prize); produced by Callistratus

413–11 *Heroes*

413–06? *Daedalus*

411 L*Lysistrata*; produced by Callistratus

411 D *Women at the Thesmophoria I*

410–09 *Triphales*

410–05 *Peace II*

410–405 *Women at the Thesmophoria II*

410 > *Lemnian Women*

409 > *Old Age*

411–09 > *Phoenician Women* (after Euripides' play)

408 *Wealth I*

ca. 408 *Gerytades*

405 L *Frogs* (1st prize); produced by Philonides; reperformed by civic decree, probably 404 L

ca. 402 *Telemessians*

< 400 *Danaids*

< 400 *Fry-Cooks*

< 395? *Aeolosicon I*

ca. 398–89 *Storks*

391 *Assemblywomen*

388 *Wealth II* (1st prize?)

387 D *Cocalus* (1st prize); produced by Araros

386 or later *Aeolosicon II*; produced by Araros (perhaps the same play as *Aeolosicon I* without the choral parts)

II. Democratic Athens

Democracy means "rule of the *demos*" (sovereign people), and in the case of fifth-century Athens this definition needs no fine print: the sovereignty of the Athenian demos was more absolute than in any other society before or since. The Athenian demos consisted of citizen males at least 18 years of age. The polis, or city-state (comprising the city of Athens, with its great harbor at Piraeus, and the surrounding territory of rural Attica), consisted of households (*oikoi*) – buildings, land, property including slaves, and money – each headed by a citizen male, whose male children (or if there were none, his closest male relatives) would inherit the *oikos*. Citizenship was by native birth, and beginning in 451 citizenship required that not only the father but also the mother be native-born. In the fifth century, the demos numbered about 30,000, who were greatly outnumbered by the rest of the Attic populace: the women, children, slaves, and resident aliens who were wards of the demos, excluded from membership and therefore from any participation in government. For the enfranchised citizens, however, the democracy was fully representative: the demos included both the wealthy classes – the landed and commercial elites, a minority known as "the few" or *hoi oligoi* – and "the many" or *hoi polloi*.

Regardless of their wealth or position, all members of the demos were equal under the law,[2] which they legislated and administered collectively and directly, and they were not only entitled but obligated to participate in government. The democratic revolution, ratified in 508 and perfected in the reforms of Ephialtes in 461, had allowed the wealthy to retain their property and various privileges in return for contributions on behalf of the polis; these included both voluntary and certain obligatory liturgies ("services"), one of which was service as *choregos* ("sponsor of a chorus") for a production at the annual dramatic festival (section III, below). Each liturgist was drawn annually by lot from a list of those socially and financially eligible to undertake a given service. In the end, democracy worked because the elite accepted that the demos would normally have a role in decision-making and so only rarely sought to limit its franchise, while the demos accepted that there would be inequality and found ways to put it to use for the general good, so only rarely sought to murder or expel the rich, or to seize their property.

All decisions affecting the governance and welfare of the polis were made by the direct and unappealable vote of the demos meeting either together in the Assembly or separately as juries in a lawcourt. There was no standing government, judges, legislators, or professional politicians: the polis was managed collectively by all members of the demos in good standing and at least 30 years of age. In addition to being able to vote in Assembly and serve as members of a jury in legal cases, members of the demos were chosen by lot from a list of those financially, mentally, and physically able to perform service in a given capacity; those allotted held office in periods ranging from one day to one year. Liturgists were similarly chosen by lot to fulfill the services befitting wealthy members of the demos. The only exceptions to this lottery system were military commanders, who were elected to one-year terms, and holders of certain ancient priesthoods, who inherited their positions.[3] The demos determined whether anyone holding any public position was qualified to do the job, and in an audit following completion of his term, whether he had done it satisfactorily. Litigants in court represented themselves: there were no attorneys or prosecutors, and the verdict of the jury, which could number in the hundreds, was final and unappealable.

By custom, though not by legal statute, all military commanders and most assembly speakers and holders of powerful allotted offices came from the wealthy classes. But their success depended on the good will of the demos as a whole, which always had the final vote. Large fines, confiscation of property, exile, enslavement, and death were punishments that the people could wield against malefactors however wealthy, just as any citizen could summons any other citizen to court. Policy was determined by a vote of the Assembly on proposals by individuals who rose to speak. By thus empowering all citizens individually to participate in managing the state, and collectively to decide between proposals and arguments made to them by ambitious, elite individuals, the democracy tried to balance egalitarianism and elitism. All members of the demos, whatever their individual differences in wealth and power, were politically and ideologically equals at the civic level, so that all could pride themselves on belonging to an exclusive and all-sovereign corporation. It was said that the demos collectively held the power once wielded by individual sovereigns – kings or tyrants – a concept central to the allegorical characterization of Demos in Aristophanes' *Knights* (Henderson 2003).[4] Like politicians and litigants, comic poets performed for the people, on whose favor they depended for success.

Drama played a unique role within the democracy. Although its traditions stretched into the remote past (section IV, below), and its producers and composers came from the ranks of the highly educated elite, drama soon became an official and very prominent element of democratic life, with distinct and important roles to play. As a festival, it attracted the largest and most representative audience to assemble during the year: no one was excluded from attending, and all categories of people were portrayed on stage, no matter that the exclusive and gender-marked civic culture of the democracy encouraged the ideological marginalization, political subordination, and public invisibility of private *oikoi*, the women who managed them, and the slaves who worked within them. In the pre-democratic period, the polis had been run by noble families, and there had been no strict dichotomy between polis and household: powerful families were members of an entitled aristocracy, and women could play important social and symbolic roles as mothers, wives or daughters eligible for dynastic marriages. Under the democracy, by contrast, "civic" (male/executive spheres) and "private" (female/family spheres) tended to be sharply distinguished, so that women were increasingly removed both physically and notionally from those civic spaces that were defined as male, and differences in wealth and pedigree were elided in a public sphere where all were legally and ideologically equal. Drama was the one communal event that could portray and appeal to polis norms and ideals older than democracy, and it remained institutionally positioned both within and outside the civic spheres of the demos. Drama could take advantage of its unique position to explore tension-points within the developing democratic dichotomies of civic and domestic, public and private, polis and *oikos*, internal and external, rich and poor, male and female, young and old, and thus provides our most detailed view of the oppositions that lay at their center.

III. The Dramatic Festivals

The word *komoidia* (comedy) means "*komos*-song" and *komikos* (comic) means "*komos*-like": the *komos* was a revel or carouse involving some solidary group of (typically young) men (a military, religious, or family group, for example), drinking and singing, who could be masked and might mock individuals or rival groups. More formally organized *komoi* were associated with the wine and fertility god Dionysus, who dwelt in the countryside. At some point before the democratic constitution was adopted in 508, *komos* had given rise to a kind of theatrical or proto-theatrical performance that was mainly choral: a group of singing dancers and their leader, plus spectators.[5] The period of organized Old Comedy at Athens began in 486, when *komoidia* became an official element of the annual festival of the Greater Dionysia, for which Dionysus was brought in a great procession from the countryside into the city to witness civic and religious pageantry in his honor, of which theatrical competitions were the main events. The *phallephoria* ("phallic parade") was a central element of the procession: celebrants wore or carried models of the ritual phallus, much as was done in the rural demes in celebrations like the one enacted in *Acharnians*. Tragedy (from *tragoidia* "goat song": original significance unclear) with its satyr drama (in which the tragic chorus impersonated satyrs), along with dithyramb (performed by a chorus of 50 including its leader), had already been staged at the festival at least since 508. By convention the Old Comic era ended ca. 386, when the last play by Aristophanes was produced. During this period some 650 comedies were produced. We know the names of some 50 comic poets and the titles of some 300 plays. We have 11 complete plays by Aristophanes, the first one (*Acharnians*) dating from 425, and several thousand fragments of other plays by Aristophanes and other poets, most of them only a line or so long, and very few from plays written before 440, when a second theatrical festival, the Lenaea, became an official annual event.

Although tragedy and comedy had earlier been performed in rural Attica, and rural theaters proliferated during the fifth century (Csapo and Wilson 2020), the principal occasions for the production of new plays were the two annual festivals of the Greater Dionysia, held in March or April and lasting six days, and the Lenaea, held in January or February and lasting four days.[6] They opened with religious and civic ceremonies, patriotic displays, and tribal competitions in dithyramb (each of the ten tribes of Attica entered a chorus of older men and a chorus of boys). On the following days came the dramas: three tragic tetralogies (each consisting of three tragedies and a satyr drama), two at the Lenaea, and then five comedies.[7] While tragic poets produced three tragedies and a satyr drama, comic poets produced only one comedy. These festivals were national holidays at once civic and religious – a dual identity that must be kept in mind, for it is important in understanding the meaning of the dramas and their functions in the polis, especially as regards political satire and criticism. The dramatic festivals were organized democratically, but because of their antiquity and panhellenic roots, they also represented older polis values that in many respects challenged democratic norms and claims, and as religious events they enjoyed a certain freedom that allowed the dramatic poets to explore social, political, and ideological tensions that would otherwise be unexplorable in a communal setting (Rhodes 2003, Henderson 2007).

The theatrical festivals in their civic aspect were officially sponsored, hosted, and regulated by the executive *demos* ("sovereign people") of Athens and were a showcase for the culture and ideology of its democracy. The theatrical productions themselves were civic competitions in which poets, dancers, actors, producers, and musicians competed for prizes, comparable in esteem to today's Academy, Grammy, and Tony Awards combined; these were awarded at the close of the festival by judges representing the people. The Greater Dionysia was held in the Theater of Dionysus on the south slope of the Acropolis, which in Aristophanes' time, at least, accommodated at least 10,000 spectators and probably several thousands more on the hillside above the formal seating area. The spectators at the Greater Dionysia included both Athenians and foreigners, while the Lenaea played mostly to local audiences, since travel in winter was difficult. Perhaps because they are so topically political, all three of the plays in this volume are Lenaean: in *Acharnians* 502–508 Aristophanes remarks that this time he cannot be accused of defaming the polis before foreigners, as had happened after *Babylonians*, his Greater Dionysian play of the previous year.

While the performances were created, organized, and performed only by men, the festival itself welcomed everyone as spectators: more of the Attic populace was gathered as an audience in one place at the same time than at any other event during the year, and participation was uniquely inclusive. Unlike such purely civic events as meetings of the assembly (accommodating up to 6,000) or the lawcourts (some 600), which only adult male citizens could attend, the Dionysia was open to anyone who could afford a seat. Uniquely in the festive calendar of the Athenians, there was a fee for admission. The price for a seat seems never to have exceeded two obols, roughly equivalent to the price of attending a major concert today and thus not an impossible annual expense for families of at least moderate means who were motivated to attend. At some point a "theoric" (spectator) fund, administered through the local demes, was created (presumably) to subsidize the attendance of citizens who could not afford a seat. This fund is not mentioned in any of our sources until 343, but a few later sources trace it back to the fifth century.

Spectators would typically arrive at the theater early each morning and spend the whole day in attendance. They included citizens, immigrants, foreigners, children, and even women and slaves (Roselli 2011). The Lenaea may have been held elsewhere in the city (if so, we do not know where) until 440, when it too was given an official dramatic contest and moved to the Theater of Dionysus. Front-row seating was reserved for important civic, military, and religious figures (including priestesses in charge of major cults) and for visiting dignitaries; there were also special sections for the 500 Councilors, newly commissioned male citizens, and war-orphans. Presumably the rest of the good seats were occupied by other male citizens and any male guests they might bring along. Women, small children, and slaves probably sat in a separate area behind the men.

The central focus of the dramatic festivals were the choruses, who with their leaders sang and danced in the *orchestra* ("dancing space") that separated the spectators from the stage on which actors performed. Fifty dancers were needed for each dithyramb, 12–15 for each tragedy, and 24 for each comedy, adding up to more than a thousand, all of them amateurs, who along with the musicians who would accompany them needed costumes (clothing and masks) and months of training before the performance. It is no wonder that one of the most important liturgies was that of *choregos* (sponsor of a dramatic chorus).[8] *Choregoi* were allotted from a list of men wealthy enough to hold this office, for they had to recruit the chorus that would perform at one of the festivals and pay for their training, costuming, and room and board. Good dancers could be compelled by a *choregos* to join his chorus and were excused from military service to do so. Being *choregos* gave a man an opportunity to display his wealth and refinement for the benefit of the demos as a whole, and to win a prize that would confer prestige on himself and his dancers. Some wealthy men therefore volunteered to be a *choregos* instead of waiting for their names to be drawn. Conversely, a man who put on a cheap or otherwise unsatisfactory chorus could expect to suffer a significant loss of public prestige. Worse, a *choregos*, like any other officeholder, could be prosecuted for failing to discharge his duties to the satisfaction of the demos: after each festival there was a public meeting at which members of the demos could lodge a complaint.

All other expenses, including stipends for the poet and his actors and for prizes, were undertaken by vote of the demos and paid from public funds. A poet got a place in the festival by submitting a draft some six months in advance to the relevant *archon* (the office-holder in charge of the festival). Ancient sources say that at least the choral parts of the proposed play had to be submitted. How much more was submitted we do not know. But revision up to the day of the performance was certainly possible, since many allusions in comedy refer to events occurring very shortly before the festival, most notably the death of the tragic poet Sophocles not long before the performance of *Frogs* in 405.

If a poet was awarded a place on the program, he would be given his stipend and assigned his actors. He and his *choregos* would then set about getting the performance ready for the big day, the poet acting as music master, choreographer, and director, the *choregos* rounding up, and paying the expenses of, the best dancers he could find. Given the large number of performers needed for these competitions, many members of the audience will have been past performers in drama themselves, like old Lovecleon, the main character in *Wasps*, who performed in tragic choruses when he was young and challenges the dancers of today to compete against him. Presumably young men danced in the dramas, since the dithyrambs, much less demanding, were reserved for old men and for boys.

IV. The Dramatic Genres

At the dramatic festivals comedy shared the theater with tragedy and satyr-drama, which like comedy had been produced in some form and in various locations since the sixth century in Attica and elsewhere. The genres are conscious of each other as poetry and theater, but they had different formative antecedents and performance traditions, and they remained fundamentally specialized (for their polarity see Taplin 1986): we know of no composer who wrote both – a feat that for Plato was only a theoretical possibility (*Symposium*, end). Performers too (*tragoidoi* and *komoidoi*) seem to have specialized in one or the other genre.

The Athenians dated their own first contest in tragedy to 534 and remembered the poet Thespis as the victor (hence "thespians" as a term for theatrical performers), but it is uncertain that this contest was held as part of the Greater Dionysia, which in any case seems to have experienced major changes after the overthrow of the Peisistratid tyranny and the establishment of democracy in 508. Tragedy dramatized stories from heroic myth, emphasizing dire personal and social events that had befallen hero(in)es and their families in the distant past (nowadays called the Bronze Age) and mostly in places other than Athens. Ordinary people and situations are rarely included. By convention, the costuming, poetry, and music of tragedy were highly stylized and archaic. Satyr-drama, which was composed by the same poets who wrote tragedy and performed as part of the tragic tetralogy, had the same features, except that the heroic stories were treated in a burlesque fashion and the chorus consisted of satyrs – mischievous followers of Dionysus who were part human and part animal, and who wore an artificial phallus as part of their standard costume (modest and erect, not an ugly dangling one, as in comedy).

All three dramatic genres were written in verse (iambic trimeter for dialogue, lyric forms for choral song and dance), but comedy differed from the other two in many of its performance conventions and characterizations, and was less restricted in its choice of linguistic and musical registers and of subjects. That is probably why the composers and performers of tragedy and satyr-drama were never the same ones who composed and performed comedy. The language of comedy was basically urbane and colloquial, though it often parodied the conventions of other (epic, lyric, and particularly tragic) poetry, and was free to use indecent, even obscene language and action (including stylized nudity male and female), which could be used as an element of characterization. Heroic personages appear only in cameos from epic or tragedy, or as burlesque: for the most part, the characters represented ordinary people and types. Standard costuming in comedy was grotesque, featuring a padded rump and stomach, with a large artificial phallus, worn by male characters and chorus-members. The music and dancing, too, tended to reflect current and popular rather than formal or "classical" styles.[9]

Unlike tragedy and satyr drama, Old Comedy was topical and self-consciously theatrical: its plots were fictional and often surreal or fantastic, though always plausible; it reflected and often portrayed the world of the audience; its performers could freely address the audience, often speaking on behalf of the poet and even, as in *Acharnians*, including the poet among the identities of a character. This was possible because the hero(in)es of Old Comedy are more than characterizations of believable individuals: they are fictional creations, neither straightforward nor consistent but complex and multiform, their personae developing and freely shifting as the thematic logic of the play proceeds. In *Acharnians*, Dicaeopolis is by turns a member of the audience; a displaced farmer; an assemblyman; an ordinary infantryman; the tragic hero, Telephus; Aristophanes as poet, citizen, and target of Cleon; and an embodiment of the Just Polis. The settings and timeframe of an Old Comedy are equally fluid: the scene shifts in *Acharnians* from theater to

Assembly to Dicaeopolis' farm (or perhaps his temporary shanty in the city: see *Acharnians* 72) to Euripides' house to Dicaeopolis' open marketplace.

Comedy also differed from tragedy in form and subject-matter. Tragedy had a more or less consistent form (episodes separated by choral songs called *stasima*), and at least after mid-century excluded topical subjects and dealt exclusively with stories from heroic (Bronze-Age) myth. Comedy developed a broad variety of forms and subjects, and prized originality and surprise. The most popular types of comedy were free-form mythological plots and myth-burlesque; golden ages or utopias and dystopias; domestic situations featuring everyday character types, including plays about *hetaerae* (geisha-like courtesans) and their lovers; the birth of gods; and (apparently beginning in the 440s) satire of people and events of current interest in the public life of the Athenians, including politics. Although Aristophanes used elements of all these types, which overlapped to various degrees, his 11 surviving comedies all fall into the last category: social and political satire.

Old Comedy in Aristophanes' day had a number of conventional features of form and structure. Typically we find: a scene in which the initial situation is revealed to the spectators (*Prologue*); the song of the chorus as it enters the orchestra (*Parodos*); a dispute leading to a formally structured debate presided over by the chorus leader (*Agon*); the self-revelation of the chorus, usually containing a speech to the spectators delivered by the chorus-leader on behalf of the poet (*Parabasis*); a series of scenes (*Episodes*) illustrating the results of the comic scheme and articulated by choral songs more or less detached from the plot, and often mocking individuals in the audience (*Songs*); and finally an exit-song by the chorus (*Exodos*). In some plays there can be a second Parabasis and/or a second Agon; in *Knights* there is a series of *agons*. Not all of these structural components are found, or found in the order given above, in each of Aristophanes' plays: during his career he creatively manipulated them for his own purposes, and as time went by, those components designed for plays featuring a prominently involved chorus (Parodos, Agon and Parabasis) tended to shrink or disappear, so that in his late play *Assemblywomen* we already see the beginnings of the comic form that was to become standard for centuries to come: Prologue followed by Episodes (later, acts) articulated by detached, and often optional, choral songs.

The chorus deserves special attention. With 24 dancers, it was considerably larger than its tragic counterpart and played a much more prominent role in the action. The typical tragic chorus possesses its emotional and gnomic authority and mediating functions by virtue of being anonymous, generic, predictable, and in terms of its dramatic status marginal or detached, helpless to affect the (often predetermined) outcome, even dispensable; it is sometimes hard to tell what connection a given tragic chorus has to the surrounding action. A comic chorus, by contrast, possesses a dramatic character unique to the play; is as prominent and active as the characters, not only reacting to but helping to invent, and as partisans often determining the success or failure of, their initiatives; its leader (or leaders, if the chorus was divided) and other members often are given names, sometimes representing actual individuals or distinct entities, and express personal recollections and opinions beyond their relationship to the plot, including opinions about working for a given poet or producer presently or in the past (these features are especially prominent in the chorus of *Knights*); it can usurp or parody other choral genres, including tragedy; in elaborate formal structures it represents both itself and the poet in direct address to the spectators and subsets thereof, variously praising, criticizing, rebuking, informing, and edifying; it is conscious of its competition with other choruses in the festival; it makes contact with gods appropriate to the play and the festival; and it moves fluidly and explicitly between topical engagement with democratic Athens (in its dramatic identity, often ironic and not always sympathetic or authoritative) and the perspective of timeless polis and theatrical values (in its authoritative identity as the traditional comic chorus).[10]

V. Performance: Actors and Chorus

Like a tragedy or a satyr drama, an Old Comedy was a *Gesamtkunstwerk*, a performance that combines all the arts: spectacle (scenery, costumes, props); poetry; music; dancing and singing solo, ensemble, and choral; acting, including the kinds of movement and gestures that are essential for a masked performance in a large outdoor amphitheater. The same theater accommodated the performances of tragedy and comedy.

The stage-area was a slightly raised platform behind the large *orchestra* ("dancing area"), which was probably circular, as it remains today, but perhaps originally (and in Aristophanes' time) rectangular. Behind it was a wooden two-story building called the *skene* ("tent," from which our word "scene"). It had two or three doors at stage-level, windows at the second story, and a roof on which actors could appear. On the roof was a crane called the *mechane* ("machine"), on which actors could fly above the stage (as gods, for example, whence the Latin expression *deus ex machina*, "god from the machine"). Another piece of permanent equipment was a wheeled platform called the *ekkyklema* ("device for rolling out"), on which actors and scenery could be wheeled on-stage from the skene to reveal "interior" action. A painted or otherwise decorated plywood facade could be attached to the skene if a play (or scene) required it, and movable props and other scenery were used as needed. Since plays were performed in daylight in a large outdoor amphitheater, all entrances and exits of performers and objects took place in full view of the spectators. All in all, more demand was made on the spectators' imagination than in modern illusionistic theater, so that performers must often tell the spectators what they are supposed to be seeing.

The actors wore masks that covered the entire head. These were typically generic (young man, old woman, etc.) but in Old Comedy they could be special, like a portrait-mask (for example, Euripides in *Acharnians*) or a caricature (for example, Cleon in *Knights*) of a prominent citizen. The costumes of tragic actors were grand, as befitted personages from heroic myth; comic costumes were contemporary and generically suited to the characters except that, wherever possible, they accommodated the traditional features of padded stomach and rump and (for men) the phallus, made of leather, either dangling or erect as appropriate, and circumcised in the case of outlandish barbarians.[11] All dramatic roles were played by men; the "naked" women who often appear were men wearing body-stockings to which false breasts and genitalia were attached. This cross-dressing was a performance convention, not a drag-show: as in Shakespeare's theater, the audience accepted the women being played by men at face value, so that no attention is ever drawn to the sex or age of the performer as distinct from his role; in ancient Greek drama this illusion was facilitated by masking. The city supplied an equal number of actors to each competing poet, probably three, and these three actors played all the speaking roles. In *Birds*, for example, there are 22 speaking roles, but the entrances and exits are so arranged that three actors can play them all. Some plays do, however, require a fourth actor in small roles; this is certainly the case in *Lysistrata* and *Frogs* and probably the case in *Acharnians* as well: it also has 22 speaking roles, but three actors could not have played them all without impossibly hectic costume-changes. It could be that in given years the allotment changed, or that poets or producers could add extra actors at their own expense, but it is more likely that novices were periodically allowed to take small parts.

In the comic orchestra was a chorus of 24 men who sang and danced to the accompaniment of an *aulos*, a wind instrument that had two recorder-like pipes played simultaneously by a specially costumed player, who could be female; and there could be other instruments as well. Like actors, members of the chorus wore masks and costumes appropriate to their dramatic identity. There could be dialogue between the chorus-leader and the actors on-stage, but the chorus as a whole only sings and dances; there was no ancient counterpart to the "choral speaking" often heard in modern performances of Greek drama. The choral songs of comedy were in music and language usually in a popular style, though serious styles were often parodied, and the dancing was expressive, adding a visual dimension to the words and music.

A fifth-century comedy was played through without intermission, the performance probably lasting about two hours.

VI. Comic Politics

The political aspects of comedy in Aristophanes' time – topical satire, burlesque, and wishful thinking; personal mimicry, mockery, and invective; criticism and advice on current issues – are certainly particular to the genre and the era, but they are similar, and perhaps related to older poetic, cultic, and carnivalesque traditions. In certain respects they also parallel the conventions of public oratory and private *symposia* ("drinking parties"). To the extent that all these shaped the experience and expectations of the audience, they must be borne in mind when evaluating comic politics.

1. Formative Traditions

As early as the Homeric period (eighth and seventh centuries) there was mythological burlesque and such proto-comedy as the Thersites-episode in the second book of the *Iliad*. Thersites, the only commoner with a speaking role in the epic, fits the persona of satirist and mocker in the traditional guise of lone and abject moralizer and critic. In the monarchic world of the *Iliad*, Thersites is beaten for his outspokenness, but he is the sort who is elsewhere deemed eligible for the "fool's privilege" to speak truth to power, a position relevant also to comic hero(in)es, who in addition to their grotesque costume typically represent ordinary, marginal, powerless, or (like Aristophanes himself, at the hands of Cleon) unfairly victimized individuals.

The iambic poets flourished in the archaic era as well. Named for the *iambos*, the characteristic rhythm of their verse, which also became the characteristic dialogue rhythm of actors in the Athenian dramatic genres, iambic poets such as Archilochus and Hipponax, who adopted a common-man persona not unlike Thersites, specialized in self-revelation, popular storytelling, parody, earthy gossip, and personal enmities, often creating fictitious first-person identities and occasionally using masks and disguise. They were credited with pioneering poetic styles of invective, obscenity, and colloquialism and seem to be associated especially with the cults of Dionysus and Demeter, whose festivals featured ritual mockery, personified in Demeter's mythology by the figure of Iambe. Comedy, the only other poetic genre to use this sort of language in the classical period, was in this respect related to iambic poetry.[12]

There was also a long tradition of wisdom poetry, which contained gnomic and philosophical criticism of society and categories of people; often enlisted mythological paradigms; offered practical and ethical advice and admonition; and sometimes singled out exemplary individuals for praise or blame, for example Hesiod's protest in *Works and Days* against the dishonesty of his brother Perses; Alcaeus' disparagement of rival political factions on Lesbos in the early sixth century; and Pindar's admonitory praise of athletic victors and their elite families. This tradition remained strong in tragic poetry, especially in the choruses, but at a more popular and immediate level, comic poets also carried it on and, unlike tragic poets, could appeal to current and historical as well as mythical exempla.

For the performance of both iambic and wisdom poetry, as well as other occasional poetry and song, the *symposion* was a prime occasion: from archaic times onward, the *symposion* was the main social gathering for men (women aside from professional entertainers, courtesans, or prostitutes were barred) and thus an occasion for personal and political back-and-forth, including mimicry and mockery, all tempered by rules of decorum intended to prevent insults and hard feelings that might lead to enmity or violence. Comedy at dramatic festivals honoring Dionysus provided a similar opportunity for controlled or artistic expression of personal and political differences. Part of the continuum was the *komos*, representing the wilder carouse following the *symposion*, which gave comedy its name. Unsurprisingly, sympotic and komastic scenes and imagery are pervasive in comedy (Pütz 2007), in our three plays most notably in *Wasps*, while in later eras comedies were often performed at *symposia*.

Then there were the various and widespread traditions of carnival, which from time immemorial and in many cultures has served as a period of ritual license, when society's normal rules and hierarchies are suspended or inverted so that ordinary people have a chance, in the "safe space" of festive enactments, to vent – or hear vented by performers who play that role – those frustrations, injustices, and hostilities that would be difficult or impossible to express with impunity on any other occasion: the oppressiveness of laws and rules, the unfairness of social hierarchies, the unworthiness or misbehavior of powerful individuals, disruptive but unactionable gossip, and the shortcomings of citizens in groups or as a whole. In this capacity carnival serves both as a social safety valve, allowing a relatively safe airing of tensions before they could become dangerous, and as a means of social communication and social control, upholding generally held norms and calling attention to derelictions. Like comedy, carnival also has a utopian dimension, allowing participants to play-act or imagine how much better life would be if reality were as most human beings would like it to be, and if there were no need for powerful authorities, rules, social distinctions, and quotidian toil. In this capacity carnival provided for utopian fantasies ("hog heaven" or "fool's paradise") that were a welcome relief from the cares, burdens, and frustrations of everyday life. Like comic fantasies and happy endings, carnivalesque inversions are implicitly or explicitly critical but also optimistic at least at the level of wish-fulfilment.[13] It did not hurt that plentiful drinking was practically a duty at festivals for Dionysus!

2. Mockery and Its Limits

Mockery and abuse thus had a very broad range including, but hardly restricted to political speech both actual and comic. In comedy, mockery and abuse are pervasive: ancient scholars noted as exceptional their avoidance by certain poets (Crates and Pherecrates, for example) as well as their absence in particular plays (Cratinus' *Odysseus and Company*, a spoof of the *Odyssey*). For the most part comic mockery was free-form and incidental, sometimes formulaic, and ranged across a broad spectrum of celebrity, from mere foibles, physical abnormalities, or character flaws – centered mainly on money, eating, drinking, and sex – to activity with political or social impact. As surveyed by Sommerstein 1996, most targets were men associated with politics and the courts, their friends and favorite courtesans, the rest mainly associated with the arts (especially theater), and the trades or professions. Personal mockery took the form mostly of drive-by jokes trafficking in the news of the day, and like tabloid scandal today might be included simply to embarrass the target, as Aristophanes says of his rivals (*Wasps* 1025–28). Such incidental mockery is only rarely part of a systematic political thrust; most often it occurs in asides, brief references, or brief songs unconnected with, or not constituting the main plot or themes of the play, and that were thus easily inserted or detached.

At the same time, however, there were guardrails in place that discouraged certain kinds of mockery and abuse.[14] Not everyone and everything was fair game: like orators (i.e., politicians) and litigants, whose modes of mockery and abuse differ from the comic mainly in sounding more decorous, the comic poets seem to have followed the rules governing all public speech. *Parrhesia* afforded citizens the right to advise, criticize, admonish, or abuse anyone, individual or collective, by telling the truth as one saw it. But there was no provision either in private or in public life either for intellectual or artistic freedom or for protected speech. Citizens were free to abuse one another publicly in virtually any terms they liked, but no one could falsely charge a fellow citizen with any of the *aporrheta* ("the unspeakable charges"), that is of being a public debtor, a parent-abuser, an evader of military service, a shield-thrower, an inheritance-squanderer, or a prostitute. These prohibitions existed not because the target's reputation would be unfairly diminished but because a citizen could lose civic rights if anyone could convince the demos that he was guilty of one of them. Thus the slander laws protected the collective demos, not the individual. None of the *aporrheta* was a standard category of abuse and only very occasionally did orators and comic poets make such charges; in each case it is clear or likely that the charge was not actionable slander but arguably true, or reflected unassailable community belief, or was otherwise unlikely to provoke legal retaliation. One or more of these exceptions apparently applied to Cleonymus, the only (but regular) target of the shield-throwing charge in comedy.[15] Otherwise the comic poets, like the orators, avoided the *aporrheta*. Nor could they mock a magistrate as he carried out his official duties, or disparage the memory of Harmodius and Aristogiton, the liberators of Athens from tyranny (see *Acharnians* 980 n.).

Comic poets, like comedians today, also seem to have respected unwritten social norms in evaluating what would or would not come off as funny. There are no accusations of murder, parent abuse, aspirations to tyranny, or offenses against the gods. Popular figures like athletes are excused, someone's married female relatives (notably wives and mothers) are mentioned only under certain protocols that applied also to orators and litigants, and no one's unmarried female relative is ever mentioned at all. Self-restraint could also be enjoined by special circumstances, for example when the political atmosphere was overheated, as the united chorus tells the audience in *Lysistrata*, a play fully engaged politically but containing only one fleeting reference to an identifiable politician (Peisander at 490).[16] The comic poets may normally have enjoyed at least some greater leeway than orators and litigants (though they never mentioned let alone invoked such a license), but when comic speech could be perceived as overstepping the bounds of law or propriety – "taking a risk beyond the pale," as Aristophanes put it in *Acharnians* 645 – it could invite the same sort of popular condemnation or retaliation as any other public speech.

Cleon's response to Aristophanic mockery shows that this risk was not merely figurative: at least twice he brought legal action against the poet, once before the Council for slandering the polis before foreigners in *Babylonians* and for falsely claiming citizenship, and again after *Knights* on personal grounds; the first case was dismissed, the second led to an agreement that Aristophanes later boasted of having finessed (*Acharnians* 377–82, 502–3, *Wasps* 1284–91). The demos could also punish comic poets by authorizing smaller stipends or by enacting laws restricting comic freedoms. One of these was enacted in 440, when Pericles led Athens to war against her own ally Samos, and another in 415, in the aftermath of the scandal involving parody of the Eleusinian Mysteries of Demeter (it is perhaps relevant that three of the men condemned in this affair seem to have been comic poets). At the same time, such restrictive measures against comedy seem to have been sporadic and short-lived, and such lawsuits against comic poets rare (could Cleon's lack of success have discouraged them?). Clearly the genre had broad support, and its transgressive elements enjoyed a wider latitude than would be allowed in venues where votes were taken and mockery could not be merely laughed off.[17]

Given these hazards it is unsurprising to find jabs at individuals or the collective that were not explicit but in the interest of deniability were indirect, figured, or rhetorically hedged. The device of *emphasis* ("innuendo" or "implication" whose implied meaning must be discovered by the audience) lay behind the use of myth to disguise an attack, as in the case of Cratinus' *Dionysalexander*, whose surviving summary states, "In the play Pericles is comedized quite skillfully through innuendo [*emphasis*] for bringing the war upon the Athenians" (for this play, see Appendix), or the use of allegory, as in *Knights*, whose portrayal of Cleon is entirely indirect, representing Cleon only as a Paphlagonian slave; Cleon is actually named only once in the play, in a detachable song by the Knights, who do not equate him with the character Paphlagon and carefully point out that they represent, and speak here on behalf of themselves and Cleon's other real-life enemies.[18] Aristophanes' excuse for such caution is humorous but acknowledges actual nervousness: "And never fear, he's not portrayed to the life: none of the mask makers had the guts to make a portrait mask. He'll be recognized all the same, because the audience is sharp" (230–33). In the event, the disguise was insufficient for deniability, and Aristophanes' fears proved to be justified, as therefore too was the pride he later expressed in having taken on Cleon, the self-proclaimed "watchdog of the demos" – unlike his rivals, who imitated Aristophanes in writing demagogue-comedies but picked on less powerful demagogues.[19] And in fact, no other comic poet did attack Cleon, and no other demagogue was portrayed in a comedy without disguise until Plato's *Peisander* of 421, after Cleon's death.

3. Political Engagement in Comedy

Routine mockery, incidental and free-form, is not the whole story of Old Comedy's personal connection with its audience: there is also political satire proper, though it was a less frequent and more specialized form of engagement.[20] A politically engaged comedy focused on current political issues; took a recognizable, detailed, and more or less coherent political stance; and while its engagement was poetic and festive, it both paralleled and expected to have an impact on real-life deliberation, which parabasis-speeches on behalf of the poets regularly assert and in at least one case succeeded: the civic crown and re-performance awarded to Aristophanes for the advice he had given in the parabasis of *Frogs* in 405, to re-enfranchise men who had colluded in the oligarchic coup of 411, an action that the Assembly approved soon thereafter. It is tempting to think that the comic festival was a good place for airing such a sensitive proposal as a trial balloon to test public sentiment. In politically engaged plays, the main thrust of the comic stance, despite its humorous or fantastic features, is always clear, and the poet's appeal to his audience almost always echoes, or is actually in accord with real-life partisan positions. Such plays were triggered by and engaged with individuals and/or civic/political issues in a sustained thematic way; criticized or admonished the spectators on those grounds; and could represent the poet himself as a partisan, at least in the case of the series of plays in this volume, which frontally attacked Cleon beginning with *Babylonians* in 426 to *Wasps* in 422, the year in which Cleon was killed in battle. Such plays also seem to have been relatively infrequent, produced by a small subset of poets and only in certain political environments; the most salient fragmentary examples are collected in the Appendix to this volume.

Since all politics are local, a brief sketch of the political landscape in Aristophanes' Athens is in order before an examination of the plays, as is a brief biography of Cleon.

Aristophanes belonged to a generation that came of age just as the long ascendancy of Pericles came to an end with his sudden death in 429 during the great pandemic that had broken out in 430. Pericles, from the ancient aristocratic family of the Alcmeonids, had championed the democratic reforms of 461, which he defended and consolidated in leading Athens through the following momentous decades. During this "Age of Pericles," Athens gradually transformed the Delian League of smaller Greek states to the east, which had been organized in 479 following the Persian invasions as a defensive bulwark against future Persian aggression, into its own tribute-paying empire. Its members were forbidden to leave and were strongly, indeed forcibly encouraged to adopt democratic governments: "nation building" as it is called today. Athens thus consolidated its position as the leading naval power in the Mediterranean, and enjoyed unprecedented prosperity, making possible Pericles' ambitious building program as well as a great artistic and intellectual flowering.

Meanwhile tensions developed between Athens and the other great power in the Greek world: Sparta with its allies (the "Peloponnesians"). Pericles and his democratic majority had always taken a tough competitive line against Sparta, and in 431 their intransigent attitude finally precipitated what is now known as the Peloponnesian War, which involved the entire Mediterranean world and was fought in two phases: the Archidamian War from 431 to the Peace of Nicias (actually a mere armistice) in 421, and the Ionian War from 413 to the unconditional surrender of Athens in 404. The Periclean war plan was defensive: the goal was to wait out the Spartans, meanwhile refraining from further imperial expansion. But following Pericles' death, political ascendancy and leadership of the war suddenly passed from men of the traditional landed elite, like Pericles, to men of the commercial elite, like Cleon, who were populists less interested in a defensive posture either politically or militarily.[21]

Thucydides paints an idealizing portrait of a Pericles firmly in control of a democratic polis, but in actuality politics in this era were sharply divided and Pericles' ascendancy vigorously challenged, as comedy amply reveals. While the traditional elite for the most part cautiously embraced democracy, a significant minority chose non-participatory quietism or grumbled about the recklessness of the masses and believed that some form of benign oligarchy was needed to temper it.[22] They resented being sidelined by the masses, who were newly empowered by the growth and growing centrality of the city, by imperial commerce and trade, and by the primacy of naval power over the traditional infantry (hoplites) and cavalry. They disapproved of Athenocentrism and democratic evangelism, which disrupted their vision of panhellenic solidarity, justified high-handed treatment of fellow-Greek allies, turned Sparta from a partner in leadership of Greece into a rival, and disrupted their international networks of friends and family connections.[23] There were also culture-wars and a generation-gap: the prosperity and security created by the labor and sacrifice of the "greatest generation" that had repulsed the Persians seemed only to empower the younger (Aristophanes') generation to jettison the old values of solidarity, discipline, religious piety, and deference to tradition in favor of selfish individualism, atheism, progressivism, intellectualism, and general enlightenment.

The outbreak of war in 431 exacerbated these tensions: the landed elite had to abandon their farms and estates and move into the city for the duration, while the Spartans invested and devastated the countryside. Suddenly empowered by Pericles' death, men like Cleon pushed a much more aggressive war policy: increasing allied tribute, taxing the wealthy, cracking down on domestic and allied disloyalty and disobedience, broadening the membership of the empire by force if necessary, and going on the offensive against Sparta. They also adopted a hard populist line, claiming to be the people's champions and encouraging suspicion that the elites were not only undemocratic but unpatriotic, immoral, atheistic, sexually deviant, and Spartan-loving, sinister plotters who aspired to tyranny. This polarization affected the arts as well, with new forms of music, song, dance, and drama becoming emblematic of political, social, and generational partisanship.[24]

Both Thucydides and Aristophanes identify Cleon as the most influential of the populists who emerged after Pericles' death. He belonged to the urban deme Cydathenaeum, as did Aristophanes. His father had been wealthy enough to undertake a successful liturgy in 460/59, and to judge from Aristophanes' sneers, the family seems to have operated a tannery and leather business. That Cleon was of barbarian (and therefore possibly slavish) ancestry – a staple of the "demagogue" caricature after the success of *Knights* – may derive from the nationality of his mother: he must have been born before the citizenship law of 451, so that she could have been non-Athenian.

Little is known about Cleon beyond the hostile portraits drawn by Aristophanes and Thucydides,[25] which are clearly biased on both political and personal grounds: Cleon pursued legal action against Aristophanes at least twice, after *Babylonians* in 426 and *Knights* in 424, and Thucydides' exile from Athens in the aftermath of his command at the battle of Amphipolis in 422 was likely at the hands of Cleon (who boasts of harrying commanders in *Knights*), as stated in Thucydides' ancient *Life*. Aristophanes caricatures Cleon as uncouth in appearance and behavior; dismissive of traditional codes of conduct for politicians; having a loud, barking voice, a blunt, harsh, and vulgar manner of speaking, a pugnacious, intimidating, and threatening posture toward opponents, and a liking for hurling insults, accusations, and lawsuits. But for all that he was detested by traditional elites, and for skeptics of popular sovereignty exemplified the unfitness of the masses for decision-making, Cleon had an innovative and successful political career as well as the greatest military triumph of the Archidamian War,[26] and he was remembered fondly, and long after his death, as a champion of ordinary people.[27]

In this social and political landscape, the stance of politically engaged comedy is clear: from the time of our first attestation of comedy ca. 440, the political plays share a consistent bias against democrats in the political mold of Pericles and his successors (such as Cleon), and almost entirely spare conservative or rightist figures, however notorious, and occasionally even defend them (as in the case of the oligarchs in *Frogs* 686–705).[28] They carefully avoid the real and always-live threat of oligarchy while instead ridiculing the populist bogey of elite tyranny.[29] At the ideological and policy level too, the political poets consistently espouse the social, moral, cultural, and political sentiments of elite conservative democrats. The wealthy as a class are never criticized, whereas the poor often are (though this attitude is mitigated in the postwar plays). Full popular sovereignty is viewed as empowering an ignorant, gullible, and impulsive majority intent on soaking the rich in Athens and the empire while rewarding the scoundrels who manipulate the Council, the Assembly, and the courts in their own self-interest. There is hostility to such leftist institutions as the subsidy (nowadays "entitlement") enabling the poor to serve on juries (but not to the equipment subsidy for the wealthy Knights). There is disagreement with the rationale behind, and the leadership of, the Peloponnesian War when (and only when) it either exposed the Attic countryside, and thus the landowners, to enemy devastation or bolstered the authority of populist leaders; when Sparta was not involved, the plays either say nothing about the war or positively support it.[30] There is disapproval of the intellectual movements associated with "sophists" (including Socrates) and of such vulgar novelties in poetry and music as those of Euripides (never Sophocles) and modern dithyrambic poets. Like Thucydides (especially 2.65), the comic poets agreed on a narrative of degeneration – the demos should, but no longer tended to, choose the best as its leaders – except that comedy did not include Pericles in the latter category.[31]

Since the comic poets were public voices competing at a democratically organized festival for prizes awarded in the name of the people, they did not – and legally could not – criticize either the democratic constitution itself or the inherent rightness of the demos' rule. If the fragmentary plays took the same line as Aristophanes, comic criticism of the democracy was framed as constructive admonition and advice, intended not to undermine the democracy but to achieve, or rather restore, a better version of it. Although Aristophanes often criticizes the demos and its institutions, and occasionally expresses views also held by oligarchs, he is careful not to blame the demos but rather its demagogic leaders (similarly Thucydides 2.65): the decline of Athens from former greatness is a recurrent theme; all would be well (again) if the demos turned once more to "the best" as its advisors, as in the good old days of Aristides and Miltiades (*Knights* 1326), before Pericles and his successors led Athens into moral, intellectual, spiritual, artistic, and military decline. In the (essentially democratic) comic view, the people are never at fault for their problems: they have simply been deceived by bad leaders or entranced by unworthy celebrities. By such portrayals the comic poets tried to persuade the actual demos, sitting among the other spectators, to rethink or even change its mind about the way it was running the polis or about issues that had been decided but might be changed, to discard dangerous novelties, and to be more critical of its populist leaders.

Plays with this engaged or forensic thrust were apparently not generically typical of Old Comedy but rather produced by a small subset of poets infrequently and only in a particular environment: when the traditional military and landed elite were politically sidelined and on the defensive, that is, when populist politicians were ascendant – Pericles and the "demagogues" who followed him – and when Athens was at war with Sparta, particularly when the fighting came to Attica. Thus we see politically engaged comedies in the periods from the late 440s up to the expulsion by ostracism of Cleon's successor Hyperbolus around 417, and then in the populist reactions of 412–11 and 405–02. In different political environments we find no comparable comedies: what satire of traditional elites we do find focused instead on their private lives. Edwards 1993 spoke of Old Comedy as an essentially carnivalesque popular genre that was "hijacked" by (what must have been) its traditional elite targets. But if there was hijacking, it was not the genre that was hijacked but rather occasional spots on its festival programs, perhaps mainly at the winter Lenaea festivals, where drama began to be produced for solely Athenian audiences around 440, just as Pericles' invasion of Samos was putting Athens on the high road to war with the Peloponnesians and the first decree is attested limiting the scope of comic topicality.[32]

The first political comedies are attested in the 430s, notably by Cratinus and Hermippus, and they focused their criticisms on Pericles: not only his character and private life – notably womanizing and in particular his relationship with his Milesian ward Aspasia, with whom he had a child – but also portraying him as an Olympian strongman whose control of the demos and ascendancy over fellow aristocrats amounted to tyranny.[33] Such plays seem to have been myth-comedies with a political slant decipherable by the spectators through the device of *emphasis*: for example, Zeus and Hera figuring as Pericles and Aspasia. The young poets who emerged after Pericles' death in 429 ushered in a transitional mode in which the criticism was more transparent, although still disguised by mythic and allegorical devices. After the death of Cleon in 422, the attacks became explicit, no longer using *emphasis* as a hedge against accountability.

Here is a roster of politically engaged comedy during its three phases: D = Dionysis; L = Lenaea; (principal target). The final two plays are named after active politicians but nothing is known about their content.

Mythical emphasis

431   Cratinus *Nemesis* (Pericles)
430   Hermippus *Moirai* (Pericles)
429   Cratinus *Ploutoi* (Pericles)
        Cratinus *Dionysalexandros* (Pericles)

Transitional

    426   Aristophanes D *Babylonians* (Cleon)
    425   Aristophanes L *Acharnians* (Cleon)
    424   Aristophanes L *Knights* and *Farmers* (Cleon)
    422   Aristophanes L *Wasps* and probably Eupolis D *Cities* (categorically)
    421   Aristophanes D *Peace* (categorically)
          Eupolis L *Marikas* (Hyperbolus)

Explicit

                    Platon L *Peisandros* (Peisander)
    420 or 419   Hermippus *Breadwomen* (Hyperbolus)
                    Platon *Hyperbolus* (Hyperbolus)
    417   Eupolis *Demes* (Hyperbolus and categorically)
    411   Aristophanes L *Lysistrata* (categorically)
    405   Aristophanes L *Frogs* (Cleophon)
                    Platon *Cleophon* (Cleophon)
    404   Aristophanes L *Frogs* restaged
    ca. 402   Archippus *Rhinon* (Rhinon)?
                    Theopompus *Teisamenus* (Teisamenus)?

After the Old Comic period, topical satire and the more transgressive elements of language and costume gradually disappeared from the comic stage: casualties of shifting audience taste as well as the social and political changes that followed Athens' loss of the Peloponnesian War, and with it their empire, in 404. The reason for the disappearance of political comedy proper is probably the same as for similar eclipses earlier: a shift in leadership back to the familiar elite and to rightist policies, which for whatever reasons were unappealing targets for the political poets. And when we ponder the role of the spectators in these trends, who were apparently content with the poets' rightist bias and did not create a demand for leftist satire, it is worth bearing in mind that in all periods of the fifth and fourth centuries, oligarchic sentiment was not confined to private clubs and dining rooms but was also a potent factor in open political life, and one with which democratic sentiment was constantly at pains to negotiate, or placate, the two sides often contesting the same patriotic vocabulary though they periodically resorted to violence.[34] It is in times of demotic self-assertion or counter-revolution that we find political comedy. Thus, it appears to have been resurrected in the fourth century in periods of democratic restoration by the comic poets Timocles, Archedicus, and Philippides (2); even the normally non-topical Menander revisits the politically charged trial scene of Euripides' *Orestes* in his *Sicyonians* (176–271).

4. *"Demagogue" Comedy*

A significant subset of politically engaged comedy is a series of plays inaugurated by Aristophanes in *Knights* of 424: there the word *demagogos* ("leader of the people"), which could apply to any democratic politician, was endowed with a meaning that suited the play's novel and influential characterization of the politicians ascendant after the death of Pericles in 429, in particular Cleon: *demagogos* now meant "leader of the mob," that is, a dishonest politician of low family background and mercenary ways who for his own profit and advancement plays to the passions and prejudices of the masses, with whom he identifies, attacking the elite and stoking partisan resentments instead of leading the whole people by virtue of his superior (or at least exemplary) stature, proven ability, and rational arguments. As one of his victims puts it, "leadership of the people (*demagogia*) is no longer a job for a man of education and good character, but for the ignorant and disgusting" (*Knights* 191–3, cf. 128–37, 213–22). *Knights* was the first play to feature a contemporary politician overtly as a central character in a plot detailing his deficiencies both personal and political and culminating in his destruction, and it established the basics of the demagogue-figure later developed by other comic poets.

In earlier comedies, as noted above, Pericles had been criticized obliquely through mythical allegory as an Olympian tyrant. To suit his immediate successors, however, the first to hail from the commercial rather than the landed and military elite, Aristophanes had to create a new kind of caricature: a rapid, pseudo-dynastic/theogonic succession of "sellers," each baser than the last, from Eucrates (hemp) to Lysicles (sheep) to Cleon (leather). Cleon is transparently portrayed as a new-bought Paphlagonian slave, and the allegory also encompasses all such "demagogues."

Aristophanes took special pride in *Knights* for its artistry, courage, novelty, and importance[35] and belittled Eupolis, Hermippus, and "all the others" (he might have added Plato Comicus) for copying his idea in plays attacking the lesser, and less dangerous, politician Hyperbolus and his mother.[36] It is true that these others did not attack Cleon (who died in 422) and that Hyperbolus had given them some sort of "handhold" (*Clouds* 551), but sole credit for the idea was contentious: Eupolis claimed to have collaborated on *Knights* (fr. 89), which Aristophanes may acknowledge when he speaks of "our *Knights*" (*Clouds* 554), and someone in Plato's *Perialges* (ca. 420–415) says "I who was the first to declare war on Cleon" (fr. 115).

Two demagogue-comedies competed at the Lenaea of 421. (1) Eupolis' *Maricas* resembled *Knights* in important respects: servile status and a fictitious name for Hyperbolus reflecting foreign origins (Persian and therefore hostile to Athens), marketplace education (frs. 194 and 208), a master (Demos?), a fateful contest including a meeting of the Assembly (fr. 192.148–50), and business with seal-rings suggesting stewardship. Eupolis seems to acknowledge a considerable debt to *Knights* but also emphasizes his independence (fr. 192.135–36, 201): new are semichoruses of rich and poor; an elite (instead of a sausage-selling) antagonist to Maricas; and an old woman representing Hyperbolus' mother, portrayed as an itinerant bread-seller (fr. 209) performing an indecent dance (*Clouds* 553–6). (2) The *Peisander* of Plato Comicus (not produced under his own name), the only poet to write more than one demagogue-comedy. *Peisander* was evidently the first to portray the demagogue not as a slave but in his own (no doubt corpulent: Plato fr. 102) person. Two other plays about Hyperbolus were produced before his ostracism ca. 417: Hermippus'

Breadwomen (probably 420), perhaps focusing on the mother (fr. 8, 9 "a worn-out sow, a common whore"), and Plato's *Hyperbolus* (probably 419), whose title character was named (fr. 182.6) so not disguised, but again of barbaric origin (this time Lydian: fr. 185), and again involved in a contest, this time in the Council against an elite antagonist (fr. 182).

After Hyperbolus' ostracism (degraded, according to Plato Comicus fr. 203, by its very use against such a man) no demagogue-comedy was produced until the Lenaea of 405, when Plato's *Cleophon* competed with Aristophanes' *Frogs*, also harshly critical of that politician (678–85, 1532–33). The "lyre-seller" Cleophon, active by the time of Hyperbolus' ostracism, in which some votes were cast against him, and the leading populist politician after the restoration of democracy in 410, was portrayed as a thief (fr. 58, 59) with a Thracian accent (fr. 61, cf. *Frogs* 678–82), and a slave and/or homosexual prostitute in his youth (fr. 60), a standard allegation against demagogues since *Knights* (167, 423–8, 878–80, 1242); his mother may have been a character in the play, since he is said to have ill-treated her (fr. 57, perhaps a new twist on the mother-theme); and the story that he appeared in the Assembly drunk and wearing a breastplate to reject a peace offer after the battle of Arginusae may derive from this play. Two other plays may have featured democratic politicians, though nothing is known of their plots: Theopompus' *Teisamenus*, probably produced around this time, featuring (though the name is not rare) the proposer of a review of the laws after the fall of the Thirty, and Archippus' *Rhinon* (ca. 402), featuring the member of the Ten who succeeded the Thirty in 403.

The comic portrait of demagogic Athens was exaggerated: the "new politicians" (Connor 1971) were not really nobodies (Cleon's father Cleaenetus, for example, was wealthy enough to be a liturgist) and their leadership did not introduce radical changes in policy. But Athenian perception of the ensemble of changes in family background, civic values, rhetorical style, and class affiliation seems real enough; it was echoed by Thucydides (especially 2.65), who speaks of Cleon (3.36.6) and Hyperbolus (8.73.3) with unusual animus, and it was also reflected even in contemporary tragedy, e.g. Euripides' *Suppliant Women* (produced in the late 420s) 399–456 and *Orestes* (produced in 408) 866–956. The idea of the demagogue would last far longer than its inaugural era and would continue to be invoked in all subsequent eras of democratic populism.

Notes

1 The polis of Attica was divided into 139 demes, semi-autonomous communities each belonging to one of ten tribes and serving as the political district of its citizens.
2 For a general introduction to the law in democratic Athens, see Gagarin 2021.
3 Citizen women (that is, the daughters, wives, or mothers of citizen men) occupied some of these religious positions, which provided their only source of public independence and visibility; before Aristophanes' *Lysistrata* (411), they are practically invisible in comedy.
4 *Knights* 1111–14 (Knights to Demos) "Demos, you have a fine rule, since all humanity fears you like a man with tyrannical power," cf. Thucydides 2.63.2 (Pericles to the Assembly) "for tyranny is the rule you now exercise," and similarly Cleon (3.37.2).

5   Performances called *komoidia* and depictions with comic features are attested outside Attica also on the mainland and in the Greek communities of southern Italy and Sicily in this period, and even earlier (Epicharmus is the best-attested Western Greek composer), but to what extent they resembled or influenced Attic comedy is unclear; Athens' neighbor Megara also claimed a native comic tradition, which was scorned by Aristophanes (e.g. *Wasps* 56 ff.): for comedy beyond Athens see now Csapo and Wilson 2020.

6   For full details and ancient testimonia about these festivals see Pickard-Cambridge 1988, Csapo 2010, Csapo and Slater 1995, Wilson 2007; for theatrical rituals, see Chaniotis 2007.

7   During the Peloponnesian War the number of comedies may have been reduced to three, though this is uncertain.

8   For a full account of the history and operation of the choregic system see Wilson 2000.

9   For obscene elements, which had roots in fertility cults (particularly those of Dionysus and Demeter), see Henderson 1991 and Robson 2009: 120–40; for the comic costume, see Compton-Engle 2015; for the abusive and satirical functions of comic language, see Edwards 1991 and Henderson 1998; for Aristophanes' language generally, see Willi 2003; for the songs, see Parker 1997.

10 For the comic chorus, especially in the plays presented in this volume, see generally Henderson 2013a.

11 The phallus, in addition to being an element of comic and satyric costumes, was a traditional symbol of fertility and masculine power, and it was especially associated with the worship of Dionysus; on the *phallephoria* see section III, above.

12 For the poetics of mockery, see Rosen 2007; for iambic poetry, see Rotstein 2010.

13 For carnival and Old Comedy, see Edwards 1993.

14 For legal restrictions, see Sommerstein 2004a; for patterns of avoidance and indirection, see Henderson 2020.

15 See further *Acharnians* n. 18. For *parrhesia* and *aporrheta*, and the many features of vituperation common to Old Comedy and forensic oratory, see Wallace 1994b, Heath 1997, Henderson 1998, Sommerstein 2004b, Lateiner 2017.

16 "We don't intend . . . to say anything about any citizen that's demeaning in the slightest, but quite the opposite: to say and do only what's nice, because you've already got more than enough troubles" (1043–49).

17 The difference between jocular and harmful was not always predictable, however: Plato in *Apology* blames Aristophanes' caricature of Socrates in *Clouds* (produced in 423) for being a major source of the false popular prejudices that influenced the jury against him at his capital trial in 399.

18 On this independent dimension of the comic chorus see Henderson 2013.

19 See for example such boasts in our extant *Clouds* 549–59 (datable to ca. 417).

20 Recent surveys of approaches to Aristophanic (and comic) politics are Olson 2010, Henderson 2013, Rosenbloom 2014, and Sommerstein 2014.

21 For Pericles' life and career, see Samons 2015.

22 See Simonton 2017. A revealing contemporary text is the disparaging analysis of democracy by the "Old Oligarch" (Pseudo-Xenophon, *Constitution of the Athenians*): see the annotated translation in Rhodes and Marr 2008.

23 Significant in this respect was the citizenship law of 451, which required both parents to be native-born Athenians.

24 For a rich survey of the era and its political and cultural tensions, see Ostwald 1986.

25 In Thucydides note especially 3.36.6, 4.27–28, 4.39.3, 5.10. For full accounts of Cleon's life and career, see Lind 1990 and Saldutti 2014; for a comparison of his comic and historical portraits, see Henderson 2017. It is highly likely that Aristophanes' portrayals, especially in *Knights*, influenced Thucydides, who was still writing his *History* after the Peloponnesian War: see Foster 2017.

26 See *Knights*, Introduction.
27 In Aristophanes, *Frogs* 569–70 (produced in 405), two female innkeepers, evidently metics (resident aliens), invoke Cleon and Hyperbolus as protectors, and in the following century Aristotle, *Rhetoric* 3.8 (1408b25) notes that when a freed slave is asked whom he would choose as a patron, the answer is always Cleon.
28 It is extremely unlikely that this pattern is merely an accident of attestation. Ancient commentators of the fourth and later centuries could still read 365 Old Comedies out of the ca. 650 produced during the fifth century, and since nearly all of our fragments are quoted from plays produced after 440 they seem to have had a practically full account of our era. If there was a leftist type of political comedy, someone would surely have written about it: ancient scholars and commentators were very alert to historical and political information in comedy and there is no conceivable reason why generations of them would deliberately ignore or suppress such instances.
29 See Henderson 2003.
30 For example, Aristophanes' *Birds* 186, 640, 813–816, 1360–1369 (produced in 414).
31 For Thucydides and the comic poets generally, see Henderson 2017.
32 See Hartwig 2015: 29–33
33 Plutarch's *Life of Pericles* provides examples of ample comic criticism, which is ignored by Thucydides (see Henderson 2017).
34 A careful recent discussion is Shear 2011.
35 See *Clouds* 546–50, *Wasps.* 1029–37, and *Peace* 748–61.
36 See *Clouds* 551–62, cf. F 58, Kyriakidi 2007; later Aristophanes would himself abuse the mother, *Women at the Thesmophoria* 844–5.

2. *Acharnians*

Introduction

Acharnians, Aristophanes' third (and earliest extant) play, and the world's earliest comedy that survives complete, was produced by Callistratus at the Lenaea of 425 and won the first prize; Cratinus was second with *Storm-Tossed* and Eupolis third with *New Moons*. *Acharnians* attacks Pericles' motives for leading the Athenians to war; the motives of current political and military leaders, particularly Cleon and Lamachus, for resisting peace negotiations; and the complacency of the Athenians for allowing their vengefulness toward the enemy to blind them to their own best interests. Its hero has a multiform identity, exemplifying the victims of wartime hardships, the people happy in peacetime, the just polis, Aristophanes unfairly attacked by Cleon, and the tragic hero, Telephus, who was similarly victimized in the archetypally unjust Trojan War of the mythical past.

The war against the Peloponnesians and the Boeotians, begun nearly six years earlier on Pericles' assurance that the Athenians would quickly prevail, was now effectively stalemated. During these years, the Athenian countryside had been devastated by annual Peloponnesian invasions and its residents – landowners large and small – had been forced to take refuge within the city walls; a debilitating plague had struck in 430, counting Pericles among its many victims, and was not yet in remission; and the Athenian financial reserves had run low by 428, so that the cost of the war was becoming an increasingly heavy burden on citizens and allies alike, not least the wealthier among them, on whom new levies were exacted. At least some Athenians continued, or had begun to question the rationale for further prosecution of the war. Nevertheless, a new breed of populist politicians, foremost among whom was Aristophanes' fellow-demesman Cleon, were successfully championing a more aggressive version of the Periclean war policy, playing on the Athenians' pride and desire for revenge and questioning the patriotism of anyone inclined toward a negotiated peace. Sparta sent emissaries, but they made little progress toward opening negotiations with Athens.

The hero of *Acharnians*, an ordinary countryman who calls himself Dicaeopolis, embodies (as his name suggests) the "just polis": what is right for the polis to be and to do, and also suggesting that he has just advice for the polis (cf. 497–501). Forced by the war to move himself and his family into poor makeshift housing

DOI: 10.4324/9781003159407-2

in Athens, Dicaeopolis dislikes the city and yearns for his farm. He is always the first to arrive at meetings of the Assembly, but he has never been allowed even to raise the subject of peace: no one else is interested. After listening with mounting agitation and disgust to a series of corrupt and deceptive speakers, Dicaeopolis decides on a radical course of action: by magical means he secures a private truce for himself and his family. Dicaeopolis' truce enables him to hold a festival for Phales/Dionysus and to resume a peacetime life. Dicaeopolis is immediately confronted by angry Acharnians, represented by the Chorus, who prepare to stone him to death for daring to make peace with the enemy, on whom they intend to take vengeance for devastating their land; in actuality, Acharnae was the largest Attic deme and the one most affected by enemy occupation.

Here Dicaeopolis stops the action and visits the tragic poet Euripides, from whom he acquires the beggarly costume of the hero Telephus. Just as in Euripides' tragedy Telephus, when unjustly condemned by fellow Greeks, had forced a hearing by taking the baby Orestes hostage and then made a persuasive speech to save himself, so Dicaeopolis, costumed as a beggar, takes a coal scuttle hostage and makes a speech defending the injustice of the war. He convinces half of the Chorus that his action was just. The other half of the Chorus, unconvinced, summon the commander, Lamachus, to help them deal with the traitor. But Dicaeopolis only mocks Lamachus: he is no longer obliged to obey military orders. Instead, he opens his own market, where he trades freely with enemy states (but not with Lamachus) for delectable foods currently contraband in Athens. He then prepares a lavish banquet, while Lamachus prepares meager rations for wintry action against Boeotian raiders. Dicaeopolis refuses to share his blessings with anyone except a young bride, "since she's a woman and does not deserve the war" (1062). In this he is hardly being selfish: participation in his market would in reality be off-limits to Athenians, who are still at war, and until they agree to end the war, they do not deserve the benefits of peace. In this Dicaeopolis resembles the heroine of *Lysistrata*, produced 14 years later, who withholds the blessings of home from a polis still committed to war. Dicaeopolis is invited by the priest of Dionysus to compete in a drinking festival (also a sign of divine approval: Dionysus is always opposed to war), which he wins (he is the sole visible contestant), and generally enjoys the wholesome pleasures of good food, drink, and sex, which the war has disrupted for everyone else. Meanwhile, Lamachus is borne in on a stretcher, having suffered an ignominious wound in battle.

To an extent the play condemns the war simply by displaying, and reminding the spectators, of the comforts and benefits that come to Dicaeopolis as a result of his truce, and by contrasting these with the hardships and dangers faced by Lamachus and the Chorus, and beyond them, the spectators, who are still committed to war. But there is more. In the prologue, the apathy of the Assembly, the arrogance of its officials, and the duplicity and self-dealing of those who address the people are sharply criticized. In his confrontation with Lamachus, Dicaeopolis (rather like Achilles in the opening action of the *Iliad*) contrasts the hard work done by the rank and file with the profits enjoyed by commanders and politicians. And in Dicaeopolis' defense speech to the Acharnians (497 ff.), we are given an account of the war's origins that are amusing, to be sure, but nonetheless reflect popular thinking,[1] and are trenchantly critical and clearly intended to be taken to heart. An unusual feature of this speech is the poet's overt self-identification with his hero, referring to his own denunciation by Cleon for "slandering the city in the presence of foreigners" at the previous year's Dionysia (in *Babylonians*) and (evidently) for being of non-Athenian birth. In the parabasis, the poet stresses the themes of freedom of speech and the value of listening even to unpopular views by boasting of his own courage in telling the Athenians unpleasant but important truths: for this he deserves not abuse but rich rewards (628 ff.).

Dicaeopolis' confrontation with the Acharnians (lines 204–625) is modelled on Euripides' lost tragedy, *Telephus*, produced in 438 and evidently already a classic.[2] Its hero, the son of Heracles and Auge, had become king of Mysia in the Troad and son-in-law of the Trojan King, Priam. When the Greek expedition against Troy mistakenly attacked Mysia, Telephus was wounded by Achilles and then informed by an oracle that his wound could be healed only by its inflictor. So much Telephus probably explained in a prologue-speech. As the action begins, Telephus is on his way to Argos in the Peloponnese, disguised as a Mysian beggar, to look for Achilles. In a speech he defends himself and the Mysians by arguing that the Greeks would have acted the same way had they suffered an unprovoked attack. He probably also questioned the Greeks' motive for the war against Troy (Paris' abduction of Helen) and urged them to consider matters from the Trojan/Mysian perspective. The Greeks' reaction to Telephus' speech is hostile, though perhaps not unanimously so, for in several fragments Agamemnon and Menelaus argue about continuing the war. When Telephus' disguise is exposed and he is threatened with death, he takes refuge at an altar, with the baby Orestes as hostage, and convinces the Greeks that he too is in fact a Greek. Achilles arrives and agrees to cure Telephus' wound. In response to another oracle, which says that the Greeks can take Troy only if a Greek leads them, Telephus agrees to guide the Greeks to Troy.

Like Telephus, Dicaeopolis disguises himself in rags, pleads his cause before a hostile audience, and takes a hostage; and his arguments against the Athenians' continuing the war against Sparta resemble Telephus' argument against the Greeks' continuing the war against the Mysians. Moreover, behind the comic hero Dicaeopolis-Telephus we are invited to see Aristophanes himself, who had been accused of treason and foreign birth by Cleon, defending his standing as an authentic and loyal Athenian (cf. esp. 366–82, 497–556, 628–64). In mounting their defense and criticizing their persecutors as well as society at large, Dicaeopolis/Telephus/Aristophanes adopt the archetypal persona of the satirist, the lone and abject figure who is present as early as the *Iliad* in the figure of Thersites (see General Introduction, Section VI.1).

In his extensive usurpation of *Telephus* Aristophanes employs, or perhaps invents (Foley 1988), a technique called "paratragedy": the incorporation or re-composition of tragic scenes in order to enhance a comedy tonally, scenically, and thematically. In the paratragedy of *Acharnians*, Aristophanes borrows the authority of tragedy, creates a play within a play (Dicaeopolis/Aristophanes as director), and constructs a complex layering of disguises that work on several levels simultaneously: Telephus vs. Greeks ~ Dicaeopolis vs. Acharnians ~ Aristophanes vs. Athenians.[3] He also calls attention to what he is up to as a playwright, thus educating the spectators about the nature of theatrical illusion and of persuasion generally. Further, by using the spectators themselves to represent the Assembly and identifying his own case with that of his hero, Aristophanes establishes a connection between theatrical and political persuasion. It is significant that when Dicaeopolis needs eloquence to make the speech that will save his life, he seeks out a poet not an orator or politician. In these ways Aristophanes, as dramatist and citizen, at once challenges the spectators to engage critically and reflectively with the theatrical event in which they are participants and invites them to be just as reflective and critical as assemblymen, when they must judge the arguments of a Cleon.

A salient feature of Aristophanic paratragedy is its incorporation (by quotation and pastiche) of tragic diction and style, whose archaic and elevated tone contrast markedly with the colloquial registers of comic speech. I have tried to reproduce this feature by rendering paratragic lines in grandiloquent English.

Characters

DICAEOPOLIS, an Attic countryman
HERALD, of the Assembly
AMPHITHEUS, treaty-fetcher for Dicaeopolis
AMBASSADOR, to the Great King of Persia
PSEUDO-ARTABAS, the Great King's Eye
THEORUS, ambassador to King Sitalces of Thrace
DAUGHTER of Dicaeopolis
SLAVE of Euripides
EURIPIDES, the tragic poet
LAMACHUS, an Athenian general
MEGARIAN
DAUGHTERS (two) of the Megarian
INFORMER
THEBAN
NICARCHUS, an informer
SLAVE of Lamachus
DERCETES, an Attic countryman
BEST MAN
FIRST MESSENGER
SECOND MESSENGER
THIRD MESSENGER

Mute Characters

PRESIDENTS (Prytaneis) of the Assembly
ASSEMBLYMEN
POLICE

AMBASSADORS
TWO EUNUCHS
ODOMANTIANS
XANTHIAS and OTHER SLAVES of Dicaeopolis
WIFE and other WOMENFOLK of Dicaeopolis
CHILDREN of Dicaeopolis
SOLDIERS with Lamachus
HISMENIAS, the Theban's slave
THEBAN PIPERS
BRIDESMAID
TWO DANCING GIRLS
CHORUS of Acharnians

SCENE: *The scene-building has a roof on which actors can appear and three doors. Onstage is a rostrum, flanked by two benches and facing the spectators. In the orchestra is a chair just in front of the spectators and facing the stage. DICAEOPOLIS, a rustic older man with a walking-stick and a knapsack, appears from the side, enters the orchestra, sits on the chair, and waits.*

DICAEOPOLIS

How often I've been bitten to my very heart!
My delights? Scant, quite scant – just four!
My pains? Heaps by the sand-grain-zillions!
Let's see, what delight have I had worthy of delectation?
I know – it's something my heart rejoiced to see: 5
those five talents Cleon had to disgorge.[4]
That made me sparkle! I love the Knights
for that deed, "a worthy thing for Greece!"[5]
But then I had another pain, quite tragic:
when I was waiting open-mouthed for Aeschylus,[6]   10
the announcer cried, "Theognis, bring your chorus on!"[7]
How do you think that made my heart quake?
But I had another delight, when once against Moschus
Dexitheus came on to sing Boeotian-style.[8]
But just this year I died on the rack to see   15
Chaeris creeping on to play the Orthian tune.[9]
        But never since I first began to bathe
have my eyebrows been as soap-stung as they are
right now, when the Assembly's on for its regular meeting
at break of day, and here's an empty Pnyx:[10]   20
they're all gossiping in the marketplace
as up and down they dodge the ruddled rope.[11]
The Presidents aren't even here. No, they'll come late,

and when they do you can't imagine how
they'll shove each other for the front row seats,   25
streaming in en masse. But making peace?
They don't care at all about that. O city, my city!
      I am always the very first to come to Assembly
and take my seat. Then, in my solitude,
I sigh, I yawn, I stretch myself, I fart,   30
I fiddle, scribble, pluck my beard, do accounts,
while gazing off to my farm and pining for peace,
loathing the city and yearning for my own deme,
that never ever cried "here's coal for sale!"
"Buy vinegar!" "Buy oil!" It didn't know from "buy."   35
It grew everything itself, that buy-man was elsewhere.
So now, in a word, I'm here, and quite prepared
to shout, to interrupt, to call the speakers out,
if anyone talks of anything but peace.

Two Presidents, the HERALD and some Police enter through the parodoi
and mount the stage. The Herald stands at the rostrum and the Presidents
sit on the benches at either side of it.

Aha, the Presidents, here they are – at mid-day!   40
What did I tell you? It's exactly as I said:
every man is jostling for the front-row seats.

HERALD

Move forward, everyone!
Move forward, inside the sacred precinct with you!

AMPHITHEUS enters from one side, mounts the stage and addresses the
Herald.

AMPHITHEUS[12]

Has anybody spoken?

HERALD

      Who wishes to speak?   45

AMPHITHEUS

I do!

HERALD

Your name?

AMPHITHEUS

Amphitheus.

HERALD

Not a human?

AMPHITHEUS

No.
I'm immortal: Amphitheus was the offspring of Demeter
and Triptolemus, and to him was born Celeus,
and Celeus married Phaenarete my grandmother,
of whom Lycinus was born, and being his son   50
I'm immortal.[13] To me have the gods commissioned
the making of a treaty with the Spartans, to me alone.
But though immortal, gentlemen, I have no travel-money.
The Presidents won't provide it.

HERALD

Call the police!

The Archers seize Amphitheus and march him to the wings.

AMPHITHEUS

Triptolemus and Celeus, will you look away –   55

DICAEOPOLIS

Esteemed Presidents, you're wronging the Assembly
by removing the gentleman who offered to make
a treaty for us and let us hang up our shields!

HERALD

Sit down and be quiet!

DICAEOPOLIS

I most certainly will not,
unless you call for a discussion about peace!   60

HERALD

The ambassadors back from the King![14]

DICAEOPOLIS

The King indeed! I'm sick of ambassadors
and their peacocks and all their bullshitting.

HERALD

Silence!

Two opulently dressed AMBASSADORS enter by a parodos and mount the stage.

DICAEOPOLIS

Wowee! Ecbatana, what a getup![15]

AMBASSADOR

(*to the audience*)
You dispatched us to the Great King,   65
on a salary of two drachmas per diem,
when Euthymenes was archon —[16]

DICAEOPOLIS

Oh dear, the drachmas!

AMBASSADOR

— and we just wore ourselves out on the Caÿstrian plains,
a-wayfaring under parasols, and reclining   70
so daintily on litters, perishing!

DICAEOPOLIS

And I must have been
on easy street — reclining in the garbage by the ramparts![17]

AMBASSADOR

And when they regaled us, they forced us to drink
from goblets of crystal and golden bowls,
fine unmixed wine.

DICAEOPOLIS

Ah, city of Cranaus![18]

75

Do you see how these ambassadors laugh at you?

AMBASSADOR

Barbarians, you see, recognize as real men
only those who can gobble and guzzle the most.

DICAEOPOLIS

While with us it's cock-suckers and candy-asses.[19]

AMBASSADOR

So, after three years we got to the royal palace,

80

but the King had gone off with an army to a latrine,
and he shat for eight whole months upon the Golden Hills –

DICAEOPOLIS

And how long til he closed up his asshole?
When the moon was full?

AMBASSADOR

– and then he departed for home.

And then he threw us a party and served us up

85

whole ox *en casserole* –

DICAEOPOLIS

And who has ever seen

ox casserole? What utter bullshitting![20]

AMBASSADOR

– and then, by Zeus, he served us up a bird
three times the size of Cleonymus;[21] he called it a gull.

DICAEOPOLIS

Because *you* were gulling *us*, drawing your two drachmas

90

AMBASSADOR

And now we're back, with Pseudo-Artabas, the King's Eye.

DICAEOPOLIS

May a crow peck it out, and yours too, Mr. Ambassador!

PSEUDO-ARTABAS enters by a parodos and mounts the stage. He has one huge eye in the center of his mask and a long scarf around his neck, and is attended by two Eunuchs.

HERALD

The King's Eye!

DICAEOPOLIS

      O holy Heracles!
Ye gods, fellow, are you giving me a shipwrecky look?   95
Or rounding a point and looking for a berth?
Is that a porthole-flap there under your eye?

AMBASSADOR

Come then, the message that the King sent you to deliver
tell to the Athenians, Pseudo-Artabas.

PSEUDO-ARTABAS

Iarta name xarxana pisona satra.   100

AMBASSADOR

You all understand what he says?

DICAEOPOLIS

      By Apollo, *I* surely didn't.

AMBASSADOR

He says the King is going to send you gold.
(*to Pseudo-Artabas*)
Speak louder and more clearly about the gold.

PSEUDO-ARTABAS

No gettum goldum, gapey-ass Ioni-o.

DICAEOPOLIS

I'll be damned, that's pretty clear!

AMBASSADOR

   Eh? What's he saying?   105

DICAEOPOLIS

Why, he says that the Ionians have gaping assholes
if they're expecting any gold from the barbarians.

AMBASSADOR

No, he says gobs of gold, no hassle.

DICAEOPOLIS

Gobs indeed! You are a big, fat bullshitter.
Away with you; I'll do the questioning myself.   110

*Dicaeopolis mounts the stage, brandishing his walking-stick. The
Ambassadors exit.*

All right you, tell me plainly, in the face of *this*,[22]
so I won't have to dye you in a bath of Sardian crimson:
does the Great King really intend to send us gold?
Then we're simply being bamboozled by our ambassadors?
These men here have a distinctly Greek way of nodding; 115
They can't but hail from this very place!
And one of these eunuchs, this one over here,
I recognize as Cleisthenes son of Sibyrtius![23]
O shaver of a hot and horny asshole,
and wearing this big beard, you monkey, do you   120
come before us appareled as a eunuch?
And this one, who is he? Surely not Strato![24]

HERALD

Sit down and be quiet!
The Council invites the King's Eye
to the Prytaneum![25]

Pseudo-Artabas and Eunuchs exit.

DICAEOPOLIS

       Isn't that a killer? 125
Then I'm supposed to cool my heels over here,
while for *their* entertainment the door is never closed?
No! I'm going to do a great and dire deed.
Where can I find Amphitheus?

Amphitheus enters from the wing.

AMPHITHEUS

       Over here!

DICAEOPOLIS

Look, do me a favor: take these eight drachmas here 130
and make a treaty with the Spartans for me alone
and for my children and the missus too.
(*to the audience*)
And *you* go on with your embassies and your gaping!

Amphitheus exits. THEORUS enters.

HERALD

Let Theorus approach, back from the court of Sitalces![26]

THEORUS

       Present!

DICAEOPOLIS

Yet another bullshitter is announced. 135

THEORUS

We wouldn't have stayed in Thrace so very long –

DICAEOPOLIS

Zeus no, if you hadn't been drawing hefty pay!

THEORUS

– if snow hadn't covered up the whole of Thrace
and the rivers froze.

DICAEOPOLIS

When Theognis was competing in this very place!   140

THEORUS

All the while I was drinking with Sitalces.
Oh he was exceedingly pro-Athenian,
and your true lover, so much so in fact
that he even wrote on the walls "Athenians are hot"![27]
And his son, whom we'd made an Athenian citizen,   145
yearned to eat sausages at the Apaturia[28]
and kept begging his father to help his fatherland.
And Sitalces poured a libation and swore he would help us
by sending an army so large that the Athenians would say,
"What a giant swarm of locusts heads our way!"[29]   150

DICAEOPOLIS

I'm damned if I believe a word of anything
you've said here, except the part about the locusts!

THEORUS

And now he sends you the most bellicose tribe
in all of Thrace.[30]

DICAEOPOLIS

                    That's clear enough, at least.

HERALD

You Thracians that Theorus brought, come forward!   155

Enter Thracian Soldiers.

DICAEOPOLIS

What the hell is this?

THEORUS

A troop of Odomantians.

DICAEOPOLIS

Odomantians indeed! Pray tell me, what's all *this*?
Dicaeopolis exposes the Odomantians' stage-phalli.
Who's clipped away the Odomantians' cocks?[31]

THEORUS

Pay these fellows a stipend of two drachmas
and they'll swash-buckle all of Boeotia.   160

DICAEOPOLIS

What, two drachmas for these abbreviated peckers?
The crowd who row our ships and defend our city
would sure yell about that![32]

The Odomantians rush Dicaeopolis and grab his knapsack.

Hey, damn it! I'm getting killed!
Plundered of my garlic by Odomantians!
Come on, drop that garlic!

THEORUS

You troublemaker!   165
Don't approach them when they're garlic-primed![33]

DICAEOPOLIS

Presidents! Were you looking away as I suffered this treatment
in my own country, and at the hands of barbarians?
I insist that the Assembly table the question
of pay for the Thracians, and I declare to you   170
we've got a sign from Zeus, and a raindrop hit me.

HERALD

The Thracians are excused, to return in two days' time.
The Presidents declare the Assembly now adjourned.[34]

All exit except Dicaeopolis.

DICAEOPOLIS

Damn it all, what a good salad I've lost.

Amphitheus enters on the run with a basket containing three libation bowls.

But here comes Amphitheus, back from Sparta! 175
Welcome, Amphitheus!

AMPHITHEUS

No welcome yet, not till I've stopped running!
I've got to run till I outrun the Acharnians!

DICAEOPOLIS

What's up?

AMPHITHEUS

        I was hurrying back here with some treaties for you
when some old men got wind of them: Acharnians, 180
sturdy geezers, tough as hardwood, stubborn
veterans of the Battle of Marathon,[35] men of maple.
Then they all started yelling, "You absolute scum!
You're bringing treaties when our vines are slashed?"
And they began to fill their cloaks with stones.
I ran away; they kept chasing me and shouting. 185

DICAEOPOLIS

Well, let them shout. Do you have the treaties there?[36]

AMPHITHEUS

I do indeed, three samples here for sipping.
This one's a five-year treaty. Have a sip.

DICAEOPOLIS

Yuk!

AMPHITHEUS

   What's the matter?

DICAEOPOLIS

　　　　　This one's not to my taste;
it stinks of pitch and battleship construction.[37]　　　　　　　190

AMPHITHEUS

Well then, here's a *ten*-year treaty for you to taste.

DICAEOPOLIS

This one stinks too, of embassies to our allies,
a sour smell, like someone being bullied.[38]

AMPHITHEUS

Well, this one here's a treaty of thirty years,
by land and sea.[39]

DICAEOPOLIS

　　　　　O holy Dionysia!　　　　　　　　　　195
This treaty smells of nectar and ambrosia,
and never dreading that "time for three days' rations!"
And it says to my palate, "go wherever you like."
I accept it; I pour it in libation; I drink it off!
And I tell the Acharnians to go have a very nice life!　　　　200

AMPHITHEUS

But as for me, I'll be getting clear of the Acharnians!

Amphitheus runs off.

DICAEOPOLIS

And as for me, free now of war and hardships,
I'm going home to celebrate the Rural Dionysia![40]

*Dicaeopolis enters the central door of the scene-building. The CHORUS
enters the orchestra.*

CHORUS LEADER

strophe
This way, everybody, chase that man, and question
every single passerby! It is a worthy cause for our city　　　　205

to arrest this man.
(*To the audience*)
                    Please let me know,
if anyone knows where on earth the man with the treaty has headed.

CHORUS

He's fled, he's gone,
he's clean away. Damn and blast
these years of mine!   210
Never in my youth,
when I could carry
a load of coal
and run just behind Phaÿllus,[41]
would this treaty-bearer,
pursued by me then,
have so easily   215
escaped or so
nimbly skipped off.

CHORUS LEADER

antistrophe
But as it is, because my shin's arthritic now
and old Lacrateides'[42] legs weigh him down,   220
he's escaped. But we must chase him! Never let him boast
that he gave us Acharnians the slip, old though we may be,

CHORUS

that man, Father Zeus
and ye gods, who's made a truce
with our foes,   225
though on my side malevolent war
waxes strong against them
on account of my lands.
Nor will I ease off, till like a reed
I impale them in revenge,   230
like a stake sharp and painful, up to the hilt,
so that never again
will they trample my vines.

CHORUS LEADER

We must hunt for the man, and look to Peltingham,
and chase him from land to land until he's found at last;   235

for never shall I have my fill of pelting him with stones.[43]

Dicaeopolis emerges from the central door with his Wife, DAUGHTER and two Slaves who carry a large phallus.

DICAEOPOLIS

Pray silence, silence!

CHORUS LEADER

Quiet, everyone! Didn't you hear the call for silence, men?
This is the very man we're looking for! This way, everyone,
out of the way; the man is coming out, to make a sacrifice, it seems.   240

DICAEOPOLIS

Pray silence, silence!
Basket-Bearer, step forward a bit![44]
Xanthias, hold that phallus up straight!
Put the basket down, daughter, so I can perform the preliminaries.

DAUGHTER

Mother, please hand me up the soup-ladle,   245
so I can pour soup over this flat-cake here.

DICAEOPOLIS

There, that's very good. O Lord Dionysus,
may my performance of this procession please you,
and may I and my household enjoy good fortune
as we celebrate the Rural Dionysia,   250
now that I'm released from campaigning, and may the treaty
turn out well for me for all its thirty years.
Now come, pretty daughter, bear the basket prettily,
and keep a lemon-sucking look on your face.[45] Ah, blessed
the man who'll wed you and get upon you a litter of kittens   255
as good as you at farting when the dawn is nigh![46]
Forward march! And in the crowd take special care
that no one steals up and pinches your bangles.[47]
Xanthias, you two must keep your phallus up,
erect behind the Basket-Bearer there!   260
I'll bring up the rear and sing the Phallic Hymn.
And you, milady, watch me from the roof. Forward!

O Phales,[48]
friend of Bacchus,
revel-mate, nocturnal rambler,
fornicator, pederast:[49]   265
after six years I greet you,
as gladly I return to my deme,
with a peace I made for myself,
released from bothers and battles
and Lamachuses.[50]   270
Yes, it's far more pleasant, Phales, Phales,
to catch a budding maid with pilfered wood –
Strymodorus'[51] Thratta from the Rocky Bottom –
and grab her waist, lift her up, throw her down
and take her cherry.[52]   275
Phales, Phales,
if you drink with us, after the carouse
at dawn you shall quaff a cup of peace;
and my shield shall be hung by the hearth.

CHORUS

That's the man! That one there!   280

All except Dicaeopolis run inside.

Pelt him, pelt him, pelt him, pelt him!
Hit him! Hit the pariah!
Come on, pelt him! Come on, pelt him!

DICAEOPOLIS

strophe
Heracles! What's going on? You'll smash my bowl!

CHORUS

No, it's you we'll stone to death, foul fellow!   285

DICAEOPOLIS

On what grounds, venerable Acharnian elders?

CHORUS

You ask that? You're

shameless and disgusting,
you traitor to your country,
the only one among us   290
to make peace, and then
you've the nerve to look me in the eye!

DICAEOPOLIS

But shouldn't you know my reasons for making peace? Please listen!

CHORUS

Listen to you? You're done for! We'll bury you under a
mound of stones!   295

DICAEOPOLIS

Don't do it, at least till you've heard me out! Come now, hold off, good sirs.

CHORUS

I will not hold off!
And don't you give me a speech;
for I hate you even more
than Cleon, whom   300
I intend to cut up
into shoe-leather for the Knights.[53]

CHORUS LEADER

I'm not going to listen as you make long speeches:
you've made peace with Spartans! So I'll punish you instead.

DICAEOPOLIS

Good sirs, forget the Spartans for a moment   305
and hear about my treaty, whether I was right to make one.

CHORUS LEADER

How can you say it's right to have any dealings at all
with people who abide by no altar, no agreement, no oath?

DICAEOPOLIS

I know that even Spartans, whom we treat too ruthlessly,
are not responsible for all our problems.   310

CHORUS LEADER

Not all of them? You criminal! You dare to say this
right to our face, and then I'm supposed to spare you?

DICAEOPOLIS

Not for all our problems, not all. But here and now I could
    make a speech
showing that, in many respects, they're the ones who are
    the wronged party.

CHORUS LEADER

What you say is truly awful and stomach-turning,   315
if you'll dare to speak to us in defense of our enemies.

DICAEOPOLIS

And what's more, if my claims aren't just and don't seem
    just to the masses,
I'll be happy to speak with my head on a butcher's block![54]

CHORUS LEADER

Tell me, why are we sparing the stones, fellow demesmen,
and not shredding the man till he's red as a scarlet cloak?   320

DICAEOPOLIS

What a dark ember blazed up in you then!
Won't you listen? Won't you really listen, sons of Acharneus?

CHORUS LEADER

No we won't.

DICAEOPOLIS

Then dire will be my suffering.

CHORUS LEADER

I'll be damned if I listen to you!

DICAEOPOLIS

Don't be like that, Acharnians!

CHORUS LEADER

Count on being an instant goner!

DICAEOPOLIS

        Then I'll bite *you*!   325
For I'll kill in return your nearest and dearest;
I've got hostages of yours; I'll fetch them and cut their throats!
Dicaeopolis goes inside.

CHORUS LEADER

Tell me, fellow demesmen, what does he mean by this threat
against us Acharnians? He hasn't got somebody's child, has he,
one of ours, locked up in there? Then why is he so cocky?   330

Dicaeopolis reappears with a large knife and a coal basket.

DICAEOPOLIS

Pelt me, if you like! And then I'll murder *this*![55]
I'll soon see which among you cares for kith and kindling!

CHORUS LEADER

Now we're done for! That coal basket is from my deme!
Don't do what you're set on doing! Don't, please don't!

DICAEOPOLIS

antistrophe
Kill I will. Shout away; I don't intend to listen.   335

CHORUS

Then you mean to kill this, my coeval, my coal-eague?

DICAEOPOLIS

You were deaf to *my* pleas just a moment ago.

CHORUS

Very well, speak your piece,
tell us here and now
in what way
the Spartan is your friend.
For this dear little basket   340
I'll never desert.

DICAEOPOLIS

Please begin by disgorging your stones on the ground.

CHORUS

There you are, they're on the ground. Now you lay down your sword.

DICAEOPOLIS

But maybe there are some stones lurking somewhere in your cloaks.

CHORUS

It's shaken out to the ground.
Don't you see it being shaken?
Come, no excuses, please,   345
just lay down that weapon;
for this is getting shaken
as I twirl in the dance.[56]

DICAEOPOLIS

So you all were getting ready to shake your shouts at me,
and some Parnasian[57] coals were very nearly killed,
and all because of their fellow demesmen's perversity.
And in its fear this basket has squirted me   350
with a load of coal-dust, like a squid.
It's terrible that the temper of gentlemen should grow
so vinegary that they throw stones, and shout,
and are unwilling to listen to something evenly balanced,
even when I'm ready to state over a butcher's block   355
everything I have to say on behalf of the Spartans,
though I do regard my own life with affection.

CHORUS

strophe
Then why don't you bring a butcher's block outside and state,
hard man, whatever this great piece is that you've got to say?
An avid longing grips me to know what's on your mind.

CHORUS LEADER

Then as you yourself prescribed for your ordeal,
place the block there and set about your speech.   365

Dicaeopolis goes inside and returns with a butcher's block.

DICAEOPOLIS

Look, now: the butcher's block's right here,
and here's the man about to make a speech, such as he is.
Don't worry: I swear to god I won't buckler myself
but will speak in defense of the Spartans just what I think.
And yet I'm very apprehensive: I know the ways   370
of country folk, how deeply delighted they are
whenever they and the city are eulogized
by some bullshitter, whether truly or falsely.
That's how they can be bought and sold all unawares.
And I know the hearts of the oldsters too,   375
looking forward only to biting with their ballots.[58]
And well I know what Cleon did to me
in my own case, because of last year's comedy.
He hauled me right into the Council chamber,
and slandered me, and tongue-lashed me with lies,   380
and roared like the Cycloborus,[59] and dressed me down,
so I nearly died in a mephitic miasma of misadventure.[60]
So now, before I make my speech, please give me permission
to array myself in guise most piteous.

CHORUS

antistrophe
Why this dodging and scheming and contrivance of delay?   385
For all I care you may get from Hieronymus
a dim dense shaggy-maned cap of invisibility.[61]   390

CHORUS LEADER

Come now, disclose your Sisyphean ruses:[62]
this case will acknowledge no mitigating circumstances!

DICAEOPOLIS

Now is the time to gain a sturdy heart,
and make a visit to Euripides.

Dicaeopolis knocks on the door of the scene-building.

Boy! Boy!

SLAVE

(*opening the door a crack*)
Who's that?

DICAEOPOLIS

                Is Euripides at home?   395

SLAVE

He's home and not at home, if you get my point.[63]

DICAEOPOLIS

Home and yet not home – how so?

SLAVE

                That's right, old sir.
His mind, being outside collecting versicles,
is not home, while he himself is home, with his feet up,
composing tragedy.

DICAEOPOLIS

                O thrice-blessed Euripides,   400
that your slave here renders you so convincingly!
Ask him to come out.

SLAVE

> Quite impossible.

DICAEOPOLIS

> Do it anyway.
The Slave shuts the door.
Well, I won't leave; I'll keep knocking on the door.
Euripides! Dear Euripides,
answer, if ever you answered any human being.   405
Dicaeopolis of Cholleidae calls you – 'tis I.[64]

EURIPIDES

(*From within*)
I've no time.

DICAEOPOLIS

> Then have yourself wheeled out.

EURIPIDES

> Impossible.

DICAEOPOLIS

> Do it anyway.

EURIPIDES

I'll have myself wheeled out; I've no time to get up.

EURIPIDES enters on the ekkyklema, *reclining on a couch.*[65]

DICAEOPOLIS

Euripides?

EURIPIDES

> Why this utterance?

DICAEOPOLIS

Composing with your feet up? 410
When they could be down? No wonder you create cripples!
And why do you wear those rags from tragedy,
a raiment piteous? No wonder you create beggars![66]
But come, I beg you by your knees, Euripides,
give me a bit of rag from that old play. 415
I've got to make a long speech to the chorus,
and it will mean my death if I speak poorly.

EURIPIDES

(*rummaging through his costumes*)
Which ragged garb? Not that in which this Oeneus,
the star-crosséd ancient, did contend?[67]

DICAEOPOLIS

No, not from Oeneus, but someone even more wretched. 420

EURIPIDES

From Phoenix, who was blind?[68]

DICAEOPOLIS

Not Phoenix, no;
There was someone else more wretched even than Phoenix.

EURIPIDES

What tatters of robing does this fellow seek?
Are you talking about those of the beggar Philoctetes?[69]

DICAEOPOLIS

No, someone far, far more beggarly than he. 425

EURIPIDES

Then do you want the foul accoutrement
that this Bellerophon, the cripple, wore?[70]

DICAEOPOLIS

Not Bellerophon, though the man I want
was also crippled, a beggar, glib, an impressive speaker.

EURIPIDES

I know the man: Mysian Telephus![71]

DICAEOPOLIS

         Yes, Telephus!   430
Give me, I entreat you, that one's swaddlings!

EURIPIDES

Boy, give him the ragments of Telephus.
They lie atop the Thyestean rags,[72]
'tween them and Ino's.[73] Here, take them.

DICAEOPOLIS

(*inspecting the rags*)
O Zeus who sees everywhere, through and under!   435
Euripides, since you've been so kind to me,
please give me what accompanies the rags:
that little Mysian beanie for my head.[74]
For the beggar must I seem to be today: 440
to be who I really am, yet seem not so.
The audience must know me for who I am,
but the chorus must stand there like simpletons,
so that with my pointed phrases I flip them off.

EURIPIDES

I'll give it, for you contrive lightly with a heavy mind.   445

DICAEOPOLIS

God bless you, and as for Telephus – what's in my thoughts!
Bravo! How I'm filling up with phraselets already!
But I really do require a beggar's cane.

EURIPIDES

Take this, and begone from these marble halls.

DICAEOPOLIS

My soul, you see how I'm driven from the halls   450
still needing many props. So now become
whiny, beggarly, and precatory! Euripides,
give me a little basket burned through by a lamp!

EURIPIDES

What need have you, poor wretch, for this wickerwork?

DICAEOPOLIS

No need at all; I want to have it anyway.   455

EURIPIDES

(*giving him the basket*)
Know you are irksome, and depart my halls!

DICAEOPOLIS

Whew! God's blessings on you – as once on your mother!

EURIPIDES

Now pray begone!

DICAEOPOLIS

No, give me one thing more,
a little goblet with a broken lip.

EURIPIDES

Take this one – to blazes! Know you are troublesome to my halls!   460

DICAEOPOLIS

(*aside*) By Zeus, you don't yet realize how much trouble *you* make!
But my dearest Euripides, give me just one thing:
that little bottle plugged up with a sponge.

EURIPIDES

Fellow, you'll make off with my whole tragedy![75]
Take this and then begone.

DICAEOPOLIS

                              I'll be taking off.   465
Wait, what am I doing? One thing's missing, which if I don't have,
I'm utterly lost. Listen, my dearest Euripides,

with this I'll go, and never come again.
Give me some withered greenery for my basket.

EURIPIDES

Blast you! Here you are. Gone are my plays!   470

DICAEOPOLIS

No more; I'll go. Indeed I am too troublesome,
though little thought I the chieftains hate me so!
Good heavens me, I'm ruined! I've forgotten
the one thing on which all my plans depend.
Euripidoodle, my sweetest and my dearest,   475
a wretched death be mine if ever again I ask
you for anything – save just one thing, this one alone:
give me some chervil from your mother's store.[76]

EURIPIDES

The man's outrageous! Batten the barriers of my domicile!

Euripides is wheeled inside.

DICAEOPOLIS

My soul, without chervil must you venture forth.   480
Don't you realize what a great contest you will soon contest,
when you speak in defense of Spartan foemen?
Forward now, my soul; there's your mark.
You hesitate? Won't you get going, after your draught of Euripides?
Bravo! Come on now, my foolish heart,   485
get on over there, and then offer up your head on the spot,
after you've told them what you yourself believe.
Be bold, go on, move out. Well done, my heart!

CHORUS

strophe
What will you do? What will you say? You must realize   490
that you are a shameless and a steely man,
you who have offered your neck to the city
and mean to speak alone against everyone.
The man does not tremble at his task. Very well: 495
since you've made the choice yourself, speak up!

DICAEOPOLIS

Do not be aggrieved with me, gentleman spectators,[77]
if, though a beggar, I am ready to address the Athenians
about the city while making trygedy.[78]
For even trygedy knows about what's right;   500
and what I say will be shocking, but also right.
This time Cleon will not go accusing me
of defaming the city in the presence of foreigners;[79]
for we are by ourselves, at the Lenaean competition,
and no foreigners are here yet; neither tribute   505
nor allies have arrived from our allied cities.[80]
This time we are by ourselves, clean-hulled.
[For I count the resident foreigners as the bran of our populace].[81]
        Myself, I hate the Spartans vehemently;
and may Poseidon, the god at Taenarum,   510
shake their houses down upon them all;[82]
for I too have had my vines cut down.
And yet – for only friends are present at this speech –
why do we blame the Spartans for all this?
For it was men of ours – I do not say the city,   515
remember that, I do not say the city –
but some trouble-making excuses for men, mis-minted,
worthless, brummagem and foreign-made,[83]
who began denouncing the Megarians' little cloaks.[84]
If anywhere they spotted a cucumber or a bunny,   520
or a piglet or some garlic or rock salt,
these were "Megarian" and sold off the very same day.
        Now granted, this was trivial and strictly local.
But then some tipsy, cottabus-playing youths[85]
went to Megara and kidnapped the whore Simaetha.[86]   525
And then the Megarians, garlic-stung by their distress,
in retaliation stole a couple of Aspasia's whores,[87]
and from that the onset of war broke forth
upon all the Greeks: from three cock-sucking sluts!
And then in wrath did Pericles, that Olympian,[88]   530
lighten and thunder and stir up all of Greece,
and started making laws worded like drinking songs,
that Megarians neither on land nor in the market
nor on sea nor on shore should any more abide.[89]
Whereupon the Megarians, starving by degrees,   535
asked the Spartans to bring about a reversal
of the decree in response to the cock-sucking sluts;
but we refused, though they asked us many times.
And then there was a clashing of the shields.
Someone will say, "they shouldn't have!" But tell me,
what *should* they have?   540

Look, if some Spartan had denounced and sold
a Seriphian puppy imported in a rowboat,[90]
would you have sat quietly by in your abodes? Far from it!
No indeed: you'd have instantaneously dispatched
three hundred ships; the city would fill up   545
with the hubbub of soldiers, clamor around the skipper,
pay disbursed, emblems of Pallas gilded,
the Colonnade reverberating, rations measured out,
wallets, oarloops, jars being bought and sold,
bunches of garlic, olives, onions wrapped in nets,   550
garlands, anchovies, flute girls, and black eyes.
And the dockyards would be full of oarspars being planed,
thudding dowelpins, oarthongs getting attached,
pipes, bosuns, whistling, and tooting too.
I know that's what you'd have done: and do we reckon   555
that Telephus wouldn't? Then we've got no brains!

LEADER OF THE FIRST SEMICHORUS

Is that so, you lousy scum of the earth?
Do you, a beggar, dare say this of us,
and scold us, if we had the odd informer?

LEADER OF THE SECOND SEMICHORUS

He does, by Poseidon, and what he says is right,   560
entirely right, and at no point does he lie.

LEADER OF THE FIRST SEMICHORUS

Even so, was he the one to say it?
He'll be sorry that he dared to make this speech.

LEADER OF THE SECOND SEMICHORUS

Hey you, where are you running? Stop, I say! Because if you hit
this man, you'll be upended yourself, and quickly!   565

FIRST SEMICHORUS

antistrophe
O Lamachus[91]
who looks lightning,
appear and help us, you of the fearsome crest!
O Lamachus, friend and fellow-tribesman!
Or if there is a taxiarch, or general,
or wall-storming champion, let him come to our aid,   570
anyone, and quickly! I'm caught in a waistlock.

LAMACHUS enters in full panoply, with Soldiers.

LAMACHUS

Whence have I heard a martial shout?
Whither must I charge? Where hurl the hullabaloo?
Who's roused my Gorgon blazon from her shield case?[92]

DICAEOPOLIS

Lamachus, hero! What crests and ambuscades!   575

LEADER OF THE FIRST SEMICHORUS

Lamachus, don't you realize that this man
has long been spewing slander at our whole city?

LAMACHUS

You there! Do you dare, beggar as you are, to say such things?

DICAEOPOLIS

Lamachus, hero, please be merciful
if, beggar that I am, I spoke and prattled some.

LAMACHUS

What did you say about me? Speak up!

DICAEOPOLIS

                    I'm not certain yet;   580
the terror of your armor makes me dizzy.
(*pointing at the Gorgon on Lamachus' shield*)
Please, take that scare-face far away from me!

LAMACHUS

(*reversing his shield*)
There.

DICAEOPOLIS

    Now lay it upside down in front of me.

LAMACHUS

There it lies.

DICAEOPOLIS

    Now hand me that plume from your helmet.

LAMACHUS

Here's a feather for you.

DICAEOPOLIS

                   Now take hold of my head,   585
so I can puke. I'm sickened by your crests!

LAMACHUS

Hey, what are you up to? Using that feather to puke?

DICAEOPOLIS

This feather here? Tell me, what sort of bird
is it from? Perhaps the roaring boastard?

LAMACHUS

Oh! Now you're doomed!

DICAEOPOLIS

                  Not at all, Lamachus!   590
It's not a matter of strength – though if you're strong,
why don't you peel my foreskin? You're well equipped![93]

LAMACHUS

Do you, a beggar, say this to a general?

DICAEOPOLIS

Me, a beggar?

LAMACHUS

                  Well, what are you then?

DICAEOPOLIS

What am I? A solid citizen, not a Mr. Placehunter,   595
but ever since the war began, a Mr. Trooper;
while you, since the war began, are a Mr. Highpay![94]

LAMACHUS

They did elect me.

DICAEOPOLIS

          Three cuckoos did![95]
That's why I was sickened and poured myself a truce,
when I saw grey-haired men in the ranks,   600
and lads like you arrantly malingering,
some drawing three drachmas' pay on the Thracian coast –
Teisamenus-Phaenippus, Scoundrel-Hipparchides –
others with Chares, others among the Chaonians –
Geres-Theodorus, Humbug from Diomeia –   605
still others in Camarina and Gela and Catagela.[96]

LAMACHUS

They did get elected.

DICAEOPOLIS

          But how comes it that
you're all drawing pay somewhere or other,
while none of these people ever does?
(*to members of the chorus*)
          Say, Marilades,[97]
ever served on an embassy, though you're a veteran greybeard?   610
He shakes his head; and yet he's solid and hard-working.
And what about Anthracyllus and Euphorides and Prinides?[98]
Any of you ever laid eyes on Ecbatana or the Chaonians?
They say no. But the son of Coesyra[99] and Lamachus have,
though just the other day, on account of dues and debts,   615
all their friends were advising them to stand back,
like people dumping the evening wash-water.[100]

LAMACHUS

Oh, Democracy! Will such talk be tolerated?

DICAEOPOLIS

No indeed, unless Lamachus draws his pay!

LAMACHUS

Whatever! I for one on all the Spartans   620
will ever make war and everywhere harass them,
with ships and foot-soldiers, with all my might.

DICAEOPOLIS

And I announce to Peloponnesians all,
to the Megarians and Boeotians too,[101]
that they may trade in my marketplace, but Lamachus not.   625

Dicaeopolis, Lamachus, and Soldiers exit their separate ways.

CHORUS LEADER

That man has won the debate, and he's changed the people's mind
about the truce. Now let's doff our cloaks and essay the anapests.[102]

Never yet, since our producer[103] first directed comic choruses,
has he come forward to tell the audience that he is brilliant.
But accused by his enemies before Athenians who jump to conclusions 630
as one who makes comedy of our city and outrages the people,
he now asks to defend himself before Athenians who change their minds.
Our poet says that he deserves rich rewards from you:[104]
he's stopped you from being deceived overmuch by foreigners' speeches,
from being cajoled by flattery, from being citizens of Simpletonia.   635
Previously, the ambassadors from our allies who meant to deceive you
would start by calling you "violet-crowned"; and when anyone said that,
those "crowns" would promptly have you sitting on the tips of your rumps.
And if anyone fawned on you by dubbing Athens "gleaming,"
that "gleaming" would get him everything – an honor fit for sardines.   640
For this he's the source of rich benefits for you,
and for exposing how the people in the allied states are
"democratically" governed.[105]
     That's why the allied emissaries who bring you their tribute
will henceforth come: they'll be eager to lay eyes on this outstanding poet
who has taken the risk of telling the Athenians what's right.   645
So far has the renown of his boldness already spread
that even the King,[106] in questioning the envoys from Sparta,
asked them first which side was stronger in ships,

and then which side this poet profusely abused;
because those folks, he said, have become far better   650
and far likelier to win the war, with him as an adviser.
And therefore the Spartans offer you peace
and ask for the return of Aegina: not that they care
about that island, but so they can steal this poet away.[107]
But never let him go, for he'll keep on making comedy of what's right. 655
He promises to give you plenty of fine direction, so you'll
      enjoy good fortune,
and not to flatter or dangle bribes or bamboozle you,
nor play the villain or butter you up, but to give you only the best direction.
That said, let Cleon hatch his plots
and build his traps against me to his utmost,   660
for Good and Right will be my allies, and never will I be caught
behaving toward the city as he does,
a coward and a giant candy-ass.

CHORUS

strophe
Come this way, refulgent Muse,[108]   665
wearing the force of fire,
ardent, Acharnian!
Even as a spark that from oaken embers
leaps aloft, excited
by a fan's fair wind,
when the herring   670
are lying there ready,
and some are mixing
the Thasian sauce with its gleaming fillet,
and others are kneading the dough: so
come, bringing with you a tempestuous,
a well-tuned, a countrified song,
to me, your fellow demesman.   675

CHORUS LEADER

We old men, the elderly, have a complaint against the city.
The care that we receive from you in our old age is unworthy
of the sea-battles we have fought; in fact you treat us terribly.
You force aged gentlemen into lawsuits
and let them be the sport of stripling speechmakers,   680
old men who are finished, soundless and played out,
men whose Poseidon Unfaltering is but their walking stick.
We approach the stand mumbling in our dotage,

seeing nothing of our case but a blur.
And the youngster, who's cut a deal to plead against the oldster,   685
quickly throws a hold on him and hits him with hard-ball phrases;
then he drags him up for questioning, sets verbal pitfalls,
harries and flusters and confounds a Tithonus of a man.[109]
And in his decrepitude he gums a reply, and leaves the court convicted.
Then he wails and weeps and says to his loved ones,   690
"The money meant to buy my coffin I end up owing in fines!"

CHORUS

antistrophe
How can that be fair?
To ruin a man old and grey,
hard by the water-clock,[110]
a man who's toiled at your side
and wiped off warm manly sweat,   695
and lots of it,
when he was a brave fighter
at Marathon, in the city's cause?[111]
What's more, when we were at Marathon
we chased the enemy;
but now we're being chased hard   700
by bad people,
and getting bagged as well.
What Marpsias will try to disprove it?[112]

CHORUS LEADER

Yes, how can it be fair that a stooped man of Thucydides'[113] age
should be destroyed in the grip of that Scythian wilderness,
this man here, Cephisodemus' son, the prattling advocate?[114]   705
I for one felt pity and wiped away a tear
at the sight of an old gentleman being confounded by a bowman.
By Demeter, when Thucydides was his old self,
he wouldn't lightly have brooked †Achaea herself†[115]
but would have first outwrestled ten Euathluses,   710
outshouted with a roar three thousand bowmen,
and shot circles round the kinsmen of the advocate's father.
But since you won't allow the old men to get a moment's sleep,
at least decree that their cases be separate; then
an old man's prosecutor would be old and toothless,   715
and the young men's would be the candy-assed, prattling son of Cleinias.[116]
From now on you should banish elderly defendants
by using elderly prosecutors, and youths by using youths.

Dicaeopolis enters with boundary-markers, leather-straps, and a table.

DICAEOPOLIS

These are the boundaries of my marketplace.
Here all Peloponnesians are free to trade,   720
and Megarians and Boeotians as well,[117]
provided they sell to me; but Lamachus is not.
As trade commissioners I hereby appoint
these three duly allotted straps from Flogwell.
Let no informer enter here   725
nor any other canary man.
I'll go fetch the pillar with my treaty inscribed,
and set it up in the market for all to see.

Dicaeopolis goes inside.
A shabbily dressed MEGARIAN with two young DAUGHTERS walks
through the orchestra and stops before Dicaeopolis' house.

MEGARIAN

(*speaking his local dialect*)
Hail, Athenian market, dear to Megarians!
By the God of Friendship, I've missed you like a mother!   730
But you, you miserable father's rotten little kids,
go up the steps there for bread, if you can find some anywhere.
(*stopping before Dicaeopolis' door*)
Now listen, give me your undivided bellies:
do you want to be sold or miserably starve?

GIRLS

Sold! Sold!   735

MEGARIAN

So say I myself. But who'd be brainless enough
to buy you two, an obvious waste of money?
No matter, I've got a real Megarian trick:[118]
I'll dress you up and say I've got some piggies.[119]
Put on these little-piggy hoofs,   740
and see that you look like a fine sow's farrow.
Because if you get home unsold, by Hermes[120]
you'll find out the hard way just what famine is!
Come on, and put these snouts on too,
and then get into this sack over here,   745

and be sure you grunt and oink
and sound like piggies at the Mysteries.[121]
And I'll call around for Dicaeopolis.
Dicaeopolis! Want to buy some piggies?

Dicaeopolis enters.

DICAEOPOLIS

What's this? A Megarian?

MEGARIAN

We've come to trade.   750

DICAEOPOLIS

How are you all doing?

MEGARIAN

We sit before the fire, fasting.

DICAEOPOLIS

Feasting, yes, that's certainly nice, if there's music.
Otherwise, how are you Megarians doing these days?

MEGARIAN

As ever.
As I was starting out on this trip
our councilmen were hard at work for the city,   755
providing for our quickest and direst destruction.

DICAEOPOLIS

Then you'll soon be rid of your troubles.

MEGARIAN

That's right.

DICAEOPOLIS

What else at Megara? How's the price of grain?

MEGARIAN

Where we are it's mighty high, like the gods.

DICAEOPOLIS

What have you got there? Must be salt.

MEGARIAN

Don't *you* all control that?   760

DICAEOPOLIS

It's garlic, then?

MEGARIAN

Garlic! Every time you invade,
you dig up the bulbs with a hoe, like field mice.

DICAEOPOLIS

What have you got, then?

MEGARIAN

I've got piggies for the Mysteries.

DICAEOPOLIS

That's fine! Let's see them.

MEGARIAN

Aren't they fine, though?   765
Have a feel, if you like. How plump and pretty she is!

DICAEOPOLIS

What's this supposed to be?

MEGARIAN

A piggy, by Zeus!

DICAEOPOLIS

What are you talking about? What sort of piggy is this?

MEGARIAN

                    Megarian.
Isn't this a piggy?

DICAEOPOLIS

                    It doesn't look like one to me.

MEGARIAN

(*to the spectators*)

Isn't this awful? Look! The skepticism of the man!   770
He says this isn't a piggy.
(*to Dicaeopolis*)
                    I tell you what:
if you like, bet me some thyme-seasoned salt
that this isn't a piggy, in the Greek sense.

DICAEOPOLIS

All right, but it belongs to a human being.

MEGARIAN

                    Yes, by Diocles:[122]
it belongs to me! Whose do you think it is?   775
Would you like to hear it squeal?

DICAEOPOLIS

                    By the gods
I would.

MEGARIAN

                    Sound off, then, little piggy.
Right now. You won't? Damn you to perdition,
you're keeping mum? By Hermes, I'll take you home again!

FIRST GIRL

Oink! Oink!   780

MEGARIAN

Is that a piggy?

DICAEOPOLIS

                              It seems like a piggy now,
but all grown up it'll be a pussy!

MEGARIAN

                              Rest assured,
in five years she'll be just like her mother.

DICAEOPOLIS

But this one isn't even suitable for sacrifice.

MEGARIAN

                              Indeed?
In what way unsuitable for sacrifice?

DICAEOPOLIS

                              It's got no wagger!   785

MEGARIAN

She's still young, but when she's grown to sowhood
she'll get a big, fat pink one.[123]

(*taking the other girl from the sack*)
But if you want to rear one, here's a fine piggy for you.

DICAEOPOLIS

Why, this one's pussy is the twin of the other one's!

MEGARIAN

Sure, she's got the self-same mother and father.   790

If she fills out and grows downy with hair,
she'll be a very fine piggy to sacrifice to Aphrodite.

DICAEOPOLIS

But a pig isn't sacrificed to Aphrodite.

MEGARIAN

A piggy not sacrificed to Aphrodite? Why, to her alone of deities![124]
What's more, the flesh of these here piggies   795
is absolutely delicious when skewered on a spit.

DICAEOPOLIS

Are they ready to eat without their mother?

MEGARIAN

Yes, and without their father, too, by Poseidon.

DICAEOPOLIS

What's their favorite food?

MEGARIAN

                        Anything you give them.
Ask them yourself.

DICAEOPOLIS

                        Piggy, piggy!

FIRST GIRL

                        Oink! Oink!   800

DICAEOPOLIS

Will you eat chickpeas?[125]

FIRST GIRL

                        Oink! Oink! Oink!

DICAEOPOLIS

Then how about Phibalean figs?

FIRST GIRL

Oink! Oink!

DICAEOPOLIS

And how about you? Will you eat them?

SECOND GIRL

Oink! Oink! Oink!

DICAEOPOLIS

How keenly you both squeal at the word "figs"!
Someone fetch some figs from inside   805
for the little piggies.
(*tossing figs to the girls*)
                    Will they eat them? Good heavens,
how they slurp them down. Holy Heracles!
Where are these piggies from? Evidently from Hungary!

MEGARIAN

Well, they didn't bolt down all the figs;
I managed to pick up this one for myself.   810

DICAEOPOLIS

By god, they're a delightful pair of creatures.
How much will the piggies cost me? Name your price.

MEGARIAN

This one here for a bunch of garlic;
the other one, if you like, for only a peck of salt.

DICAEOPOLIS

I'll take them. Wait here.

MEGARIAN

All right.   815
Dicaeopolis goes inside.
Hermes of Traders, may I sell that wife of mine
on such terms, and my own mother too!
Enter INFORMER

INFORMER

Your nationality, sir?

MEGARIAN

                       Megarian, a piggy-dealer.

INFORMER

In that case, I shall expose these piggies here
as contraband, and you as well!

MEGARIAN

                       Here we go again,   820
back to where our troubles first began!

INFORMER

You'll regret that Megarian talk. Surrender that sack!

MEGARIAN

Dicaeopolis! Dicaeopolis! I'm being exposed!

DICAEOPOLIS

(*running out*)
By whom? Who's exposing you?
(*flicking his straps*)
                       Market Commissioners,
why don't you keep these informers out of here?   825
(*to the Informer*)
Who taught you to expose without a wick?[126]

INFORMER

I'm not to expose our enemies, then?

DICAEOPOLIS

You'll regret it
if you don't run off and do your informing elsewhere.

INFORMER runs away.

MEGARIAN

What a curse this is in Athens!

DICAEOPOLIS

Never mind, Megarian. Take this garlic and salt,   830
the price you asked for the little piggies,
and best of luck to you.

MEGARIAN

Luck's not native to us.

DICAEOPOLIS

If I was being meddlesome, let it be on my head.[127]

MEGARIAN

Little piggies, even without your father, try
to get salt with the loaf you gobble, if anyone gives you one.   835

Exit Megarian; Dicaeopolis takes the girls into his house.

CHORUS[128]

The man is truly blessed. Didn't
you hear how his enterprising plan
is progressing?
The man will reap a bumper crop
by sitting in his market.
And if some Ctesias intrudes[129]
or any other informer,   840

he'll be sorry if he hangs around.
Nor will anyone else vex you
by cutting into the queue,
nor will Prepis[130] smear off
his candy-assedness on you,
nor will you bump into Cleonymus;[131]
wearing a bright cloak, you'll saunter through,   845
and Hyperbolus[132] won't run into you
and infect you with his lawsuits.

Nor in your market will you meet
Cratinus[133] strolling about
with an adulterer's cut[134]
done with a straight razor,
an Artemon "the miscarried," [135]   850
too hasty with his poetry,
his armpits smelling nasty,
son of a father from the Goat d'Azur.

Nor again in your market
will the thoroughly depraved Pauson[136] ridicule you, nor will
Lysistratus,[137]
the disgrace of Cholargus,   855
soaked in the slough of despond,
ever freezing and starving
more than thirty days
in every month.

Enter a THEBAN with his slave Ismenias, both carrying wares and
accompanied by Pipers.

THEBAN[138]

Heracles bear witness, my shoulder's damned weary.   860
Put the pennyroyal down easy, Ismenias.
And all you pipers who are here with me from Thebes,
puff on those bones to the tune of "The Dog's Asshole."

Dicaeopolis enters.

DICAEOPOLIS

Stop, damn you! Away from my doorway, you hornets!
Where did these dadblasted buzz-pipers   865
fly to my door from, these sons of Chaeris?[139]

THEBAN

By Iolaus,[140] you've done me a favor there, friend.
All the way from Thebes they've been puffing behind me
and blowing my pennyroyal blossoms to the ground.
But if you like, buy some of the goods I've got,   870
some fowl or some four-wingers.

DICAEOPOLIS

Welcome, my baguette-eating Boeotian!
What have you got?

THEBAN

               Just everything good that we Boeotians have:
marjoram, pennyroyal, rush mats, lamp wicks,   875
ducks, jackdaws, francolins, coots,
wrens, grebes.

DICAEOPOLIS

               Then you've hit my market like a fowl nor'easter!

THEBAN

And yes, I've also got geese, hares, foxes,
moles, hedgehogs, cats, badgers,
martens, otters – and Copaic eels.[141]   880

DICAEOPOLIS

O you who bring mankind's most delectable cutlet,
permit me to greet the eels, if you've got them!

THEBAN

(*producing an eel*)
Most venerable mistress of fifty Copaic maidens,[142]
step forth here and grant your favors to our host!

DICAEOPOLIS

O dearest one, and one so long desired,   885
you have come, the heart's desire of trygic choruses[143]
and dear to Morychus![144] Servants, fetch
me forth the brazier and the fan.

These are brought out, followed by Dicaeopolis' children.

Children, look at the excellent eel
that's arrived after six years, so sorely missed.   890
Say hello to her, kids, and I'll provide coals
for you in honor of this lady guest.[145]
Now place her on her bier, "for not even in death
may I ever be parted from you," enshrouded in beet![146]

THEBAN

And how am I going to be paid for her?   895

DICAEOPOLIS

I guess you'll give her to me as market tax.
But if you're selling any of these other things, speak up.

THEBAN

I'm selling everything here.

DICAEOPOLIS

                    All right, name your price.
Or would you rather take some barter back home?

THEBAN

                    I will!
Something that's found in Athens but not among Boeotians.   900

DICAEOPOLIS

You'll probably want to trade for Phalerian sprats,
or pottery.

THEBAN

                    Sprats or pottery? We have them back home.
No, something that's absent among us, but plentiful here.

DICAEOPOLIS

I've got it! An informer: pack him up
like crockery and export him.

THEBAN

Twin Gods, 905
I'd surely make a sizeable profit by importing one,
one filled with lots of deviltry, like a monkey.

DICAEOPOLIS

And look here: Nicarchus[147] is coming to denounce us.

Enter NICARCHUS

THEBAN

He's not very big.

DICAEOPOLIS

But every inch of him's bad!

NICARCHUS

These wares, whose are they?

THEBAN

These are mine, 910
from Thebes, as Zeus is my witness.

NICARCHUS

In that case,
I hereby expose them as contraband.

THEBAN

What's the matter with you,
declaring war and battle upon my birdies?

NICARCHUS

And in addition, I shall denounce *you*.

THEBAN

What have I done?

NICARCHUS

I'll explain it to you for the bystanders' benefit.   915
You're importing lamp wicks from hostile territory.

DICAEOPOLIS

So you're actually denouncing him because of a lamp wick?

NICARCHUS

Yes, this could set the shipyard afire!

DICAEOPOLIS

A wick, a shipyard?

NICARCHUS

                          I reckon.

DICAEOPOLIS

                          In what way?

NICARCHUS

A man from Boeotia could put it on a beetle's back,   920
light it and send it into the shipyard
through a water main, waiting for a stiff north wind.
And once the fire caught hold of the ships,
they'd be ablaze in no time.[148]

DICAEOPOLIS

                          Damn and blast you,
they'd be ablaze from a beetle and a wick?   925
Hits him with the straps.

NICARCHUS

I call witnesses!

DICAEOPOLIS

                          Put his mouth under arrest.
Give me some sawdust so I can pack him like pottery
before I hand him over, so he won't get broken in transit.

CHORUS LEADER

strophe
Dear fellow, pack the merchandise
nicely for our foreign friend,   930
so that he can carry it
without breaking it.

DICAEOPOLIS

I'll take care of that, because
– listen – it makes a chattering
and fire-cracked noise,
altogether godforsaken.

CHORUS LEADER

Whatever will he use it for?   935

DICAEOPOLIS

It will be a pot for every purpose:
a bowl for mixing evils, a mortar for pounding lawsuits,
a lampstand to expose outgoing officials,
and a cup for blending trouble.

CHORUS LEADER

antistrophe
But how could anyone feel safe   940
using a pot like this
around the house,
when it's always making so much noise?

DICAEOPOLIS

It's sturdy, sir, so
it will never get broken,
even if it's hung head-downwards
by its feet.   945

CHORUS LEADER

(*to the Theban*)
You're all set now!

THEBAN

I'll surely rake in a profit!

CHORUS LEADER

Rake away, most excellent guest;
toss him onto your load
and take him wherever you want, 950
an informer for every occasion.

DICAEOPOLIS

I had my hands full packing up the blasted wretch.
Now take your pottery and load it up, Boeotian.

THEBAN

Come here and get your shoulder under it, Ismenichus.

DICAEOPOLIS

Make sure you carry him back with care. 955
You certainly won't be carrying anything wholesome, but no matter.
And if you make a profit importing this shipment,
you'll make a fortune in the informer trade!

THEBANS depart; enter SLAVE.

SLAVE

Dicaeopolis!

DICAEOPOLIS

        What? Why are you yelling for me?

SLAVE

      Why?
Lamachus orders you, for this drachma here, 960
to give him some of your thrushes for the Pitcher Feast,[149]
and he orders a Copaic eel for three drachmas.

DICAEOPOLIS

Which Lamachus is it who orders the eel?

SLAVE

The awesome, the tough-as-leather, who brandishes
the Gorgon as he shakes "three o'ershadowing crests"![150]   965

DICAEOPOLIS

No deal, by Zeus, not even if he gave me his shield.
Let him shake those crests of his for salt-fish.[151]
And if he squawks about it, I'll summon the commissioners.
Slave runs away.
I'll take this load for myself and go inside,
lofted on wings of thrushes and blackbirds.   970
DICAEOPOLIS goes inside.

CHORUS

strophe
Have you seen him, all you people, the smart
and exceedingly sagacious man,
seen what fine merchandise, thanks to his truce,
he's got for sale?
Some of his things are useful
around the house, while others   975
should be eaten hot.

CHORUS LEADER

To this man all bounties are supplied spontaneously.
I will never welcome the War God into my house,
nor will he ever sing the Harmodius Song[152]   980
reclining at my side, for he is an unruly fellow drunk.
When we enjoyed every bounty, he crashed our party
and inflicted all kinds of damage, upending, spilling,
and fighting; and the more I kept inviting him
"to drink, recline, take this cup of fellowship,"   985
the more he kept setting our vine props afire
and violently spilling the wine from our vines.

CHORUS

antistrophe
He's in flight to his dinner
and grand indeed are his thoughts;
as a token of his life style

he's tossed out these feathers before his door.
O Reconciliation, companion
of Aphrodite the fair
and the beloved Graces,

CHORUS LEADER

I didn't realize what a lovely face you have!   990
How I wish that some Eros could bring you and me together,
like the one in the painting who wears a garland of rosettes![153]
Or perhaps you think I'm an absolute geezer?
Ah but if I got hold of you, I think I could still strike home three times.
First, I'd shove in a long rank of tender vines,   995
and beside that some fresh fig-shoots,
and thirdly a well-hung vine branch – this oldster would! –
and, around the whole plot, a stand of olive trees,
so that you and I could anoint ourselves for the New Moon feasts.[154]

Enter HERALD.

HERALD

Hear this, people! According to ancestral custom, drink your pitchers   1000
when the trumpet sounds; and whoever is the very first to drink it off
will win a wineskin the size of Ctesiphon![155]
*The eccyclema is rolled out, revealing Dicaeopolis' Slaves and Womenfolk
as they prepare the feast. Dicaeopolis enters from the house.*

DICAEOPOLIS

You slaves, you women, didn't you hear?
What are you doing? Don't you hear the herald?
Braise the hare-fillets, roast them, turn them, pull them   1005
off the skewers quickly, string the garlands.
Hand me the skewers, so I can spit the thrushes!

CHORUS

strophe
I envy you your well-laid plan,
and more so your well-laid table,
sir, here before us.   1010

DICAEOPOLIS

What will you say when you see
the thrushes being roasted!

CHORUS

You're right about that too, I think.

DICAEOPOLIS

Start poking up the fire!

CHORUS

Did you hear how master-chef-ily,   1015
how subtly and how gourmettily
he takes the job in hand?
Enter DERCETES.[156]

DERCETES

O woe is me!

DICAEOPOLIS

                        Heracles! Who's this?

DERCETES

A man ill-fated!

DICAEOPOLIS

                        Then keep it to yourself.

DERCETES

Dear friend, since you've got a truce all to yourself,   1020
measure out some peace for me, even if for five years.

DICAEOPOLIS

What's the matter?

DERCETES

I'm shattered; I've lost my pair of oxen!

DICAEOPOLIS

Where?

DERCETES

At Phyle; the Boeotians rustled them.[157]

DICAEOPOLIS

Thrice ill-fated man! And you're still wearing white clothes?

DERCETES

And by god, those two oxen supported me   1025
with all the manure I could want!

DICAEOPOLIS

So what do you want now?

DERCETES

I've ruined my eyes, sobbing for my oxen.
But if you care at all for Dercetes of Phyle,
anoint my eyes with some peace, right away!

DICAEOPOLIS

You rascal, I don't happen to be a public doctor!   1030

DERCETES

Come on, I'm begging you; then maybe I could recover my oxen!

DICAEOPOLIS

It's impossible. Go squawk to Pittalus' people.[158]

DERCETES

No, please drip me just one drop of peace
into this fennel stalk right here!

DICAEOPOLIS

Not even a teensy peep! Go and grieve somewhere else.   1035

DERCETES

Ah, poor me! My little beasts of burden!
Dercetes trudges off.

CHORUS

antistrophe
The man's discovered in his treaty
something delightful, and evidently
won't share it with anyone.

DICAEOPOLIS

You, pour the honey on the sausage;   1040
grill the squid.

CHORUS

Did you hear his ringing tones?

DICAEOPOLIS

Broil the eels.

CHORUS

You'll kill us with hunger,
me and my neighbors, with the smell,   1045
and with your voice too, shouting such orders.

DICAEOPOLIS

Broil these here, and grill these nicely.
Enter a BEST MAN with a Bridesmaid.

BEST MAN

Dicaeopolis!

DICAEOPOLIS

                        Who's that? Who's that?

BEST MAN

A bridegroom has sent you these cuts of meat
from his wedding feast.

DICAEOPOLIS

A fine gesture, whoever he is.   1050

BEST MAN

And he asks you, in return for the meat –
so he won't have to go on campaign but can stay home and screw –
to pour just one spoonful of peace into this tube.

DICAEOPOLIS

Take the meat back, take it back and don't offer it to me!
I wouldn't pour a drop for a thousand drachmas.   1055
But who's this girl here?

BEST MAN

                    The bridesmaid,
who wants to give you a private message from the bride.

DICAEOPOLIS

Well, now, what's your message?

(*she whispers in his ear*)

                    Dear gods, how droll
the bride's request is! Her very earnest request to me is,
that the bridegroom's cock be allowed to stay at home![159]   1060
Bring the treaty over here; I'll give some to her and her alone,
since she's a woman and doesn't deserve the war.
Hold the tube over here, this way, ma'am.
Do you know how it's done? Tell the bride this:
whenever they call up troops, with *this*   1065
she should rub her husband's cock at night.
Best Man and Bridesmaid depart.
Take the treaty away. Bring me the wine ladle,
so I can draw wine and pour it into the pitchers.

CHORUS LEADER

But look, a man speeds toward us with furrowed brows,
as if he has some dire news to report.   1070

Enter FIRST MESSENGER.

FIRST MESSENGER

Ah, hardships and battles and Lamachuses!

LAMACHUS

(*emerging from his door*)
Who makes a racket round my bronze-bossed halls?

FIRST MESSENGER

The generals have ordered you this very day,
to take your crests and your ambuscades on the double
and march out in the snow to guard the passes.   1075
They've received a report that, around the time of the Pitchers and Pots,
Boeotian bandits plan to stage a raid.

Exit First Messenger.

LAMACHUS

Oh generals more numerous than capable!
Isn't it terrible that I'm not even allowed to join the feasting?

DICAEOPOLIS

Hooray for the polamical expedition!   1080

LAMACHUS

Alas and damn the luck, are you now mocking me?

DICAEOPOLIS

(*picking up a locust from the table*)
Would you like to fight, you four-feathered Geryon?[160]

LAMACHUS

Alas,
what an order the messenger messaged me!

DICAEOPOLIS

Alas, what is this second messenger running up to tell me?

Enter SECOND MESSENGER.

SECOND MESSENGER

Dicaeopolis!

DICAEOPOLIS

What is it?

SECOND MESSENGER

Go along to dinner   1085
right away, and take your hamper and your pitcher;
the Priest of Dionysus is inviting you!
But hurry; you've held up dinner a long time.
Everything else is standing at the ready:
couches, tables, pillows, coverlets,   1090
garlands, perfume, tasty tidbits; the whores are there;
cakes, pastries, sesame-crackers, rolls,
dancing-girls, Harmodius' beloveds,[161] pretty ones!
But hurry up, as fast as you can!

Exit Second Messenger.

LAMACHUS

I'm under a bad sign!

DICAEOPOLIS

It serves you right, for signing up with a big Gorgon!   1095
(*to a slave*)

Close up, and someone pack my dinner!

LAMACHUS

Boy, boy, bring my mess kit out here to me.

DICAEOPOLIS

Boy, boy, bring my picnic basket out here to me.

LAMACHUS

Get the seasoned salt, boy, and the onions.

DICAEOPOLIS

For me the fish-fillets; I'm sick of onions.   1100

LAMACHUS

Bring me a fig-leaf, boy, full of stale salt fish.

DICAEOPOLIS

And you can bring me a stuffed fig leaf; I'll cook it when I get there.

LAMACHUS

Bring here the twin plumes from my helmet.

DICAEOPOLIS

Bring me the pigeons and the thrushes.

LAMACHUS

So fair and white the ostrich plume!   1105

DICAEOPOLIS

So fair and brown the pigeon meat!

LAMACHUS

Mister, stop laughing at my weapons.

DICAEOPOLIS

Mister, please stop looking at my thrushes.

LAMACHUS

Bring out the crest case with the triple crests.

DICAEOPOLIS

And give *me* a casserole with the hares' meat.   1110

LAMACHUS

What, have moths consumed my crests?

DICAEOPOLIS

What, am I to eat the hare stew before dinner?

LAMACHUS

Mister, will you please stop addressing me.

DICAEOPOLIS

I'm not; my boy and I have been having an argument for a while now.
(*to his slave*)
Do you want to bet, and have Lamachus decide it,   1115
whether locusts are tastier, or thrushes?

LAMACHUS

Oh! What impudence!

DICAEOPOLIS

He's strongly for the locusts.

LAMACHUS

Boy, boy, take down my spear and bring it out here.

DICAEOPOLIS

Boy, boy, you take the sausage off and bring it here.

LAMACHUS

Come, let me draw the case off my spear.   1120
Ready, hold on, boy.

DICAEOPOLIS

And you, boy, hold on to *this*.

The slave holds the skewer while Dicaeopolis removes the sausage.

LAMACHUS

Bring me the staves, boy, to support my shield.

DICAEOPOLIS

Bring out the baguettes to support mine (*rubbing his belly*).

LAMACHUS

Bring hither my buckler round and Gorgon-bossed.

DICAEOPOLIS

And give me a flat-cake round and cheese-bossed.   1125

LAMACHUS

Isn't this what men call flat insolence?

DICAEOPOLIS

Isn't this what men call delicious cake?

LAMACHUS

Boy, you pour on the oil.
(*buffing his shield*)
                    In this bronze
I see an old man about to be prosecuted for cowardice.

DICAEOPOLIS

And you pour on the honey.
(*gazing into the cake*)
                    Here too an old man is visible,   1130
telling Lamachus, son of Gorgasus,[162] to go to hell!

LAMACHUS

Hand hither, boy, my warlike corslet.

DICAEOPOLIS

Boy, fetch me forth a corslet too – my pitcher.

LAMACHUS

In this I bolster me to meet the foe.

DICAEOPOLIS

In this I bolster me to meet my fellow drinkers.   1135

LAMACHUS

Boy, bind my bedding to the shield.

DICAEOPOLIS

Boy, bind my dinner to the picnic basket.   1138

LAMACHUS

And I shall carry the mess kit by myself.   1137

DICAEOPOLIS

And I'll grab my cloak and be leaving.

LAMACHUS

Enclasp and raise the shield, boy, and be off.   1140
It's snowing! Brrr, I've wintry business!

Exit Lamachus in one direction.

DICAEOPOLIS

Pick up the dinner, I've festive business!

Exit Dicaeopolis in the other direction.

CHORUS LEADER

Good luck on your expeditions!
How dissimilar the paths you travel:
he'll wear a garland and drink;   1145
you'll stand watch and freeze.
He'll be sleeping
with a blooming girl,
getting his thingum squeezed.

CHORUS

strophe
Antimachus son of Drizzler,[163]   1150
the drafter of bills,
the composer of bad songs:

to put it bluntly,
may Zeus terribly eradicate him!
He's the one who, as producer[164]
at the Lenaea,
unkindly dismissed me[165]
without dinner.   1155
May I yet see him hungry for squid,
and may it lie grilled and sizzling by the shore
and make port safely at his table;
and then, when he's about
to grab it, may a dog snap it up   1160
and run away with it!

antistrophe

That's one curse for him; and here's another,
to happen to him in the night.
As he walks home shivering
after galloping his horse,   1165
I hope some drunkard –
mad Orestes![166]
knocks him on the head;
and when he wants to grab a stone
I hope in the darkness
he grabs in his hand a fresh-shat turd,   1170
and holding that glittering missile
let him charge at his foe, then miss him
and hit Cratinus!

A THIRD MESSENGER rushes in and bangs on Lamachus' door.

THIRD MESSENGER

Ye vassals of the house of Lamachus,
water, heat water in a little basin,   1175
make ready linen strips, wax salve,
oily wool, a bandage for his ankle!
The man's been wounded by a stake, jumping over a trench,
and twisted his ankle backwards and dislocated it,
and fractured his head by falling on a stone,   1180
and waked the sleeping Gorgon from his shield!
And <when he saw> the great plume had fallen <from his helmet>
against the rocks, he voiced a direful cry:
"O brilliant visage, now for the very last time
do I behold you, light of mine; I am no more!"   1185

This he said when he fell into a drainage ditch;
then he stood up and faced his fleeing men,
as he pressed and routed the brigands with his spear.

Enter Lamachus, wounded and bedraggled, supported by two SOLDIERS.

And here he is himself! Come, open the door!

LAMACHUS

Oh oh! Ah ah! 1190
Hateful as hell these icy pains; wretched am I!
I am undone, by foeman's spear struck down.
But it would be true agony 1195
if Dicaeopolis should see me wounded
and jeer at my misfortunes.

Enter Dicaeopolis, intoxicated, supported by two dancing girls.

DICAEOPOLIS

Oh oh! Ah ah!
What tits! How firm, like quinces!
Kiss me softly, my two bangles, 1200
one with open mouth, one with plunging tongue.
Because I'm the first to drain my pitcher!

LAMACHUS

O lamentable conjunction of my woes!
Ah, ah, my afflictive wounds! 1205

DICAEOPOLIS

Hey, hey! Hello there, little Lamachippus!

LAMACHUS

Accursed am I!

DICAEOPOLIS

                    (*to one girl*)
Smooching me, eh?

LAMACHUS

Beleaguered am I!

DICAEOPOLIS

(to the other girl)
Nibbling me, eh?

LAMACHUS

Woe is me, what a costly fray!   1210

DICAEOPOLIS

What, somebody made you defray their expenses at the Pitcher Feast?

LAMACHUS

Oh, oh, Healer, Healer!

DICAEOPOLIS

But it's not the Healer's Festival today.

LAMACHUS

Hold, o hold this leg of mine! Ouch!
Take hold, my friends!   1215

DICAEOPOLIS

And you two hold the thick of my cock;
take hold, my girls!

LAMACHUS

I reel, my pate smitten by a stone,
and swoon in darkness.

DICAEOPOLIS

I too want to go to bed; I have a hard-on,   1220
and want to fuck in darkness.

LAMACHUS

Bear me off to Pittalus' clinic,
with healing hands.

DICAEOPOLIS

Take me to the judges. Where's the King?[167]
Give me the wine-skin!   1225

LAMACHUS

A lance has pierced me through,
most woefully, to the bone!

Lamachus is borne away.

DICAEOPOLIS

(*holding up his pitcher*)
Look, this pitcher's empty!
Hail the Champion!

CHORUS LEADER

Hail then – since you bid me,
old sir – the Champion!

DICAEOPOLIS

And what's more, I poured the wine neat
and chugged it straight down!

CHORUS LEADER

Then Hail, old chap!
Take the wineskin and go.   1230

DICAEOPOLIS

Then follow me, singing
"Hail the Champion"!

CHORUS

Yes, we'll follow, in your honor,
singing "Hail the Champion"
for you and your wineskin.

Dicaeopolis leads the Chorus off in song.

Notes

1   The account of the war's origins in Thucydides is quite different, but the comic record in *Acharnians* and other plays reflects popular belief and attitudes: see Henderson 2017.

2   Fragments of *Telephus* are available in Collard and Cropp 2009.

3   Disguise physical and rhetorical is an important theme running through the play: the phony speakers of the Assembly scenes, the *Telephus* paratragedy, the Megarian's daughters disguised as piglets, the uniform and weapons of Lamachus, the multiform identity of Dicaeopolis himself.

4   The nature of this incident, variously explained by ancient commentators, is obscure; Aristophanes alludes to it again in 299–302, and it is assumed as a given in *Knights*. It was evidently a legal dispute and must have involved official misconduct on the part of Cleon and/or the Knights, but since we hear of no trial, Cleon may have "disgorged" the money by the settlement-procedure called *probolê*. Some think that the incident was not historical but happened in a comedy (*Babylonians*?), but the Knights seem to have played no role in comedy before *Knights* in 424 (cf. 377 ff., *Knights* 507 ff.) and the logic of the comic attacks depend on topical circumstances known to the audience.

5   Quoting Euripides, *Telephus* (fr. 720), where the preceding words were "he would perish wretchedly."

6   The great tragic poet and Marathon veteran (see n. 32), who had died about thirty years earlier, was a favorite of older men like Dicaeopolis; as a character in Aristophanes' *Frogs* (Lenaea 405) he represented the good old days, when Athens had defeated the Persians and built the empire. By special decree, his plays could be reproduced at the dramatic festivals and thus became the first "classic" repertoire.

7   The comic poets called this "frigid" tragic poet "Snow," cf. 138–40.

8   Or "once upon a calf" if Moschus is not a proper name; Dexitheus was a lyre-player known to have won a musical contest at the Pythian games.

9   A lyre player and piper often ridiculed in comedy for poor technique.

10 A hill west of the Acropolis that was the normal venue for Assembly meetings, which could accommodate as many as 6,000 citizens; in *Knights* the allegorical character Demos is represented as living there.

11 Citizens marked with the dye, as being late to enter or leave the Assembly, were liable to a fine.

12 The name, which appropriately means "divine on both sides of the family," is rare in Attica but attested in a contemporary list of members (*Inscriptiones Graecae* ii² 2343) of a private cult of Heracles in Cydathenaeum, Aristophanes' and Cleon's deme, along with Philonides (producer of several of Aristophanes' plays), Simon (one of the Knights in *Knights*, 242), and Antitheus, the father of Critylla, a character in *Lysistrata* (323) and *Women at the Thesmophoria* (cf. 898).

13 The genealogy suggests an association with the important cult of Demeter and Kore at Eleusis, which was centrally concerned with agricultural fertility.

14 Both Athens and Sparta sought money from the Great King of Persia, but old soldiers like Dicaeopolis will have despised him as a barbarian and as their one-time enemy.

15 The capital of Media and summer home of the Great King.

16 In 437/6, eleven years earlier; the one-year terms of archons were used to designate official years.

17 Common soldiers stood watch at the walls (Thucydides 2.13), while refugees from the countryside "took up quarters in the towers along the walls or indeed wherever they could find space to live in" (2.17).

18 A mythical king of Athens, punning on "unmixed" (*akraton* < *kerannumi*).

19 "Candy-ass" translates *katapygon*, literally a man who receives anal penetration; comic poets routinely assumed that political leaders had prostituted themselves for advancement. The term is also used more generally of cowardice and depravity.

20 Herodotus 1.133 does report that on their birthdays rich Persians might be served an ox, horse, camel, or donkey baked whole.

21 A populist politician of Cleon's type, regularly ridiculed by comic poets as a fat glutton, a coward, and (in comedies after *Acharnians*) a shield-thrower. The latter charge (unique in comedy) was serious, tantamount to desertion, though Cleonymus was evidently never officially charged. Probably the mockery recalls the general Athenian retreat at Delium in 424, when Cleonymus' fatness made him conspicuous and thus a suitable scapegoat.

22 His fist, to judge by the pronoun's gender.

23 Cleisthenes is ridiculed elsewhere as beardless and (therefore?) effeminate, and Strato as his lover. He was politically prominent and may be the Cleisthenes who presided over the trials of the oligarchic plotters of 411 (Lysias 25.25). If Sibyrtius, who ran a wrestling-school, was not really Cleisthenes' father, the joke may be sarcastic (wrestling being a manly activity) or may suggest that Sibyrtius had also enjoyed Cleisthenes sexually.

24 Beyond his relationship with Cleisthenes (cf. also *Knights* 1374), nothing is known about Strato.

25 The Prytaneum, a building in the agora, was used to entertain, at public expense, foreign ambassadors and Athenians returning from embassies. For exceptionally great services to the state, citizens could be rewarded with meals there for life.

26 The King of the Odrysai in Thrace, who had aided the Athenians in an abortive invasion of Macedonia four years earlier (Thucydides 2.95–101). Theorus is mentioned elsewhere as a crony of Cleon. Sitalces' son, Sadocus, had been made a citizen in 431 (Thucydides 2.29).

27 Taking literally, and in a pederastic sense, a familiar democratic metaphor that citizens should "fall in love with Athens," attested first in 458 (Aeschylus, *Eumenides* 852) and famously in Pericles' funeral oration (Thucydides 2.43). The pederastic formula "X is *kalos*" was inscribed on courtship gifts to boys.

28 The festival where children and new citizens became members of Athenian kinship-groups; here there may be a pun on *apate* ("deceit").

29 No co-operation of Sitalces with Athens is recorded after the Macedonian operation, and when he died later in this year he was succeeded not by his son Sadocus but by his nephew Seuthes, an ally of Macedonia.

30 For the savagery of Thracian mercenaries see Thucydides' account of their attack on Mycalessus in 413 (7.29).

31 The Greeks, in contrast to barbarians, did not practice circumcision. Since actual Odomantians were also uncircumcised, Dicaeopolis is simply being insulting or (more likely) exposing Theorus' troop as barbarian (and therefore contemptible) imposters; if so, they wore the large, circumcised phallus that in *Clouds* 537–39 Aristophanes lists among trite ways to raise a laugh.

32 Rowers on Athenian warships were paid one drachma per day.

33 As were fighting cocks.

34 Apparently this Assembly is as eager to adjourn as it was reluctant to convene. Although official business could be adjourned at a sign of divine displeasure, an individual's motion at a single drop of rain would in reality not suffice.

35 Veterans of the battle of Marathon in 490, who would have been at least 82 years old at the time of the play, were the oldest living generation and regarded as the greatest: they had repulsed the numerically superior Persians (fighting alongside the Spartans, it will have been remembered), established the democracy, and acquired the empire.

36 In this scene, Aristophanes makes a metaphor concrete, combining the literal meaning of the word *spondai* ("libations of wine") with its metonymic meaning "treaty": libation was part of the ceremony by which treaties were ratified.

37 Pitch was used to caulk ships and to flavor wines; *retsina* is still a popular and inexpensive Greek table wine.

38 Official delegations from Athens threatened allies inclined to revolt from the empire with severe punishment, like that meted out to the people of Mytilene in 427, although it was not as extreme as Cleon had urged (Thucydides 3.1–50).

39 The standard duration specified for treaties but not always attained: the thirty-year peace of 446 with Sparta lasted fifteen years, and the fifty-year treaty ratified in 421 would last barely six.

40 Festivals for Dionysus, celebrated in individual demes at various times and in various ways, began with a procession and featured musical (sometimes dramatic) events, dancing, and drinking. Because of the war, Dicaeopolis (like many of the spectators) had been unable to celebrate such a festival for six years. Here the scene is understood to change from the Pnyx to Dicaeopolis' farmhouse, or perhaps his temporary shanty in the city (see 72, with n.).

41 This famous athlete from Croton in Southern Italy commanded his city's ship at the battle of Salamis in 480.

42 The name (meaning "Son of Great-Strength") was borne by an archon of the Persian-War era and by a political enemy of Pericles (Plutarch, *Pericles* 35). As in satyr drama (but not in tragedy), members of a comic chorus can have names either generic or actual.

43 Punning on Pallene (an Attic deme) and *ballein* "pelt."

44 Marriageable girls were chosen by the community to be basket-bearers in processions, a great distinction that conferred honor upon the whole family: Dicaeopolis already benefits from his sole possession of peace.

45 That is, a solemn expression, as if there were the usual festival crowd (here there are only the spectators in the theater).

46 Such good-natured ribaldry was common in wedding ("hymenaeal") contexts. Here "farting" (implying laziness) is substituted for "fucking."

47 Girls in procession wore finery that might attract thieves; here *chrysia* (jewelry) puns on *cysos* (female genitals).

48 Personification of the large wooden phallus carried in Dionysiac processions.

49 Classical Greek men regarded the desire to sexually penetrate both boys (but not grown men) and women as normal, but they strongly disapproved of passive roles (oral or anal) for men.

50 *Lamachōn* (the name Lamachus, relatively rare, means "Great Battler") jingles with *machōn* "battles" but also alludes to the actual general Lamachus, who exemplifies the "hawkish" city, probably because of his name, but it was also convenient that his deme was Acharnae, cf. 568. He will appear later in the play (566 ff.) as the antagonist of Dicaeopolis, who exemplifies the city at peace.

51 A rare name at Athens but given to members of the chorus in *Wasps* and *Lysistrata* (in both cases representing very old men); the name is attested at the island of Aegina, however, with which Aristophanes had a connection (see 652–64).

52 Rape of someone else's slave was legally a form of assault, but trespassing and theft on the slave's part were mitigating factors; images of the phallic god Priapus, who guarded gardens and orchards, frequently bore inscriptions threatening rape as a punishment.

53 Speaking not as Acharnians (who have no reason to hate Cleon) but as Aristophanes' own chorus, they advertise his following year's Lenaean play, *Knights*, with a jibe at Cleon's trade. Similarly, Dicaeopolis can speak as actor (416) and on behalf of Aristophanes (377 ff., 496–508).

54 Literalizing a metaphor from Euripides' *Telephus* (fr. 706), where the hero tells Agamemnon that he will not withhold a just reply "even if a man with an axe were about to strike my neck."

55 For the parody of the hostage-scene in *Telephus* see Introduction.

56 For Greeks ancient and modern, "shaking out" one's clothing expresses or reinforces a remonstration, curse, or threat.

57 A spur of Mt. Parnes extended into Acharnae and furnished the wood burned to make Acharnian charcoal.

58 Referring to the popular courts, whose jurymen tended to be elderly and poor and were often suspected by wealthy litigants of voting vindictively from class bias, especially at the instigation of populists like Cleon. The court system and its jurymen are satirized in Aristophanes' *Wasps*.

59 An Attic stream noted for its loudness when in spate.

60 For Cleon's action against Aristophanes following the production of *Babylonians* see Introduction.

61 A tragic and dithyrambic poet with long hair and thus capable of hiding himself as effectively as the mythical "cap of Hades" (the name means "unseen"), which made its wearer invisible (like the Tarnhelm of Norse mythology).

62 Sisyphus, a mythical king of Corinth, was proverbial for cunning.

63 Among tragic poets Euripides was especially fond of such paradoxical phrases, here comically true also of his doorman.

64 Here we first learn the hero's name. The deme Cholleidae was not far from Acharnae; why Dicaeopolis is associated with it is unclear. It may simply pun on *cholos* "lame;" although that theme has yet to be introduced (line 411), it may have been a standing joke about Euripides.

65 The *eccyclema* was a platform which could be wheeled out of the stage-building to represent its interior.

66 In his plays Euripides often upended conventional notions about outward status and inward virtue, including the portrayal of noble personages in desperate circumstances. Dicaeopolis' inability to recall Telephus in particular allows Aristophanes to review examples; more were to come as Euripides' career continued, indicating their continuing popularity with audiences.

67 Oeneus, King of Calydon, deposed by his nephews in favor of his brother Agrius, became an impoverished exile. In Euripides' lost play, Oeneus is returned to power by his grandson Diomedes.

68 Phoenix was falsely accused by his father's concubine of trying to seduce her, made an unconvincing defense speech, and was blinded and exiled.

69 Euripides had portrayed the castaway Philoctetes dressed in animal skins and living on the charity of the Lemnians.

70 Bellerophon tried to scale Olympus on the winged horse, Pegasus, but was thrown and crippled when Zeus sent a gadfly to vex the horse.

71 For the play see Introduction.

72 Referring probably to *Thyestes*, in which the title character is banished for seducing the wife of his brother, Atreus.

73 In *Ino*, the title character disappears in the mountains while serving as a bacchant and is later retrieved by her re-married husband, Athamas, and brought home disguised as a captive.

74 This prop will keep the issues of identity and foreignness visually before the spectators.

75 Implying that the spectacle was more impressive than the poetry.

76 Aristophanes, for reasons unclear, often refers to Euripides' mother as an impoverished hawker of wild herbs. In the fourth century, this kind of insult would be legally forbidden (see General Introduction, Section VI.2).

77 The speech of Dicaeopolis (overtly channeling Aristophanes' own case) is modelled on Telephus' speech to the Greeks, in which he claims that the Mysians were justified in defending themselves and so could not be charged with treason; see Introduction.

78 A portmanteau word combining *tragoidia* "tragedy" and *trygan* "harvest" (especially of new wine, *tryx*) and used to designate comedy that somehow incorporates or contrasts with tragedy.

79 In the prior year's comedy, *Babylonians*, which was produced at the Greater Dionysia.

80 Tribute payments from Athens' subject allies were presented at the Greater Dionysia in the spring, when allied troops would be mustered for the campaign season.

81 The line is baffling in context, unless there was a joke whose meaning is irrecoverable: Greek *achyra* means "chaff" (inedible discard, implying that metics were not present, which is very unlikely as well as pointless) or possibly "bran" (an inferior product of grain, and thus a gratuitous insult). Wilson 2007 therefore deletes the line as an intrusive quotation.

82 An allusion to the great earthquake that devastated Laconia ca. 464 and that many attributed to the anger of Poseidon following the Spartans' execution of some members of their subject population (helots), who had taken refuge in his temple at Cape Taenarum at the south-western tip of the Peloponnese.

83 The metaphor from counterfeit coin amounts to an accusation that the men in question were not native Athenians and therefore not entitled to citizen rights, such as denouncing black marketeers. Such "informers" (*sycophantai*) would operate not from civic duty but as extortionists and blackmailers; such an informer is portrayed later in the play (818 ff.).

84 On the suspicion that they had been imported without payment of duties.

85 The game of cottabus, in which drinkers tossed wine-lees at a target, was associated with dissolute behavior.

86 Women-stealing as a *casus belli* is a motif found in the mythology of the Trojan War (e.g. the *Iliad* and the Cyclic Epics) and the Persian War (cf. Herodotus' *Histories* book 1), and it may have figured in the *Telephus* too. That Aristophanes names the prostitute, however – a lover of Alcibiades (716 n.), according to the scholia – suggests that this incident had some basis in reality.

87 Popular gossip held that Aspasia, an immigrant citizen of Miletus who lived with Pericles as his unmarried wife and bore him a son, procured free-born women, or even groomed prostitutes, for him. In Aristophanes' *Peace* 603–15 a different personal motive for starting the war is attributed to Pericles.

88 Pericles' detractors, comic poets among them (see Appendix for further examples), regarded Pericles' power as tyrannical and compared him to Zeus. Here the war is attributed to very personal motives, much as in 440 Pericles' enemies had accused him of siding with the Milesians in their war against Samos in order to please Aspasia, a Milesian native.

89 For this decree of 432 see Thucydides 1.39, 67, 144 (also mentioned in Aristophanes' *Peace* 609); Aristophanes models his parody of the decree on a "drinking song" by Timocreon of Rhodes (*PMG* 731).

90 Seriphus, a small cycladic island, was one of the least important Athenian allies, and indeed proverbial for insignificance.

91 See 270 n. Lamachus plays the part of Achilles in *Telephus* versus Dicaeopolis' Telephus.

92 The Gorgon was a mythical female monster whose face literally petrified anyone who saw it.

93 A double insult: in one sense "skin my cock" means "circumcise me with your sword" (for this barbaric practice see 158 n.), in another it means "make my foreskin retract" by stimulating an erection (Dicaeopolis sarcastically claims to find Lamachus' stage phallus arousing).

94 Lamachus was the least wealthy of contemporary commanders and thus a good choice to exemplify the theme of corruption: promoting the war for personal gain.

95 Here, as in the opening scene, is the theme of civic apathy: poor attendance at Assembly (there was no official quorum in this period).

96 None of the men mentioned here is certainly identifiable, though the only political figure from Diomeia known in this period is the Philoxenus ridiculed in Aristophanes' *Clouds* 686 and *Wasps* 84. The name of the Chaonians, a warlike people of Epirus, is used here and elsewhere in comedy to pun on Greek *chaos* "void" or *chaskein* "gape." Camerina and Gela (suggesting *gelos* "laughter") were Sicilian towns; Catagela is a comic coinage suggesting *katagelos* "a joke."

97 "Coalson": the Acharnians are given invented names appropriate to charcoal burning, their chief local industry.

98 "Ember," "Totewell," and "Oakson."

99 Evidently referring to Megacles, who like Pericles was of the Alkmaeonid family and thus typified the bluest blood; here he is so identified in order to emphasize his non-Athenian ancestry on his mother's side (she was Eretrian).

100 Lamachus' debts will have resulted from his poverty, Megacles' from his extravagance.

101 Since both Megara and Boeotia were enemies of Athens, none of their goods could be imported or traded. But this restriction no longer applies to Dicaeopolis, and we will presently see him trading with them.

102 The verse form in which the speeches of a parabasis (see General Introduction, Section IV) were most often written, and the usual way to refer to its speech on behalf of the poet, for which the Chorus apparently "doffed" (actually or metaphorically) their play-specific character.

103 Here referring to the poet, as the following lines make clear; the actual producer (i.e. trainer of the chorus) was Callistratus.

104 Perhaps, with Bentley's emendation, "the source of rich rewards for you" (cf. 641).

105 Referring to misadministration by the Athenians rather than local corruption, which would have been insulting to the allies in attendance and thus contradict the claim made in the following lines.

106 The Great King of Persia (cf. 61 n.); for these contacts cf. Thucydides 4.50.

107 By the terms of the treaty of 445 Aegina, hitherto an ally of Athens, was guaranteed autonomy (Thucydides 1.67); on the eve of the war the Spartans accused the Athenians of violating the guarantee (ibid. 1.139). In 431 the Athenians settled the island with their own colonists, expelling the Aeginetans (ibid. 2.27), who were finally restored by the Spartans in 405 (Xenophon, *HG* 2.2.9). Our passage suggests that Aristophanes had a connection to Aegina (family or property), which Cleon may have used to question his Athenian citizenship.

108 Appeals to divinities to join a dance are typical of all Greek choral poetry. Here the Muse is invited to bring musical and poetic inspiration appropriate to the imagined occasion (preparing a feast in the Acharnian countryside), and therefore is singular and personalized rather than plural or generic.

109 Tithonus, mortal husband of the goddess Dawn, asked Zeus for immortality but forgot to include agelessness, so that he eventually withered away to a mere squeaking voice.

110 The device used in lawcourts to time each litigant's speech.

111 See 182 n.

112 The name, meaning "grappler," appears also in Eupolis' comedy *Spongers* (fr. 179) as a hanger-on of Callias, but is unattested outside comedy; it may be a nickname, or generic for litigators.

113 Thucydides, son of Milesias, at this time nearly 80 years old, had been Pericles' principal rival until he was exiled for ten years in 443. Upon his return he tried to make a comeback by prosecuting Pericles' friend, the philosopher Anaxagoras. But his career came to an end in the trial mentioned here, when he became tongue-tied during his defense speech.

114 Cephisodemus' son, Euathlus, is mentioned elsewhere in comedy as a zealous prosecutor (e.g. *Wasps* 592); apparently there was an Asiatic on his mother's side of the family, non-Athenian women having been eligible for marriage before the enactment of the citizenship law of 451 (see General Introduction, Section II). Scythians were familiar barbarians at Athens, where because of their skill as archers many were owned by the city and used as policemen.

115 A cult-title of Demeter, whose relevance to this context is hard to discern; evidently an original allusion to someone Thucydides could have out-wrestled in his prime has somehow been replaced in the transmitted text.

116 Alcibiades, nephew of Pericles, was in 425 only 25 years old; he would later become one of the leading generals and politicians of the Peloponnesian War period, and one of its most notorious personalities.

117 See 624 n.

118 The Athenians regarded Megarians as crude bumpkins, and their local style of comedy as reliant on low-brow humor (see *Wasps* 57 n.).

119 The following exchange plays on the double sense of Greek *choiros* = "pig(let)" (a staple meat and sacrificial animal) and "hairless/young vulva" (cf. 781–82); compare English "pussy" and (regional American slang) "pigmeat" (virgin).

120 A god associated with both trade and trickery.

121 At Eleusis, where initiands brought suckling pigs with them to sacrifice in the preliminary ceremonies.

122 A Megarian hero who had an annual festival there.

123 In Greek "tail" was slang for penis (cf. German *Schwanz*).

124 At Athens Aphrodite did not normally receive piglets as sacrificial offerings (in mythology her lover, Adonis, had been killed by a boar); but the Megarian is thinking of her in her capacity as the goddess of sexual enjoyment, continuing the double meaning of *choiros*.

125 The following items of food have phallic double meanings.

126 Perhaps referring to the Informer's lack of a comic phallus, marking him as unmanly.

127 Interference in other states' internal affairs was a common criticism of Athens.

128 After the parabasis it was normal for the Chorus, between episodes, to mock individual spectators.

129 A common name in Athens, probably chosen because it can mean "Grasper," cf. "Marpsias" at 702.

130 A Prepis, son of Eupherus, served as Council Secretary in 422/1.

131 See 89 n.

132 The first datable reference to Hyperbolus, owner of a lamp-making business, who after Cleon's death in 422 would replace him as the leading populist politician.

133 The leading comic poet of the generation before Aristophanes, now elderly but still active: he was competing in this very festival with his play *Stormtossed*, which won second prize behind *Acharnians*.

134 Referring either to a style fashionable among young roués or to one of the degrading forms of depilation meted out to adulterers.

135 Artemon was a contemporary of the sixth-century poet Anacreon, who for some reason assigned him the epithet *periphoretos* "borne in a litter" or "notorious" (F 372 and 388), which Aristophanes transforms into *periponeros* "very wicked."

136 An impoverished painter known for caricatures, jokes, and riddles.

137 Of several known contemporaries by this name the likeliest candidate is the politician Lysistratus mentioned in *Knights* 1266 and *Wasps* 787–95, 1308–13 as a poor man (or as affecting the plain Spartan style of dress) and a jokester.

138 Like the Megarian, the Theban (also from an enemy state, though this time a prosperous one) speaks in his native dialect.

139 See 16 n.

140 Heracles' nephew and fellow hero.

141 From Lake Copais in NE Boeotia, and a great delicacy.

142 Adapted from an address to Thetis in Aeschylus' *Award of the Arms* (F 174).

143 Parodying tragic scenes of reunion, suitably to the moment, when Dicaeopolis' wartime deprivations are past.

144 A wealthy gourmand.

145 Dicaeopolis seems to tease his children: instead of a real treat, they get to set up the grill.

146 "for not even . . ." is quoted from Euripides, *Alcestis* 367–8 (Admetus to his dying wife), with "enshrouded in beet" substituted for "the woman who alone has been faithful to me."

147 Otherwise unknown.
148 For a Boeotian incendiary device actually deployed in the following year, see Thucydides 4.100.
149 The Pitcher Feast (Choes) was celebrated on the second day (of three) of the Anthesteria, a great mid-winter festival honoring Dionysus. The pitcher in question (the *chous*) held about three quarts. Among the many festivities were drinking contests and a state banquet to which guests were invited by the priest of Dionysus. Also relevant to our play, with its quasi-hymeneal ending, was the sacred marriage between the wife of the King Archon (the official in charge of the state religion) and Dionysus.
150 The phrase is taken from Aeschylus, *Seven Against Thebes* 384, where it refers to Tydeus, after whom Lamachus apparently named his own son.
151 Among the cheapest foods.
152 A traditional patriotic drinking song celebrating Harmodius and his friend Aristogeiton, who in 514 assassinated Hipparchus, the brother of the last Athenian tyrant, Hippias, an act recalled as having paved the way for democracy; four versions are preserved.
153 A painting by the great Zeuxis, a contemporary of Aristophanes, "in the temple of Aphrodite at Athens," according to the scholia.
154 The first day of a new month was the occasion for religious and social festivities.
155 Evidently this man (otherwise unknown) had a belly of impressive size.
156 The name (very rare) means "bright-eyes" and so has comic point, but there was in fact a contemporary Dercetes of Phyle (see 1028), no doubt a supporter of the war.
157 A rural Attic deme on Mt. Parnes (348 n.) near the Boeotian frontier; it is the setting for Menander's *Dyscolus*.
158 Pittalus, mentioned also in *Wasps* 1432, evidently held an appointment as a public doctor, paid by the city to treat the indigent.
159 Dicaeopolis' own report of the request: in actuality, a respectable woman would not use obscenity in the presence of a man unrelated to her.
160 The winged monster Geryon, slain by Heracles, was traditionally triple-bodied.
161 Punning on the opening words of the Harmodius song (see 980 n.) and casting Harmodius as an active heterosexual and not the junior partner in a pederastic relationship (for which see Thucydides 6.54).
162 A jocular play on "Gorgon": the real Lamachus was the son of Xenophanes.
163 Otherwise unknown; the scholia say that "son of Drizzler" refers to Antimachus' habit of spraying saliva when he talked.
164 A producer was expected to hold a banquet for his troupe after the competition.
165 They speak as the generic comic chorus.
166 That is, someone like the mythical hero who wandered insane to Athens after killing his own mother.
167 I.e., the judges of the drinking contest, perhaps with an allusion to the dramatic judges as well. For the King (Archon) see 961 n.

3. *Knights*

Introduction

Knights was produced at the Lenaea of 424 and, like *Acharnians* the year before, won the first prize; Cratinus (ridiculed as a has-been in the play) placed second with *Satyrs*, and Aristomenes third with *Porters*. *Knights* was the first play that Aristophanes produced in his own name; to the many who asked why he had waited so long he replies that he had wanted to feel fully prepared artistically (512–50). With *Knights* Aristophanes made good his promise at the previous year's Lenaea to "cut Cleon up into shoe-leather for the Knights" (*Acharnians* 299–302), thus pursuing the feud[1] that had begun with Cleon's judicial retaliation after *Babylonians* in 426 (*Acharnians* 378–82, 502–7). *Knights* would provoke further retaliation, which was subsequently settled by an agreement that Aristophanes later boasted of having finessed (*Wasps* 1284–91). Unfortunately for his detractors, however, Cleon watched *Knights* from the front row as a new national hero, more powerful than ever, this time for having overseen, and successfully taking credit for, a pivotal victory at Pylos that changed the course of the war (see Thucydides 4.1–41).

In the preceding summer, Athenian troops under the command of the general Demosthenes had stranded a force of Spartan infantrymen on an island off Pylos in the western Peloponnese, and there followed a strategic and diplomatic impasse: the Athenians hesitated to attack the island because the Spartans had a reputation for invincibility on land, and the Spartans hoped to retrieve the infantrymen somehow. Cleon rose in the Assembly and challenged the generals to attack the Spartans; when Nicias, a veteran commander and spokesman for the generals, demurred, the Assembly invited Cleon to assume Nicias' authority over the Pylos campaign. Cleon accepted, vowing to kill or capture the Spartans within three weeks, and then fulfilled his vow, returning to Athens with 120 Spartan hostages. This was a key victory for Athens: it diminished the legend of Spartan invincibility on land, and the hostages could be used to force an end to the annual invasions of Attica. It also made a hero of Cleon, who was honored with a civic crown, lifetime meals in the Prytaneum (see 168 n.), and front-row seating at festivals and in the theater. And it seemed to vindicate Cleon's warlike policies, so that the Athenians now rejected out of hand all proposals to negotiate a peace treaty and

DOI: 10.4324/9781003159407-3

instead embarked on an ambitious and aggressive series of campaigns. One of these, which involved Nicias and the Knights, is invoked in the play as a counterbalance to Cleon's victory at Pylos (595–610).

Knights is a remarkably savage indictment, both personal and political, of Cleon[2] and the other populist politicians who succeeded Pericles upon his death in 429 and hailed from the commercial not the landed or military elite, and also of the complacency of the demos in following their self-serving advice. In Aristophanes' eyes, Cleon and his ilk were crude and dishonest but cunning tradesmen of questionable ancestry, who had made their way into politics as blackmailers and malicious prosecutors; who stoked partisan division and distrust, particularly by attacking, and falsely impugning the morality and patriotism of the well-to-do and better educated; who claimed to fight for the people but instead deceived them into authorizing the sort of reckless military and imperialistic adventures that would enable them to enrich themselves by embezzlement, extortion, and bribe-taking; who impoverished both rich and poor by their rapacity; who corrupted the morals of the young; and who tarnished the glory, and were threatening the future, of Athens. The play resounds with the noise, the vulgarity, the violence, and the selfish cynicism that for Aristophanes typified the new, populist style of Athenian leadership. As for the victory at Pylos, Cleon had simply stolen the credit from the real generals.

To dramatize these spacious themes Aristophanes devised, with brilliant economy of means, an allegorical plot as simple as a folk tale. Paphlagon, a new-bought barbarian slave (transparently representing Cleon)[3] has gained control of the house (Athens) of Master Demos, a decrepit old man. This Paphlagon has entranced Demos with lies, petty gifts (e.g. jury-pay), fawning, and flattery, while hoarding Demos' wealth to himself and, by slander (in the courts) and extortion, alienating the home-bred slaves (traditional elite leaders) from Demos, whom they had loyally served. Two of these Slaves (unnamed, but suggesting Demosthenes and Nicias, the other two principals in the Pylos action) hit on the idea of stealing Paphlagon's oracles, where among his phony oracles they discover an authentic one, stating that he is but the latest in a succession of sellers (demagogues), each worse than the last.[4] This oracle predicts that Paphlagon, a tanner, is to be overthrown by someone who outdoes him at his own villainous methods: a sausage seller.[5] Such a Sausage Seller appears as if by divine providence, and the Slaves recruit him by promising power and the wealth that it brings, and reassure him by promising that as allies he will have not only the Knights ("fine gentlemen a thousand strong, who detest him") but "all fine and upstanding citizens, and every one of the spectators who is smart, and myself along with them, and the god will lend a hand" (225–29).

There follows a series of contests in which the Sausage Seller outdoes Paphlagon at his own demagogic techniques: the initial rounds, overseen by the First Slave and the Chorus of Knights (303–460), verify Sausage Seller's ability to outdo Paphlagon, and the later rounds, staged for Demos on the Pnyx, culminate, as divinely predicted, in Paphlagon's dismissal in favor of Sausage Seller. In a private duet with the Knights, Demos claims not to be as gullible as he seems

(1111–50), but in fact he does not return to his senses until Sausage Seller magically restores him to his youthful prime, revealing him as he was in the days of Marathon and Salamis when he, and the Athenians, were at the pinnacle of their greatness. Guided by the now-honest Sausage Seller, Mr. Demos promises never to repeat his recent mistakes, and in traditional comic fashion he is sent back to his farm with a "well-hung boy" and two girls, who represent peace-treaties. The caricature of Demos, which includes extensive ridicule and criticism of the actual demos, is elitist but not (at least straightforwardly) oligarchic: Demos' misrule is the fault of the wicked-slave demagogues and does not disqualify him to be master: his temporary enthrallment is cured when he is rejuvenated, and he seems ready to carry on as he had in the past, when he was more the kind of partner that the elites hoped for when they embarked on the democratic experiment.

Knights differs from *Acharnians* and *Wasps* in featuring a Chorus that is both the hero's supporter and defender from the start, and that articulates its own reasons for joining the action, as do the Slaves who initiate it.[6] Their partnership with the lowly Sausage Seller demonstrates that everyone, rich and poor alike (223–24), would be better off without Paphlagon/Cleon, who has no supporters onstage, and it enables Aristophanes to level every charge or complaint against him that might appeal to any segment of the audience. The Knights, never before represented as a chorus, are happy to join in because Cleon had attacked them too (507–11): their enmity, assumed, not part of the allegory or fantasy, had already been mentioned in *Acharnians* (5–8, 299–302). As in *Acharnians* Aristophanes aligns himself with his hero, as a young and inexperienced poet and civic champion ready to take the measure both of Cleon and of rival poets (507–50).

The Knights (two are named: 242–43) attack Paphlagon (and the actual Cleon by name: 976) independently of Sausage Seller and the First Slave. Their role is to defend the elite, that is, Cleon's wealthy victims (247–48, 258–65, 326–27, 973–84), and to celebrate Athens' military valor, claiming to "want only to fight nobly in defense of the city and its native gods" (565–77, cf. 597). They offer as an example their own recent victory at Solygeia under Nicias (595–610, cf. Th. 4.42–45), which even Paphlagon unwittingly admits showed courage (267–68), and for which, unlike Cleon's victory at Pylos, the Knights can honestly claim credit. Otherwise the war, which had been the main focus in *Acharnians*, is only tangentially noted (792–804 Cleon's intransigence; 805–9 the hoped-for return to the countryside; 1388–94 provision of peace treaties), while the play's attack focuses on demagogic leadership.

In subsequent years Aristophanes expressed greater pride in *Knights* than in any other of his plays, for its artistry, courage, novelty, and importance (*Nu.* 546–50, *Ve.* 1029–37, *Pax* 748–61), claiming to have inaugurated a new genre of "demagogue comedy"[7] and boasting of his own personal courage, and success, in attacking the most dangerous of the demagogues (see esp. *Clouds* 549–62). Despite Eupolis' counter-claim that he had shared in the composition of *Knights* (fr. 89), Aristophanes' pride seems justified on both counts. Subsequent "demagogue" comedies by rival poets do seem to have followed the template of *Knights*, and they were produced only after Cleon's death and against lesser targets. And although the play's allegorical mode of attack has its own artistic advantages (Cleon could be portrayed as even more horrible than he actually was, and his demagogic character could be generalized as a new type of politician), the fact that no character is explicitly identified with an actual person – Cleon is named only once in the play (976) in a choral song expressing the Knights' own feelings and is not explicitly associated with the character Paphlagon – suggests fear of retaliation. In the event, Cleon did retaliate, indicting Aristophanes a second time (see *Acharnians*, Introductory Note), this time settling out of court (*Wasps* 1284–91).

Knights did not turn the demos against Cleon in that year's election of generals, as Aristophanes had hoped (*Clouds* 581–7) – after his success at Pylos, Cleon could hardly be denied a command – but it did win the first prize, and in concentrating its fire not on Cleon's military ability but on his deficiencies in leadership and character, the poet's attack may well have drawn blood.

Characters

FIRST SLAVE of Demos
SECOND SLAVE of Demos
SAUSAGE SELLER
PAPHLAGON, steward of Demos
DEMOS of Pnyx Hill

Mute Characters

SLAVE BOY
PEACE TREATIES, two girls
SLAVES of Demos
CHORUS of Athenian Knights

The scene building represents the house of Demos.

FIRST SLAVE rushes from the house.

FIRST SLAVE

Yow, ow ow ow! Damn it all! Yow ow ow!
That damn new-bought slave Paphlagon,[8] damnably
may the gods destroy him, him and all his schemes!
Ever since he turned up at our house,
he's been getting the home-bred servants beaten nonstop.   5

SECOND SLAVE comes out of the house.

SECOND SLAVE

Yes, most damnably of all Paphlagons,
him and all his slanders!

FIRST SLAVE

Poor fellow, how goes it?

SECOND SLAVE

Damn badly, just like you.

FIRST SLAVE

Then join me over here,
so we can wail a tune by Olympus[9] as a wind duet.

FIRST AND SECOND SLAVES

Boo hoo hoo hoo hoo hoo hoo!   10

FIRST SLAVE

Why are we standing here wailing? Shouldn't we be looking
for some way out of this, instead of just sobbing on?

SECOND SLAVE

All right, what way? Do tell.

FIRST SLAVE

No, you tell me;
I don't want to squabble about it.

SECOND SLAVE

Not me, by Apollo, no!

FIRST SLAVE

Come on, out with it; then I'll tell you.   15

SECOND SLAVE

"Could you but say for me what I must say!"[10]

FIRST SLAVE

But I haven't got an inkling.

SECOND SLAVE

> All right, how can I possibly
express it in smart Euripidean fashion?

FIRST SLAVE

Please don't, please don't, don't chervil me over![11]
Just think of some kind of shimmy away from the master!　　　　20

SECOND SLAVE

Very well, say "wall lets," and put it together like this.

FIRST SLAVE

All right, "wallets."

SECOND SLAVE

> Now next,
after "wallets," say "go way."

FIRST SLAVE

> "Go way."

SECOND SLAVE

> Very good!
Now, as if you were masturbating, slowly say
"wallets" first, then "go way," and then start speeding it up.　　　　25

FIRST SLAVE

Wallets, go way, wallets go way, lets go AWOL!

SECOND SLAVE

> There,
wasn't that nice?

FIRST SLAVE

> Zeus yes, except I'm afraid this doesn't bode well
for my skin.

SECOND SLAVE

How so?

FIRST SLAVE

Because masturbators get their skins peeled off.

SECOND SLAVE

Well then, our best option, given the circumstances,   30
is to make for some god's image and kowtow.

FIRST SLAVE

What do you mean, "immmage?" Say, do you really believe in the gods?

SECOND SLAVE

Sure.

FIRST SLAVE

What's your evidence?

SECOND SLAVE

Because I'm godforsaken. Isn't that enough?

FIRST SLAVE

You've certainly convinced me. But we should consider alternatives.   35
Would you like me to explain the situation to the spectators?

SECOND SLAVE

Not a bad idea. But let's ask them one favor:
to make it obvious to us by their expressions
whether they're enjoying our dialogue and action.

FIRST SLAVE

Now I'll tell them. We two have a master   40
with a farmer's temperament, a bean chewer, prickly in the extreme,
known as Mr. Demos of Pnyx Hill,[12] a little codger cranky

and half-deaf. Last market day this fellow
bought a slave, Paphlagon, a tanner,
an arch criminal, and an absolute slanderer.   45
He sized up the old man's character,
this rawhide Paphlagon did, and crouching before the master
he flattered and fawned and toadied and swindled him
with odd tidbits of waste leather, saying things like,
"Mr. Demos, do have your bath when you've tried but one case."   50
"Here's something to nibble, wolf down, savor: a 3-obol coin."[13]
Shall I serve you a snack?" And then Paphlagon swipes
whatever one of us prepared and presents it to the master
with his compliments. Why, just the other day
when I'd whipped up a Spartan cake at Pylos,[14]   55
by some very dirty trick he outmaneuvered me, snatched the cake,
and served it up himself – the very one *I'd* whipped up!
He shuts us out and won't allow anyone else to court the master;
no, when master's having supper he stands by
with a leather swatter and bats away the politicians.   60
And he chants oracles; the old man's crazy about sibyls.
And since he sees that the master's a mooncalf,
he's devised an artful technique: he tells outright lies
about the household staff; then we get whippings,
and Paphlagon chases after the servants,   65
shaking us down, shaking us up, demanding bribes, making threats
like:
              "See how I got Hylas that whipping?
You'd better be reasonable or you've lived your last day!"
And we pay the price, because if we don't, we get pounded
by the master till we shit out eight times as much.   70
(*to Second Slave*)
So now, my friend, let's figure out quick
what sort of path we ought to take, and to whom.

SECOND SLAVE

Our best option, my friend, is that "go way."

FIRST SLAVE

But nothing at all can get past Paphlagon;
he keeps an eye on everything. He's got one foot   75
in Pylos, and his other foot in the Assembly.
He's got his legs spread out so far apart
that his asshole's smack dab over Buggerland,
his hand's in Shake Downs, and his mind's on Crimea.

SECOND SLAVE

Then our best option is death.

FIRST SLAVE

           Well, figure out   80
what would be the most manly death for us.

SECOND SLAVE

Let's see then, what would be the most manly?
Our best course is to drink bull's blood:
we should choose the death Themistocles chose.[15]

FIRST SLAVE

God no, we should toast the Good Genie with neat wine instead![16]   85
Maybe that way we might think up a good plan.

SECOND SLAVE

Listen to him, neat wine! You're always looking for an excuse to drink.
But how could a tipsy person think up a good plan?

FIRST SLAVE

Oh, is that right? You babbling bucket of bilgewater!
How dare you cast aspersions on the creative power of wine?   90
Can you come up with anything more effective than wine?
Don't you see, it's when people drink that they
get rich, they're successful, they win lawsuits,
they're happy, they can help their friends.
So quick, go in and fetch me a jug of wine;   95
I want to water my wit and come up with something smart.

SECOND SLAVE

Oh dear, what are you and your drink going to get us into?[17]

FIRST SLAVE

A good spot! Now go in and get it.
First Slave goes inside.
I'm going to stretch out on the ground,
because if I get drunk I'm going to spatter everything
with bits of plans and thoughts and ideas.   100

Second Slave returns with a jug, a cup, and a garland.

SECOND SLAVE

It's a lucky thing I wasn't caught in there
swiping the wine!

FIRST SLAVE

Say, what's Paphlagon doing?

SECOND SLAVE

That devil's been licking the sauce off confiscated goodies,[18]
and now he's belly-up drunk on his hides, snoring away.

FIRST SLAVE

Come on then, slosh me the wine neat, a double   105
libation.

SECOND SLAVE

Here you are; now pour one for the Good Genie.

FIRST SLAVE

Down the hatch, down goes the libation for the Pramnian Genie![19]
Oh Good Genie, that idea's yours, not mine!

SECOND SLAVE

Tell me, please, what idea?

FIRST SLAVE

Quick, go steal Paphlagon's oracles   110
and bring them out here while he's still asleep.

SECOND SLAVE

OK, but I'm afraid I may transform our Genie from Good to Bad.

Second Slave goes inside.

FIRST SLAVE

Well then, I'll just pass myself the jug,
to water my wit and come up with something smart.

Second Slave returns with a scroll.

SECOND SLAVE

Paphlagon's snoring and farting so loud,   115
he didn't notice when I grabbed his holy oracle,
the one he most closely guarded.

FIRST SLAVE

                    You're a genius!
Give it here, so I can read it. And you pour me a drink
pronto. Let's have a look; what's in here then?
What prophecies! Give me the cup, give it here quickly!   120

SECOND SLAVE

Here. What's the oracle say?

FIRST SLAVE

                    Pour me a refill!

SECOND SLAVE

In the prophecies it says "pour me a refill"?

FIRST SLAVE

Oh Bacis![20]

SECOND SLAVE

                    What is it?

FIRST SLAVE

                    Quick, give me the cup!

SECOND SLAVE

Bacis certainly made use of that cup!

FIRST SLAVE

Paphlagon, you scum! So that's what you were guarding all that time: 125
you scared shitless about the oracle concerning yourself!

SECOND SLAVE

               Why?

FIRST SLAVE

Herein lies the secret of his own destruction!

SECOND SLAVE

Well? How?

FIRST SLAVE

               How? The oracle explicitly says
that first of all there arises a seller of hemp,
who will be the first to manage the city's affairs.[21]   130

SECOND SLAVE

That's one seller. What's next? Tell me!

FIRST SLAVE

After him there's another one again, a seller of sheep.[22]

SECOND SLAVE

That makes a pair of sellers. And what's in store for him?

FIRST SLAVE

To hold power, until another champion more disgusting
than he arises, whereupon he perishes.   135
For his successor is a seller of hides, our Paphlagon,
a robber, a screamer, with a voice like the Cycloborus in spate.

SECOND SLAVE

So the sheep seller was fated to perish at the hands
of a hide seller?

FIRST SLAVE

That's right.

SECOND SLAVE

Heaven save us!
If only one more seller would appear somehow!   140

FIRST SLAVE

There *is* one still to come, with an extraordinary trade.

SECOND SLAVE

Tell me, please, who is it?

FIRST SLAVE

You want me to tell you?

SECOND SLAVE

Certainly!

FIRST SLAVE

The man who shall destroy this one is a sausage seller.

SECOND SLAVE

A sausage seller! Holy Poseidon, what a trade!   145
Come on, where will we find this man?

FIRST SLAVE

Let's look for him!

SECOND SLAVE

Wait, here he comes,
On his way to market, as if by providence!²³

Enter SAUSAGE SELLER carrying his stand and paraphernalia.

FIRST SLAVE

O blessed
Sausage Seller, step this way, this way, dear fellow,
the city's savior and ours now come to light!

SAUSAGE SELLER

What is it? Why are you hailing me?

FIRST SLAVE

Come over here and find out   150
how fortunate you are, how greatly blessed.

SECOND SLAVE

All right then, take his stand off of his hands
and brief him on the gist of the god's oracle;
I'll go in and keep Paphlagon under surveillance.

Second Slave goes inside.

FIRST SLAVE

Now then, first put down that gear of yours,   155
then kowtow to the earth and to the gods.

SAUSAGE SELLER

Very well; what's it all about?

FIRST SLAVE

You're lucky! You're rich!
You're nothing now, but tomorrow supremely great!
You're the captain of flourishing Athens!

SAUSAGE SELLER

Look, mister, why don't you let me soak my tripe   160
and hawk my sausages, instead of making fun of me?

FIRST SLAVE

Tripe, you idiot? Look out there:
do you see the ranks of this assembled host?[24]

SAUSAGE SELLER

I do.

FIRST SLAVE

You're going to be top dog of them all,   165
of the market, the harbors, and the Pnyx![25]
You'll trample the Council, dock the generals,
put people in chains and lock them up, suck cocks in the Prytaneum![26]

SAUSAGE SELLER

Me?

FIRST SLAVE

Yes, you! And that's not all.
Here, climb higher up, on this stand,
and survey all the islands[27] panoramically.   170

SAUSAGE SELLER

I see them.

FIRST SLAVE

What else? Ports and cargo ships?

SAUSAGE SELLER

Sure.

FIRST SLAVE

Then how can you deny that you're flourishing?
Here then, swivel your right eye toward Caria
and your other eye toward Carthage.[28]

SAUSAGE SELLER

I'll really flourish if I swivel myself wall-eyed!   175

FIRST SLAVE

No, the point is that all this is yours to buy and sell!
You're going to be a tremendous big shot;
this oracle here says so.

SAUSAGE SELLER

Tell me, just how
does a sausage seller like me become a big shot?

FIRST SLAVE

That's precisely why you are going to be great,   180
because you're loudmouthed, low class, and down market.

SAUSAGE SELLER

Even I don't think I deserve great power.

FIRST SLAVE

Uh oh, what makes you say you don't deserve it?
You sound as though you've got something good on your conscience.
Don't tell me you come from a distinguished family!

SAUSAGE SELLER

Heavens no,   185
they're nothing if not low class.

FIRST SLAVE

Congratulations, what blessed luck!
Right there you've got a fine start in politics.

SAUSAGE SELLER

Look, mister, I'm not even educated
except for reading and writing, and I'm damn poor at those.

FIRST SLAVE

The only thing that hurts you there is that you're only damn poor.   190
No, leadership of the people is no longer a job
for a man of education and good character,
but for the ignorant and disgusting. Please don't throw away
what the gods are offering you in their prophecies!

SAUSAGE SELLER

What does the oracle say, then?

FIRST SLAVE

By heaven,   195
it's a good one, rather intricate and subtly enigmatic:
"Yea, when the crook-taloned rawhide eagle shall snatch
in its beak the dimwitted blood-guzzling serpent,
even then shall perish the garlic brine of the Paphlagons,[29]
while to tripe sellers the god grants great glory,   200
unless they choose rather to sell sausages."

SAUSAGE SELLER

Well, how does this apply to me? Clue me in.

FIRST SLAVE

(*pointing to Cleon, sitting in the front row*)[30]
This Paphlagon here is the rawhide eagle.

SAUSAGE SELLER

And what's crook-taloned?

FIRST SLAVE

That's pretty self-explanatory:
with crooked hands he gets things by grabbing.   205

SAUSAGE SELLER

And what about the serpent?

FIRST SLAVE

That's quite obvious:
the serpent's long, and so is a sausage long;
and both sausage and serpent are blood guzzlers.
So the oracle says that the serpent will soon overpower
the rawhide eagle, if he isn't first melted by verbiage.   210

SAUSAGE SELLER

The prophecies are flattering, but it's an amazing idea,
me being fit to supervise the people.

FIRST SLAVE

Nothing's easier. Just keep doing what you're doing:
make a hash of all their affairs and turn it into baloney,
and always keep the people on your side   215
by sweetening them with fine gourmet bons mots.
You've got everything else a demagogue needs:
a repulsive voice, low birth, marketplace morals –
you've got all the ingredients for a political career.
Plus, the oracles and Delphic Apollo agree.[31]   220
(*extending the cup and garland*)
So put on this garland, pour a libation to the god Dimwit,
and see that you settle the man's hash.

SAUSAGE SELLER

                And who will be my ally?
He makes the rich tremble and the poor folk shit their pants.

FIRST SLAVE

But there are the Knights,[32] fine gentlemen a thousand strong,   225
who detest him and will rally to your side,
and all fine and upstanding citizens,
and every one of the spectators who is smart,
and myself along with them, and the god will lend a hand.
And never fear, he's not portrayed to the life: 230
none of the mask-makers had the guts
to make a portrait mask. But all the same,
he'll be recognized, because the audience is smart.

SECOND SLAVE

(*within*)
Heaven help me, Paphlagon's coming out!
Enter PAPHLAGON

PAPHLAGON

By the Twelve Gods, you two won't get away   235
with your unending plots against the people![33]
What's that Chalcidian cup doing here?[34]
It can only mean you're inciting the Chalcidians to revolt![35]
You two are goners, done for, you utter scum!

SECOND SLAVE

Hey, why are you running away? Please stay! O worthy   240
Sausage Seller, don't betray the cause!
Gentlemen of the cavalry, ride to our aid; now's the time!

Enter the CHORUS.

Simon,[36] Panaetius,[37] drive for the right wing!
(*to the Sausage Seller*)
The troops are nearby. Now turn back around and put up a fight!
The dust cloud's plain to see as they come closer,   245
galloping to the fray. Come on, put up a fight! Chase him! Repulse him!

First Slave and Sausage Seller join the attack.

CHORUS LEADER

Hit him, hit the scoundrel, the harrier of the horse troops,
the tax farmer, the chasm and Charybdis[38] of rapacity,
the scoundrel, the scoundrel! I'll keep calling him that,
because he acts the scoundrel many times each day.   250
Come on, hit him, pursue him, shake him up, mix him up,
loathe him as we do, give out with a war cry as you attack him!
Take care he doesn't get away; he knows the routes
Eucrates took to decamp straight to the hemp market![39]

PAPHLAGON

Elders of the jury courts, brethren of the three obols,[40]   255
to whom I cater by loud denunciations fair and foul,
reinforce me: I'm being roughed up by enemy conspirators!

CHORUS LEADER

And rightly so, since you gobble public funds before you're
      allotted an office;[41]
and like a fig picker you squeeze magistrates under review, looking to see
which of them is raw, which ripe or still ripening;   260
yes, and what's more, you scan the citizenry for anyone who's
      an innocent lamb,   264
rich and innocuous and afraid of litigation.   265
And if you hear of anyone who's apolitical and naive,   261
you drag him back from the Chersonnese,[42] trip him up with
      your slanders,   262
then twist his shoulder back and stomp on him.   263

PAPHLAGON

Are you Knights joining the attack on me? But gentlemen,
    it's on your behalf 266
that I'm being pummeled: I was just about to move a decree
    declaring it right for the city
to erect a monument in honor of your courage![43]

CHORUS LEADER

What a phony! Smooth as calfskin! See how far he'll go to get around us
and bamboozle us as if we were mere codgers? 270
Well, if he tries to <escape> this way, he'll get hit with *this*;
and if he tries to duck out that way, he'll butt against a leg!

PAPHLAGON

Ah, city! Ah, people! What sort of beasts are punching me in the guts?

SAUSAGE SELLER

There you go shouting, just as you're always turning the city upside down!

PAPHLAGON

Well, you're the first one I'm going to rout with that very shout! 275

CHORUS LEADER

Well, if you manage to beat him with your shouting, you're the
man of the hour;
but if he outdoes you in brazenness, we take the cake.

PAPHLAGON

I denounce this man here and accuse him of smuggling
plank steaks for Spartan triremes![44]

SAUSAGE SELLER

And I denounce this man, by Zeus, for running into the Prytaneum 280
with an empty gut and running out again with a full one![45]

FIRST SLAVE

Damn right, and for smuggling out what he shouldn't – bread, meat,
a fish fillet – goodies that Pericles[46] himself was never awarded.

PAPHLAGON

You two are dead meat now!

SAUSAGE SELLER

I'll shout three times as loud as you!   285

PAPHLAGON

I'll outbellow you with my bellowing!

SAUSAGE SELLER

I'll shout you down with my shouting!

PAPHLAGON

I'll slander you if you become a general!

SAUSAGE SELLER

I'll beat your back like a dog's!

PAPHLAGON

I'll harass you with quackeries!

SAUSAGE SELLER

I'll cut off your escape routes!   290

PAPHLAGON

Look at me without blinking.

SAUSAGE SELLER

I was raised in the markets too!

PAPHLAGON

One peep from you and I'll rip you apart!

SAUSAGE SELLER

Any blather from you and I'll cart you off like a load of dung!   295

PAPHLAGON

I admit I'm a thief; you don't.

SAUSAGE SELLER

I do so, by Hermes of the Markets![47]
And even when people see me do it, I swear I didn't!

PAPHLAGON

Then you're stealing someone else's tricks!
And I expose you to the Officers   300
for possession of sacred tripe belonging to the gods,
and with failure to pay the tithe on it.[48]

CHORUS

strophe
You filthy disgusting shout-downer, your brazenness
fills the whole land, the whole Assembly,   305
the taxes, the indictments and lawcourts,
you muckraker, you who have thrown our whole city
into a sea of troubles,   310
who have deafened our Athens with your bellowing,
watching from the rocks like a tuna fisher for shoals of tribute!

PAPHLAGON

I know where this long-term conspiracy was cobbled up!

SAUSAGE SELLER

If you don't know cobbling, I don't know sausage making.   315
You're the one who used to slant-cut the hide of a low-grade ox
so it looked thick and sell it to the farmers at a dishonest price;
before they'd worn it a day, it was two handbreadths wider!

FIRST SLAVE

By Zeus, he pulled that one on me too! It made for a huge laugh
at my expense from friends and fellow demesmen,   320
when I started swimming in my shoes before we got as far as Pergase![49]

CHORUS

So then, didn't you from the very start display
Shamelessness, that sole bulwark of politicians?   325
Trusting in her, you pluck the most fruitful foreigners,
second to none, while Hippodamus' son can only look on and shed tears.[50]
Ah, but another man has shown up,
much slimier than you, I'm delighted to say,
one who from the word go is obviously going to stymie and outdo you   330
in villainy and brazennesss
and flimflammery!

CHORUS LEADER

(*to Sausage Seller*)

Very well, since you were bred where men are what they are,
show us now what nonsense a decent breeding is.

SAUSAGE SELLER

Sure! I'll tell you what sort of citizen this one is.   335

PAPHLAGON

You still won't let me speak first?

SAUSAGE SELLER

Certainly not, because I'm sleazy too.

FIRST SLAVE

And if that doesn't make him yield the floor, tell him your ancestors
were sleazy too.

PAPHLAGON

You still won't let me speak first?

SAUSAGE SELLER

               Certainly not!

PAPHLAGON

               Certainly yes!

SAUSAGE SELLER

By Poseidon, no!
First to speak? I'll fight you for that here and now!

PAPHLAGON

I'm going to burst my seams!

SAUSAGE SELLER

I said, I won't let you. 340

FIRST SLAVE

Good heavens, let him! Let him burst his seams!

PAPHLAGON

Just what makes you so sure you're fit to speak against me?

SAUSAGE SELLER

Because I can speak too, and make a stew of everything.

PAPHLAGON

Speak, ha! A pretty speech you'd make if you stumbled into a case
you received fresh slaughtered; you'd take it in hand like a pro! 345
Want to know my opinion? The same as happens to most people
    has happened to you.
You probably spoke well in a bitty lawsuit against an immigrant foreigner,
after droning your speech all night long, babbling it to yourself
    in the streets,
swearing off wine, and rehearsing with your friends till you
    got on their nerves,
and then you started thinking you're a powerful speaker. You fool,
    what a delusion![51] 350

SAUSAGE SELLER

And what do *you* drink, to have fixed it so the city's now
gagged speechless by the thrust of your tongue, and yours alone?

PAPHLAGON

I'd like to know who in the world you compare me with! Me,
I'll polish off a plateful of hot tuna right now, wash it down with a pitcher
of neat wine, and then screw the generals at Pylos![52] 355

SAUSAGE SELLER

And as for me, it's cow belly and hog tripe that I'll
gobble down, and drink up the gravy, and then without washing my hands
I'll throttle the politicians and harass Nicias![53]

FIRST SLAVE

I like most of what you said, but one thing doesn't sit well with me,
that you mean to slurp up the political gravy all by yourself.   360

PAPHLAGON

But you won't eat up the Milesians' big fish and then run
    roughshod over them.[54]

SAUSAGE SELLER

But I will eat sides of beef and buy mining leases.[55]

PAPHLAGON

I'll jump into the Council and stir it up with brute force.

SAUSAGE SELLER

And I'll stuff your asshole like a sausage skin.

PAPHLAGON

And I'll drag you outside by the butt, upside down.   365

FIRST SLAVE

By Poseidon, if you drag him you'll have to drag me too!

PAPHLAGON

How I'll enjoy clamping you in the stocks!

SAUSAGE SELLER

I'll prosecute you for cowardice!

PAPHLAGON

Your hide will end up on my tanning bench!

PAPHLAGON

I'll use your skin for a loot bag!   370

PAPHLAGON

You'll be stretched out on the ground and pegged!

SAUSAGE SELLER

I'll make mincemeat of you!

SAUSAGE SELLER

I'll tweeze off your eyebrows!

SAUSAGE SELLER

I'll crop out your gizzard!

FIRST SLAVE

And by god, we'll jam   375
a peg in his mouth like butchers,
and yank out his tongue
and take a good brave look down to his
gaping   380
asshole, to see if he's measly![56]

CHORUS

antistrophe
So there really are temperatures hotter than fire, and speeches
more brazen than the brazen speeches heard in the city.   385
And our job turns out to be nothing so trifling <or slight>!
Attack him and make his head spin; don't set your sights low,
for now you've got him around the middle.

CHORUS LEADER

That's right, if you soften him up now in the first onslaught,
you'll find he's a coward; I know his character.   390

SAUSAGE SELLER

He's been that sort of character his whole life long,
and then he passes for a real man by reaping another man's harvest.[57]
And now those ears of corn he brought back with him,
he's clamped them in the stocks for parching, in hopes of selling them back.[58]

PAPHLAGON

I'm not afraid of you people, as long as the Council lives   395
and Demos's booby face gawps from his seat!

CHORUS

See how he keeps up his boundless brazenness
without even changing his usual color!
If I don't hate you, may I turn into a blanket in Cratinus' house[59]   400
and be coached by Morsimus
to sing in a tragedy![60]
Oh, you're everywhere, in everyone's business,
lighting on bribery's blossoms;
I hope you throw up your mouthful as easily as you found it.
Then I'll sing nothing but   405
"Drink, Drink on a Happy Occasion!"[61]

CHORUS LEADER

And I imagine Ulius, the old grain ogler,
would whoop a paean of joy and sing the Bacchebacchus.[62]

PAPHLAGON

By Poseidon, you aren't going to outshoot me in brazenness,
or I hope never again to share in the feast of Marketplace Zeus![63]   410

SAUSAGE SELLER

So help me the punches and blows from barber's shears
I've taken many times in many places since childhood,[64]
I'm sure I will overshoot you in all this, or else
I've grown this big on a diet of sops for nothing.

PAPHLAGON

Sops, like a dog? How can a total loser like you   415
eat dogfood and expect to fight a dog-faced baboon?

SAUSAGE SELLER

I swear, when I was a boy I had a lot more monkey-tricks.
I used to fool the butchers by saying things like,
"Look, boys, don't you see? Spring is here, there's a swallow!"
And just when they were looking up, I swiped some meat.   420

FIRST SLAVE

A most meaty machination; smart planning!
You got your booty, like eating nettles before the swallows come.

SAUSAGE SELLER

And I never got caught in the act, because if any of them spotted me,
I'd stash it up my crotch and swear to god I'm innocent.
So when one of the politicians saw me doing that he said,   425
"There's no way this boy won't someday govern the people."

FIRST SLAVE

That was a good guess! But it's obvious how he figured it out:
you perjured yourself about a robbery and took meat up your ass.

PAPHLAGON

I'll put a stop to your insolence, and I mean both of you.
I'll hit you like a hurricane, awesome and strong,   430
roiling land and sea every which way!

SAUSAGE SELLER

But I'll furl my sausages and let myself run fairly
before the waves, after bidding you fare-ill.

FIRST SLAVE

And I will man the bilges in case of a leak.

PAPHLAGON

By Demeter, you won't get away with the huge pile of money   435
you've filched from the Athenians!

FIRST SLAVE

                          Ahoy there, slacken the sheets!
He's ready to blow up a nor'easter, or a frame-upper.

SAUSAGE SELLER

I know all about the ten talents you got out of Potidaea.[65]

PAPHLAGON

What about it? Want to take one of those talents to keep quiet?

FIRST SLAVE

The gentleman would be glad to! Slacken the ropes;   440
the wind's dropping.

PAPHLAGON

You'll face charges <of bribe-taking,>
four of them at a hundred talents each!

SAUSAGE SELLER

And you'll face twenty for draft-dodging,
and more than a thousand for embezzlement!

PAPHLAGON

I say that you're descended from   445
the polluters of our Goddess![66]

SAUSAGE SELLER

And I say your grandfather was
among the bodyguards –

PAPHLAGON

                    What bodyguards? Go on.

SAUSAGE SELLER

– of Hippias' wife, Pursine![67]

PAPHLAGON

                    You scamp!

SAUSAGE SELLER

You crook!   450

FIRST SLAVE

Hit him a good one!

PAPHLAGON

    Ow! Help!
The conspirators are beating me!

FIRST SLAVE

Hit him a really good one!
Belly-punch him with your guts
and your tripe,   455
and see that you give the man his comeuppance.

CHORUS-LEADER

You're a prime cut of meat and surpass all men in guts,
appearing as savior to our city and us her citizens!
How well and adroitly you've mounted your verbal attack!
How can we find the praise to match our delight?   460

PAPHLAGON

By Demeter, I wasn't unaware how all this business
Was fabricated; no, I knew all along
how all of it was being bolted and glued!

SAUSAGE SELLER

And I'm on to what you're up to in Argos.   465
He pretends he's making the Argives our friends,   466
but he's down there cutting his own deal with the Spartans![68]   467

FIRST SLAVE

Uh oh, hadn't you better use some jargon from the blacksmith's?   464

SAUSAGE SELLER

And I know the design for this welding of his: 468
he's forging it on the men in irons.

FIRST SLAVE

That's good, that's good: meet his gluing with forging!   470

SAUSAGE SELLER

And men on the other side are helping him hammer it out.
And *you* may offer me bribes of silver or gold,
or send your colleagues around to visit,
but you won't talk me out of revealing all this to the Athenians.

PAPHLAGON

Quite the reverse: I'm off to the Council this very minute   475
to inform on all of you for your conspiracies,
your nocturnal meetings against the city,
all your plots with the Medes and their King,[69]
and that cheesy business with the Boeotians.[70]

SAUSAGE SELLER

So, what *is* the price of cheese in Boeotia?   480

PAPHLAGON

Oh by Heracles, I'll knock you flat!

EXIT Paphlagon.

FIRST SLAVE

Alright then, what's your idea? What's in your plan?
You'll show it to us now, if you really did hide
that meat up your crotch that time, as you claim you did,
because you've got to run in a flash to the Council Hall;   485
he's going to charge in there slandering
all of us and screaming that scream of his.

SAUSAGE SELLER

I'm off, then. But first I'll leave my tripe
and my butcher's knives right here.

FIRST SLAVE

Here now, smear this on your neck,   490
so you can slip out of his slanders.[71]

SAUSAGE SELLER

That's good, that's spoken like a coach!

FIRST SLAVE

Here now, take this and bolt it down.

SAUSAGE SELLER

How come?

FIRST SLAVE

You'll fight better, my boy, if you're primed with garlic.[72]
Now off with you!

SAUSAGE SELLER

I'm gone!

FIRST SLAVE

Now remember: 495
bite him, slander him, gobble up his comb,
and make sure you chew off his wattles before you return!

Sausage Seller runs off in the same direction as Paphlagon.

CHORUS

Go, and good luck, and may you accomplish
our aims, and may Zeus of the Marketplace
watch over you![73] I hope you're victorious there,   500
and come back to us
spangled with crowns!
But now we ask that you all listen
to our anapests,[74] you who are in your own right
well versed   505
in every kind of art.

CHORUS LEADER

If any old-time comic producer had tried to force us
to face the theater in a parabasis and make a speech,
he wouldn't easily have succeeded. But today our poet deserves it,
because he hates the same people we do, and dares to say what's right,   510

and nobly strides forth against the typhoon and the whirlwind.[75]
As to what he says surprises many of you and has you coming up
    to ask him about –
why he's waited so long to apply for a chorus in his own name –
he's authorized us to explain that to you. The gentleman says
that he wasn't lingering in that position out of thoughtlessness,
    but in the belief   515
that producing comedies is the hardest of all tasks,
for while many have courted this muse, few have enjoyed her favors;
and he was long aware that your tastes change every year,
and that you abandoned his predecessors as they grew older.
He knew what happened to Magnes as soon as the grey hairs appeared,   520
the poet who'd posted so many victories over his rivals' choruses:
though he vocalized all kinds of sounds – strumming, flapping,
singing Lydian, buzzing, dying himself green as a frog –
it wasn't enough; in his old age, though never in his prime,
he was booed, veteran that he was, because his power to mock
    was gone.[76]   525
Then he recalled Cratinus,[77] who once rode the high wave
    of your applause
and coursed through the open plains, from their moorings sweeping
oaks, plane trees, and enemies, and bearing them off uprooted.
At a party there was no song but "O Bribery Shod With Impeach Wood"
and "Builders of Handy Hymns," so lush was his flowering![78]   530
But now you see him driveling around town, his frets falling out,[79]
his tuning gone and his shapeliness all disjointed, but you feel no pity;
no, he's just an old man doddering about, like Conn-ass[80]
wearing a withered crown and perishing of thirst,
who for his earlier victories should be getting free drinks in the
    Prytaneum,[81]   535
and not driveling but sitting pretty in the front row next to Dionysus.
And what violent rebuffs Crates had to endure at your hands,[82]
who used to send you home with a low-cost snack,
baking up very witty ideas from his dainty palate.
And he merely survived, sometimes losing, sometimes not.   540
In dread of all that our poet kept delaying, and in addition, he held
that one should be an oarsman before handling the tiller,
and from there take charge of the bow and watch the weather,
and only then become a pilot in one's own right. So for all these reasons,
that he acted responsibly and didn't mindlessly leap in spouting
    rubbish: 545
raise a big wave of applause for him, and give him an eleven-oar cheer[83]
worthy of the Lenaea,
so that our poet may go away happy
and successful,
his shining head gleaming![84]   550

CHORUS

strophe
Poseidon, Lord of Horses,[85]
thrilling to the ring of horses' hooves
clashing like bronze, and their neighing,
and to the swift triremes   555
with their blue rams and their payloads,
and to the contest of youths
in their chariots, heading for the heights of glory
or the depths of ill fortune,
come join our dance, god of the golden trident,
master of dolphins at Sunium,[86]   560
son of Cronus at Geraestus,[87]
dearest of gods to Phormio[88]
and the Athenians
in time of war!

CHORUS LEADER

We want to praise our forebears for being   565
gentlemen worthy of this land and of the Robe,[89]
who in infantry battles and naval expeditions
were always victorious everywhere and adorned our city.
For not one of them ever reckoned the enemy's numbers,
but as soon as he saw them his spirit was defiant.   570
If in any battle they happened to fall on their shoulder,
they would slap off the dirt, deny they'd fallen,
and get back into the match. And not a single general
of old would have applied to Cleainetus[90] for a state subsidy;   575
whereas now if they don't get front row seats and free meals,
     they refuse
to fight. But we want only to fight nobly for the city and
     its native gods.
We ask nothing more, except for only this much:
if peace ever comes and we cease from toils,
don't begrudge us our long hair and fancy bathing kits.[91]   580

CHORUS

antistrophe
Pallas,[92] City Guardian,
mistress of the land
that is the holiest of all
and the most successful in war, poets,
and power,   585

come join us, and bring
our helper
in expeditions and battles,
Victory, our companion in choral dances,
who sides with us against our enemies.   590
Come then, appear to us, for you should
by all means bestow victory
on these gentlemen,
now if ever before!

CHORUS LEADER

We want to praise what we saw our horses accomplish.[93]   595
They deserve our eulogy, for a great many hardships
they have borne with us, invasions and battles too.
But we aren't too amazed at their actions on land,
considering how they jumped manfully aboard the horse transports
after buying canteens and rations of garlic and onions,   600
then sat to their oars like we humans,
dipped their blades, and raised a snort of "Heave Horse!
    Who'll dip his blade?
stroke harder! What are we doing? Pull harder, S-Brand!"
They jumped ashore at Corinth, and then the colts
made dugouts with their hooves and foraged for fodder.   605
Instead of mede clover they ate crabs,
whenever any crawled ashore and even fishing them from the deep.
So Theorus[94] claims a Corinthian crab declared:
"Lord Poseidon, it's awful if neither in the deep
nor on shore nor at sea will I succeed in escaping the Knights!" 610
Enter SAUSAGE SELLER.
My dearest and lustiest of men,
you had us so worried while you were gone!
Now that you've come safely back,
tell us how you fared in your contest.

SAUSAGE SELLER

How do you think? I'm a real Nicobulus![95]   615

CHORUS

strophe
Now that deserves from everyone
a shout of thanksgiving!
Ah, you've brought fine news
and done deeds far finer still,
so please tell me

the whole story plainly,
for I think   620
I'd travel a long way
to hear it. Very well, my
excellent fellow, speak boldly,
since we're all enjoying this!

SAUSAGE SELLER

Yes, the story of these events is certainly worth hearing.
I took right off from here, hot on his heels,   625
and there he was inside, breaking out thunderous phrases
and assaulting the Knights with his bombast,
launching mountainous tirades and calling them conspirators,
most persuasively. The ears of the whole Council
were as quickly overgrown by his lies as by weeds,   630
their eyes looked mustard, and their brows were knitted together.
When I saw that they were swallowing his story
and being fooled by his flimflammeries,
"Come on, you demons of Puffery and Quackery," I said,
"Come on, Foolery, Chicanery and Debauchery,   635
and you Marketplace where I was reared as a boy,
now give me boldness, and a ready tongue,
and a shameless voice!" As I was pondering this prayer,
some bugger validated it by farting on my lucky side.[96]
I kowtowed, then striking the turnstile with my ass   640
I knocked it from its hinges, and opening my mouth wide
I bellowed, "Councilmen, I've got good news
and want to be the first to announce it to you:
never since the war broke out upon us
have I ever seen sprats sold for cheaper prices!"   645
Right away their expressions turned sunny,
and they moved to crown me for my glad tidings. And I recommended
to them, making it their state secret,
that to be able to buy lots of sprats for a penny: immediately
confiscate all the bowls in the potters' market.   650
They applauded loudly and gaped at me in admiration.
But he caught on, that Paphlagon, knowing of course
the sort of line that especially pleases the Council,
and he made a proposal: "Gentlemen, I recommend,
in view of the happy events just reported,   655
a glad-tidings sacrifice of a hundred cows to the Goddess!"[97]
The Council switched its allegiance back to him.
When I realized I was being outplayed by his cow dung,
I raised his bid to two hundred cows
and advised that a thousand goats be vowed   660
to the Wild Maiden the very next day,[98]

if anchovies should sell for a hundred a penny.
The Council swung their heads back to me again.
He was stunned to hear it and started babbling away.
Then the magistrates and the policemen started to drag him away,   665
and the Councillors stood up hollering about the anchovies.
He kept begging them to hold on a moment
"until you find out what the Spartan herald has to say,"
says he, "because he's here to discuss a peace treaty!"
But all of them yelled back as from one mouth,   670
"A peace treaty now? How convenient, sir,
when they've just heard that anchovies are a bargain here!
We don't need a peace treaty; let the war drag on!"
And they hollered for the magistrates to adjourn,
then started jumping over the turnstiles every which way.   675
I cut ahead of them and bought up all the coriander
and as many leeks as there were in the marketplace,
then handed them out to the councilors
as a free gift when they needed seasoning for the sprats.
And they all praised and cheered me so extravagantly   680
that I've returned with the whole Council in my pocket
for a penny's worth of coriander.

CHORUS

antistrophe
Your fortune has been all
that defines the successful man,
and that rascal has met
another who far excels him
in greater rascality,   685
and intricate schemes,
and wheedling words.
But mind you plan how best to fight
the remaining rounds;
you've long known that in us
you have partisan allies.   690

Enter Paphlagon.

SAUSAGE SELLER

And here comes that very Paphlagon now,
driving a long ground swell and chopping and churning,
no doubt intent on pulling me under. What a brassy devil!

PAPHLAGON

If I'm the liar that I used to be, and still
can't destroy you, let me be blown to bits!   695

SAUSAGE SELLER

Your threats are music to my ears! Your fuming boasts
make me laugh, dance the shimmy, and crow!

PAPHLAGON

I won't go on living, by Demeter I won't,
if I don't devour you right off this earth!

SAUSAGE SELLER

If you don't devour me? Same goes for me if I don't   700
guzzle you down, even if swallowing you makes me burst!

PAPHLAGON

I'll destroy you, so help me the front row seat I won at Pylos!

SAUSAGE SELLER

Oho, front-row seat! How I'll love seeing you
exchange that seat for one in the very last row!

PAPHLAGON

By heaven, I'll clamp you in the stocks!   705

SAUSAGE SELLER

What a cranky temper! Here, what'll I give you to eat?
What's your favorite snack? Wallet?

PAPHLAGON

I'll rip out your guts with my fingernails!

SAUSAGE SELLER

I'll scratch out your free dinners in the Prytaneum!

PAPHLAGON

I'll haul you into court and get justice from you!   710

SAUSAGE SELLER

And I'll haul *you*, and out-slander you too!

PAPHLAGON

But Demos doesn't listen to anything you say, you creep,
whereas I can make a fool of him as much as I want.

SAUSAGE SELLER

You're pretty sure you've got Demos in your pocket.

PAPHLAGON

That's right; I know the sort of tidbits that he likes.   715

SAUSAGE SELLER

Sure, you feed him, just like the nannies: badly!
You chew some food and feed him a little morsel,
after you've bolted down three times as much yourself.

PAPHLAGON

And what's more, by god, thanks to my dexterity
I can make that Demos expand and contract.

SAUSAGE SELLER

Even my asshole can pull that very same trick!   720

PAPHLAGON

Mister, you won't get credit for putting me down in Council.
Let's go before Demos.

SAUSAGE SELLER

                    Nothing's stopping us.
All right, move along; don't let anything keep us.

Paphlagon knocks on Demos' door.

PAPHLAGON

Oh, Demos, come out here!

SAUSAGE SELLER

             Yes, sir,   725
do come out!

PAPHLAGON

            My dearest darling Demos,
come out and see what outrageous insults I endure!

DEMOS

(*within*)
What's all the shouting? Get away from my door!

DEMOS opens the door.
You've battered my harvest-wreath all to bits!
Paphlagon, who's doing you wrong?

PAPHLAGON

            For your sake,   730
this guy here and these young bloods are beating me up.

DEMOS

Why?

PAPHLAGON

Because I adore you, Mr. Demos, and because I'm your lover![99]

DEMOS

(*to Sausage Seller*)

And tell me, who are you?

SAUSAGE SELLER

            His rival for your love,
one who has long lusted for you and wanted to treat you right,
like many other fine upstanding people.   735

But because of him, we can't. You see,
you're like the boys who attract lovers:
you say no to the fine upstanding ones,
but give yourself to lamp-sellers[100] and cobblers
and shoemakers and leathermongers.   740

PAPHLAGON

Because I treat Demos right!

SAUSAGE SELLER

                    How so? Let's hear it.

PAPHLAGON

How? I got the jump on the general from Pylos,[101]
sailed down there and brought the Spartans back.

SAUSAGE SELLER

And when I was strolling around, I entered a shop
and filched a pot someone else had on the boil.   745

PAPHLAGON

I suggest you hold an Assembly right away,
Mr. Demos, to find out which of us is more
devoted to you, and decide, so you can cherish that one.

SAUSAGE SELLER

Yes, yes, do decide between us, but not on the Pnyx.

DEMOS

I wouldn't sit myself down anywhere else.   750
Forward, then! All be in attendance on the Pnyx!

All move into the orchestra, where Demos takes a seat on a rock.

SAUSAGE SELLER

(*aside*)

Oh blast my luck, I'm finished! When he's at home
the old fellow is the very shrewdest of men,
but whenever he's sitting upon that rock,
he gapes like someone chewing on dried figs!   755

CHORUS

strophe
Now you must spread all the sail you have,
and convey a commanding spirit and irresistible arguments,
with which to overthrow him. For your foe is wily,
good at working out what works in unworkable situations.
So advance on your man with the full force of a storm!   760

CHORUS LEADER

Now keep your eyes open, and before he attacks, you hoist
your dolphins[102] to the yardarms and lay your boat alongside.

PAPHLAGON

To Lady Athena, our Mistress of the City
I pray: if in service to the Athenian Demos
I have been the leading man, after Lysicles,[103] Cynna, and
    Salabaccho,[104]   765
may I continue to dine in the Prytaneum for doing nothing;
but if I hate you and don't stand alone in the forefront to fight for you,
may I perish, sawn in two and sliced up for harnesses!

SAUSAGE SELLER

As for me, Demos, if I don't love and cherish you, may I be sliced up
and boiled with mincemeat; and if you don't believe it,   770
may I be grated on this very table in pesto with cheese,
and be dragged by the balls with a meat hook to Potters' Field!

PAPHLAGON

Just how could any citizen cherish you more than I do, Demos?
First of all, when I was a Councillor,[105] I showed record profits
in the public accounts by racking people, or throttling them,
    or demanding a cut,   775
without regard for anyone's personal situation, so long as I could
    gratify you.

SAUSAGE SELLER

Demos, that's nothing to brag about; I'll do the same thing for you.
I'll snatch other people's loaves and serve them to you.
My first lesson to you is that he's not your friend or your partisan,
save only that he enjoys relaxing by your fire.   780
At Marathon you outdueled the Medes in defense of our country,[106]
and your victory bequeathed to our tongues matter for minting
    great phrases.
But he doesn't care if you have to sit like that on the hard rocks,
unlike me, who bring this cushion I've had made for you. Here,
    get up a moment;
now sit back down comfortably, so you don't chafe what sat to the
    oar at Salamis.[107]   785

DEMOS

Who are you, my man? Not a descendant of Harmodius'
    famous family, are you?[108]
All I can say is, this act of yours is truly outstanding and Demos-spirited!

PAPHLAGON

With that paltry bit of fawning you're suddenly his partisan!

SAUSAGE SELLER

Well, you hooked him with much paltrier baits than that.

PAPHLAGON

I say the man has never appeared who stuck up for Demos
    better than me,   790
or cherished you more, and I don't mind staking my head on it!

SAUSAGE SELLER

Just how can you claim to cherish him, when you've seen him
    living in barrels
and shanties and garrets for eight years now and feel no pity,[109]
indeed shut him in and rifle his hut? And when Archeptolemus[110]
    brought us
a peace proposal, you tore it in pieces; and the embassies that
    offered a treaty,   795
you kicked their butts and drove them from the city.

PAPHLAGON

Yes, so he could rule over all Greeks! It's right in the oracles:
one day this Demos shall draw five obols[111] to hear cases in Arcadia,[112]
if he stays the course; in any event, I'll nourish and cater to him,
finding him his three obols by any means, fair and foul.   800

SAUSAGE SELLER

You certainly aren't figuring how he can rule Arcadia,
but how you can steal and take bribes from the allied cities,
and how Demos can be blinded to your crimes in the fog of war,
while mooning at you from necessity, deprivation, and jury pay.
But if Demos ever returns to his peaceful life on the farm,   805
and regains his spirit by eating porridge and chewing the
        fat with pressed olives,
he'll realize the many benefits you chiseled him out of with your state pay;
then he'll come after you, a fierce farmer hunting a ballot against you.
You're aware of this, so you keep fooling him and rigging up
        dreams about yourself.[113]

PAPHLAGON

Isn't it really awful that you presume to say such things and to
        slander me   810
before the Athenians and Demos, after my many fine services –
many more, by Demeter, than Themistocles ever did for the city?[114]

SAUSAGE SELLER

"City of Argos, hearken to his words!"[115] Are you matching yourself
        with Themistocles?
He found our city's cup half-full and filled it the rest of the way
and on top of that, he baked the Piraeus as dessert for her lunch,[116]   815
and added new seafood dishes to her menu while taking away
        none of the old;
whereas you've tried to turn the Athenians into tiny-townies
by building partitions and chanting oracles. Themistocles' match!
And he's exiled from the country,[117] while you wipe your fingers
        with baguettes![118]

PAPHLAGON

Isn't it awful to hear him say these things about me, Demos,   820
just because I cherish you?

THE DEMOS

> Shut up, shut up, you, and stop your sleazy mud-slinging!
You've been getting away with hoodwinking me for far too long already.

SAUSAGE SELLER

He's utter scum, my precious Demos, and a champion evildoer.
While you're gawking into space, he breaks the choicest stalks
off the audits of outgoing office holders   825
and gulps them down, and with both hands
sops the gravy from the people's treasury.

PAPHLAGON

You won't get the last laugh; I'll indict you
for stealing thirty thousand drachmas!

SAUSAGE SELLER

Why slap the water with the flat of your oar,   830
when you've treated the Athenian people
in the scurviest fashion?
And by Demeter and hope to die,
I'll prove you took a bribe from Mytilene
of over forty minas![119]   835

CHORUS

antistrophe
O paramount benefactor of all mankind revealed,
I envy you your ready tongue! Keep thrusting forward this way,
and you'll be the greatest man in Greece, hold sole power in the city,
and rule over the allies, in your hand a trident
for shaking them and quaking them and making lots of money.   840

CHORUS LEADER

And don't let your man off the hook, now that he's let you
    get a grip on him;
you'll put him down easily, with a chest like yours!

PAPHLAGON

No, gentlemen, we haven't reached that point quite yet, by Poseidon.
For I've accomplished a deed quite great enough
to put a gag bit in the mouths of all my enemies,   845
as long as there's anything left of those shields from Pylos![120]

SAUSAGE SELLER

Hold it: those shields have given me an opening.
If you really cherish the people, you shouldn't have
deliberately let those shields be displayed with their handles still on.
That, Demos, is a stratagem designed to frustrate   850
any punishment you may want to mete out to this guy.
You see what a pack of young leather sellers surround him,
and around them live the honey sellers
and cheese sellers. They're all in this together.
So if you start growling and look to be toying with ostraca,[121]   855
they'll take those shields down by night
and in a flash seize the entrances to our grain market!

DEMOS

Dear me, their handles are still on? You sneak,
how long have you been gouging me like this by short-changing
    the people?

PAPHLAGON

My dear sir, don't believe the last thing you hear,   860
and don't think you'll ever find a better friend than me,
who singlehandedly put a stop to the conspirators. And nothing
gets plotted in the city that I'm not onto and immediately screaming
    about.

SAUSAGE SELLER

Yes, you act just like the eel fishermen.
When the lake is still, they catch nothing;   865
but if they stir the mud up and down,
they make a catch. You also make a catch if you stir up the city.[122]
Answer me just one question: though you sell so much leather,
and profess to cherish Demos, have you ever given him
a free patch for his shoes?

DEMOS

        No, by Apollo, he never has!   870

SAUSAGE SELLER

So now do you recognize him for what he is? I, on the other hand,
have bought you this pair of shoes here to wear: my present!

DEMOS

I judge you, of all the men I know, the finest servant
of Demos and the most devoted to the city and my toes!

PAPHLAGON

But isn't it shocking that a pair of shoes counts for so much,   875
while you've quite forgotten all I've done for you? It was I who
put a stop to the buggers by striking Grypus from the citizen rolls.[123]

SAUSAGE SELLER

Well, isn't it shocking that you should pursue this asshole sleuthing
and try to stop the buggers? There's no question that you stopped them
out of rivalry, for fear they'd become politicians![124]   880
And though you see Demos here without a tunic – at his age! –
you've never thought he deserves a tunic with two sleeves
to wear in winter; (*to Demos*) whereas I'm giving you this one.

DEMOS

Themistocles never thought of this kind of thing!
I grant you the Peiraeus was clever too,[125] but to my way of thinking   885
that wasn't a greater piece of policy than this tunic.

PAPHLAGON

Damn it all, what monkey tricks you harass me with!

SAUSAGE SELLER

No, I'm just borrowing your methods, as a man at a drinking-party
borrows slippers when he needs to shit.

PAPHLAGON

Well, you can't outdo me when it comes to fawning.   890

(*taking off his jacket*)
I'm going to put this on him too, and you can eat your heart out, creep!

DEMOS

                    Ugh!
Get the hell away from me with your terrible stink of rawhide!

SAUSAGE SELLER

And he tried to make you wear that thing deliberately, to suffocate you!
He pulled the same trick on you before. Remember when
asafetida stalks were such a bargain?

DEMOS

Sure I remember   895

SAUSAGE SELLER

He deliberately fixed the price at a bargain,
so that everybody would buy and eat them, and then in court
the jurors would fart each other to death!

DEMOS

By Poseidon, that's exactly what I was told by a man from Dungstown!

SAUSAGE SELLER

And didn't you all fart each other brown?   900

DEMOS

God yes, and a real Brown Shirt tactic it was, too.[126]

PAPHLAGON

You bastard, what clownish antics you use to fluster me!

SAUSAGE SELLER

Well, the Goddess told me to beat you with flim-flammeries.

PAPHLAGON

But you won't beat me! I assure you, Demos, for doing absolutely nothing
I'll provide you with a bowl of state pay to lap up.   905

SAUSAGE SELLER

And here's a little jar of ointment from me,
to rub into the blisters on your shins.

PAPHLAGON

And I'll pluck out your white hairs and make you young.

SAUSAGE SELLER

Here, take this bunny tail and dab your darling eyes.

PAPHLAGON

Blow your nose, Demos, and wipe your hand on my head.   910

SAUSAGE SELLER

No, on mine.

PAPHLAGON

         No, on mine!
I'll put you in command of a trireme
at your own expense,
an ancient hulk
that you'll never stop pouring money into   915
and refitting, and I'll fix it
so you get rotten sails!

SAUSAGE SELLER

The man's blowing his top – stop, stop! –
he's boiling over! We've got to pull out   920
some of that kindling and skim off
some of those threats; use this!

PAPHLAGON

You'll pay me a pretty penalty:
when I crush you with tax bills.
Because I'll fix it so   925
you're registered among the rich![127]

SAUSAGE SELLER

I'll make no threats,
but I wish you this:
your squid is sizzling in the pan

when you're scheduled to make a motion   930
about the Milesians[128] and stand
to make a talent
if you get it passed,
and you're hurrying
to stuff yourself with the squid   935
in time to get to Assembly,
and before you can eat it
a man comes to fetch you,
and you're so eager to get the talent
that you choke to death on your meal!   940

CHORUS LEADER

That's a good one, by Zeus, Apollo, and Demeter!

DEMOS

I agree, and think that in general he's obviously
a good citizen; it's been quite some time
since the dime-a-dozens have had such a man on their side.   945
But you, Paphlagon, have ruffled my feathers with your claims
    of affection for me.
Now return my ring, because you're no longer
my steward!

PAPHLAGON

        Here, take it; but you can be sure of this much:
if you won't let me be your steward, someone
more villainous will materialize in my place.   950

DEMOS

There's no way that this ring here can be mine;
it seems to have a different seal.
Or maybe it's my eyesight.

SAUSAGE SELLER

        Let's have a look. What was your seal?

DEMOS

A pea pulse sandwich, steaming hot.

SAUSAGE SELLER

Not on this ring.

DEMOS

No sandwich? Then what?   955

SAUSAGE SELLER

A large-mouthed seagull on a rock haranguing the people.

DEMOS

How revolting!

SAUSAGE SELLER

What's the matter?

THE DEMOS

Get it out of my sight!
He wasn't wearing my ring, but Cleonymus'.[129]
But here's another; take it and be my steward.

PAPHLAGON

Not quite yet, master, I'm begging you now,   960
at least not until you've listened to my oracles!

SAUSAGE SELLER

And mine too, then.

PAPHLAGON

Well, if you listen to him,
you'll surely become a mere balloon.[130]

SAUSAGE SELLER

And if you listen to him,
you'll surely get your cock skinned back to the short and curlies![131]

PAPHLAGON

But I've got oracles predicting that you shall rule   965
over every land, and wear a crown of roses.

SAUSAGE SELLER

And mine predict that you shall wear a diadem
and a robe spangled with crimson, and ride in a golden chariot,
and chase Smicythe and master into court.[132]

DEMOS

Very well, go and get them, so this guy   970
can hear them.

SAUSAGE SELLER

        Sure thing!

DEMOS

        And you get yours.

PAPHLAGON

OK!

SAUSAGE SELLER

        OK it is! What are we waiting for?

Sausage Seller and Paphlagon go inside.

CHORUS[133]

strophe
Bright and joyful that day
will be, for residents
and visitors alike,   975
if Cleon is destroyed!
And yet I heard some
litigious old fogeys
in the lawsuit market
arguing the case   980

that if he hadn't become
a big shot in the city, we wouldn't
have had two useful utensils:
a pestle and a ladle.

antistrophe
I also wonder at this   985
part of his education
as a swine: the boys
who were his classmates
say that often he would tune
his lyre only in the Dorian mode   990
and refuse to learn another;
and then the music teacher
angrily had him expelled
"because this boy
can't learn any mode   995
but the Quid Pro Quorian."[134]

Enter Paphlagon with a load of scrolls.

PAPHLAGON

Look at these, and that's not all of them!

Enter Sausage Seller with a bigger load.

SAUSAGE SELLER

Oh dear, I'm about to shit, and that's not all of them!

DEMOS
What's all this?

PAPHLAGON

                    Prophecies.

DEMOS

                    All of them?

PAPHLAGON

                    Surprised?
By Zeus, I've still got a locker full of them!   1000

SAUSAGE SELLER

And I've got an attic and two tenement buildings full of them!

DEMOS

Let's see. Who could be the source of these oracles?

PAPHLAGON

Mine are from Bacis.[135]

DEMOS

             And what about yours?

SAUSAGE SELLER

From Glanis, the older brother of Bacis.[136]

DEMOS

             And what are they about?

PAPHLAGON

             About Athens, about Pylos,   1005
about you, about me, about everything.

DEMOS

And what about yours?

SAUSAGE SELLER

             About Athens, about lentil soup,
about the Spartans, about fresh mackerel,
about grain dealers in the market who give short measure,
about you, about me. He can go suck himself!   1010

DEMOS

Well then, both of you expound them to me,
including the one about myself that I so enjoy,
that I shall become an eagle in the clouds.[137]

PAPHLAGON

Then listen, and give me your full attention.
"Mark well, son of Erechtheus,[138] the path of the prophecies,
    which Apollo   1015
sent shrieking to you from his sanctum through the priceless tripods.
He bids you keep safe the holy saw-toothed watchdog,[139]
who yawns at your feet and by barking terribly on your behalf
provides you with pay, which if he cannot do, he'll die;
for many are the jackdaws that in their hatred croak against him."   1020

DEMOS

By Demeter, I don't know what that one means.
What's Erechtheus got to do with jackdaws and a dog?

PAPHLAGON

I'm the dog, because I howl on your behalf;
and Phoebus[140] is telling you to keep me, your dog, safe.

SAUSAGE SELLER

That's not what the oracle says. This dog here   1025
is treating your prophecies like gruel, sneaking bites.
I've got the right reading about this dog.

DEMOS

Let's hear it then. But first I'll grab a stone
in case the oracle about the dog tries to bite me.

SAUSAGE SELLER

"Mark well, son of Erechtheus, the dog Cerberus, trafficker in
    bodies,[141]   1030
who wags his tail at you when you're dining and watches,
and when you happen to gape in another direction, eats up your entree,
and at night steals into your kitchen all unseen, and doglike
licks clean the plates and the islands."

DEMOS

By Poseidon, that's much better, Glanis!   1035

PAPHLAGON

Listen, sir, before you render your verdict:
"There is a woman who shall bear a lion in holy Athens,
who will fight for Demos against a swarm of gnats
as stalwartly as for his cubs; keep him safe,
building a wooden wall and iron towers."[142]   1040
Do you know what that means?

DEMOS

                    By Apollo, not I.

PAPHLAGON

The god was clearly advising you to keep me safe,
because I stand for the lion you're to get.

DEMOS

And just how did you come to stand for lyin' behind my back?[143]

SAUSAGE SELLER

One detail in the prophecy he purposely isn't explaining to you: 1045
what the one wall is that's made of iron and wood,
where Loxias[144] ordered you to keep this guy safe.

DEMOS

Well then, what did the god mean by that?

SAUSAGE SELLER

                    This guy
he was ordering you to clamp in the five-holed wooden pillory.

DEMOS

I think that prophecy will very soon come true!   1050

PAPHLAGON

Trust it not; for jealous are the ravens that squawk against me.
"Rather keep in your thoughts the hawk and cherish him,
who brought you in fetters the Spartan ravenfish."[145]

SAUSAGE SELLER

The fact is, Paphlagon was drunk when he took that bold gamble.[146]
"Ill-advised scion of Cecrops,[147] why do you think this a great deed?   1055
Even a woman can bear a burden should a man put it on her,
but fight she cannot, for if she should fight she would shit."

PAPHLAGON

But ponder this, what the god's said about Pylos before Pylos:
"there's a Pylos before Pylos . . ."

DEMOS

What does he mean, "before Pylos"?

SAUSAGE SELLER

He says he shall pillage a pile of tubs from the bath house.   1060

DEMOS

And I'm supposed to go bathless today?

SAUSAGE SELLER

That's because he's made off with the tubs.
Now here's the oracle about the fleet for you,
so you should pay very close attention to it.

DEMOS

I will; but mind you start by expounding   1065
just how my sailors are going to get their pay.

SAUSAGE SELLER

"Scion of Aegeus,[148] ponder the fox-dog lest he beguile you;
he's treacherous, swift of foot, a wily trickster, and very crafty."
Do you get that one?

DEMOS

The fox-dog is Philostratus.[149]

SAUSAGE SELLER

That's not it; no, this one regularly demands   1070
swift ships for collecting revenue;
Loxias is warning you not to give them to him.

DEMOS

How can a trireme be a fox-dog?

SAUSAGE SELLER

        How?
Because both triremes and dogs are fleet.

DEMOS

And how come "fox" is added to the dog?   1075

SAUSAGE SELLER

Soldiers are compared to fox cubs
because they both eat grapes in the farmlands.[150]

THE DEMOS

        Aha.
And where's the pay for these fox cubs?

SAUSAGE SELLER

I'll provide it, and that within three days.[151]
But listen also to this, the oracle wherein Leto's son   1080
bids you shun the wiles of Crookhaven."

DEMOS

Crookhaven?

SAUSAGE SELLER

The verse properly refers to this guy's hand as Crookhaven,
because he says, "put something in my crooked hand."

PAPHLAGON

He's got it wrong: by "Crookhaven" Phoebus'actually
meant to allude to the hand of Diopeithes.[152]   1085
But here, I've got an oracle about you, a winged one,
that you are to become an eagle, and the king of every land.

SAUSAGE SELLER

Me too: over the earth and the Red Sea too,
and that you'll judge cases in Ecbatana,[153] nibbling canapés.

PAPHLAGON

Wait, I've had a dream: I saw the Goddess[154] herself   1090
pouring healthy wealthiness over Demos with a big ladle.

SAUSAGE SELLER

By god I've had one too: I also saw the Goddess herself,
coming from the Acropolis with an owl sitting on her helmet;
then down she poured a pitcher of ambrosia over your head,
and over his a pitcher-full of garlic sauce.   1095

DEMOS

Ha ha!
There's really nobody more ingenious than that Glanis!
I hereby request that you be my own steward,
"to guide me in my old age and retrain me."[155]

PAPHLAGON

Not yet, I beg you! Please hold off, so that I   1100
may provide you with barley grain and a daily livelihood.

DEMOS

I can't stand to hear about barley grain!
You and Thuphanes[156] have cheated me once too often.

PAPHLAGON

All right, I'll supply barley meal already processed.

SAUSAGE SELLER

And I'll supply barley cakes ready made,   1105
and the hot meal too; all you have to do is eat.

THE DEMOS

Then you two get on your marks and go to it,
because to the one who treats me best
I intend to award the reins of the Pnyx.[157]

PAPHLAGON

I'll run inside first!

SAUSAGE SELLER

           Oh no, I'm first!   1110

Sausage seller precedes Paphlagon into the house.

CHORUS

Demos, you have a fine
rule, since all humanity
fears you like
a man with tyrannical power.[158]
But you're easily led astray: 1115
you enjoy being flattered
and thoroughly deceived,
and every speechmaker
has you gaping. You've a mind,
but it's out to lunch.   1120

DEMOS

There's no mind under your long hair,
since you consider me stupid;
but there's purpose
in this foolishness of mine.
I relish   1125
my daily pap,
and I pick one thieving
political leader to fatten;
I raise him up, and when he's full,
I swat him down.[159]   1130

CHORUS

In that case you'll do well;
and your character really does
contain, as you claim,
very deep cunning,
if you deliberately fatten these men,   1135
like public victims,
on the Pnyx, and then
when you chance to lack dinner,
you sacrifice one who's bloated
and have yourself a meal.   1140

DEMOS

Just watch me and see if I don't
ingeniously trick them,
those who think they're smart
and that I'm their dupe.
I monitor them all the time,   1145
pretending I don't even see them,
as they steal; and then I force
them to regurgitate
whatever they've stolen from me,
using a verdict tube[160]
as a probe.   1150

Enter Sausage Seller and Paphlagon, each carrying a large basket.

PAPHLAGON

Get out of the blessed way!

SAUSAGE SELLER

　　　　　　　　　You get out of the way, creep.

PAPHLAGON

Oh Mr. Demos, I've been sitting here for triennia,
ready and willing to give you beneficence.

SAUSAGE SELLER

And I've been ready for decennia,
dodecennia, millenia, millenni-enni-ennia.   1155

DEMOS

And I've been waiting for billionennia,
and getting sick of you both for millenni-enni-ennia.

SAUSAGE SELLER

Do you know what you should do?

DEMOS

If I don't, you'll tell me.

SAUSAGE SELLER

Start me and this guy off from the same gate,
so we have an equal shot at serving you.

DEMOS

That's what we should do.   1160
Go to the gate!

SAUSAGE SELLER and PAPHLAGON

Ready!

DEMOS

Go!

SAUSAGE SELLER

No cutting in!

Sausage Seller and Paphlagon race into the house.

DEMOS

By god, my lovers are certainly going to make me
blissfully happy today, if I play hard to get.

Sausage Seller and Paphlagon emerge.

PAPHLAGON

Look! I'm the first to fetch you something – a stool!

SAUSAGE SELLER

But not a table; I'm firster with that!   1165

PAPHLAGON

Look, I've got this cookie for you,
made from grain imported from Pylos.

SAUSAGE SELLER

And I've got this spoon bread, indented
by the ivory hand of the Goddess.

DEMOS

Sovereign Goddess, you must have a very big finger!   1170

PAPHLAGON

I've got pea soup, fragrant and fine.
And it was stirred by Athena Battler at the Pylisades.[161]

SAUSAGE SELLER

Demos, the Goddess manifestly watches over you.
Just now she's holding over your head a potful of beef broth.

THE DEMOS

Of course; do you think there'd still be a city here,   1175
if she didn't visibly hold her pot over us?[162]

PAPHLAGON

This fish fillet here is the gift of Athena Chiller of Armies.

SAUSAGE SELLER

And from Athena Strong Like Her Father, beef boiled in broth
and a good cut of tripe and paunch.

DEMOS

Nice of her to remember the Robe we gave her![163]   1180

PAPHLAGON

Athena of the Ghastly Plumes bids you taste this fine
roll, so our oarsmen can *row well*.

SAUSAGE SELLER

Then take these, too.

DEMOS

                Just what am I supposed to do
with these belly tripes?

SAUSAGE SELLER

                They're shipped to you
from the Goddess to use in the bellies of our triremes;   1185
she obviously watches over the fleet.
Have a drink, too, mixed two parts wine to three of water.

THE DEMOS

It's good, by god, and takes the three parts nicely!

SAUSAGE SELLER

Sure: Athena Tritogenes tritogenated it.[164]

PAPHLAGON

Now have a slice of luscious cheesecake, with my compliments.   1190

SAUSAGE SELLER

And with my compliments, have this whole cheesecake.

PAPHLAGON

But you don't have a source for hare's meat to give him; I do.

SAUSAGE SELLER

(*aside*)

Damn! Where will I come up with hare's meat?
It's time, my soul, to think up some tomfoolery.

PAPHLAGON

(*producing a hare*)

Take a look at this, you loser!

SAUSAGE SELLER

                    I don't care,   1195
because here come some ambassadors
with bags of silver, to visit me!

PAPHLAGON

(*dropping the hare*)
                    Where? Where?

SAUSAGE SELLER

What's it to you? Why don't you leave the foreigners alone?
(*picking up the hare*)
My precious Demos, see the hare's meat I've got for you?

PAPHLAGON

Damn it all, you pinched my hare! That's unfair!   1200

SAUSAGE SELLER

By Poseidon, it isn't: just what you did with the men from Pylos!

DEMOS

Tell me, please, where you got the idea of pinching that?

SAUSAGE SELLER

The Goddess thought it up, I pulled the job.

PAPHLAGON

But it was I took the risk, and I that roasted the meat!

DEMOS

Go on! Nobody but the server ever gets thanked.   1205

PAPHLAGON

Great heavens me, I'm going to be out-brazened!

SAUSAGE SELLER

Why not decide once and for all, Demos, which of us
is the better man for you and for your stomach?

DEMOS

Well, what do you think the audience would accept
as evidence of a smart decision on my part?   1210

SAUSAGE SELLER

I'll tell you: just go pick up my basket, don't
say a word, and examine what's inside of it;
Paphlagon's too. Don't worry, you'll make a good decision.

DEMOS

(*opening the Sausage seller's basket*)
Let's see now, what's in it?

SAUSAGE SELLER

                    Daddy, don't you see it's empty?
I brought everything to your table.   1215

DEMOS

Say, this is a basket with Demos' interests at heart!

SAUSAGE SELLER

Now come over here to Paphlagon's.

(*opening it*)
See this?

DEMOS

                    My goodness, it's crammed; look at all the goodies!
Have a look at the cheesecake he's put aside for himself!
And he cut me off a slice no bigger than this!   1220

SAUSAGE SELLER

That's what he was doing to you all along,
tossing you a petty piece of his profits
and putting away the lion's share for himself.

DEMOS

You scum, is that how you robbed me blind?
And me that crowned and endowed you?[165]   1225

PAPHLAGON

But I was stealing for the good of the city!

DEMOS

Lay down that crown this instant; I'm going
to put it on *his* head.

SAUSAGE SELLER

                              This instant, you scamp!

PAPHLAGON

No! I have in my possession a Pythian oracle
specifying the only one destined to defeat me.   1230

SAUSAGE SELLER

Specifying my name, and with perfect clarity.

PAPHLAGON

Well then, I'd like to examine you to see
whether you match up with the god's prophetic utterances.
First, let me put to you this relevant question:
when you were a boy, whose school did you attend?   1235

SAUSAGE SELLER

The school of hard knocks, in the slaughterhouse district.

PAPHLAGON

What's that you say? (*aside*) How the oracle bites me to the quick!
Now then: at the wrestling school, what technique did you learn?

SAUSAGE SELLER

When stealing, to look them in the eye and swear I didn't do it.

PAPHLAGON

(*aside*)
"Phoebus Apollo of Lycia, what do you mean to do to me?"[166]   1240
And when you were becoming a man, what sort of trade did you follow?

SAUSAGE SELLER

I sold sausages, and now and then I also sold my ass.

PAPHLAGON

(*aside*) Oh, I'm damned! This is the absolute end of me!
There's but a splinter of hope keeping me afloat.
And it's this: tell me, did you sell sausages   1245
in the marketplace or at the city gates?

SAUSAGE SELLER

At the city gates, where they sell cheap fish.

PAPHLAGON

Ah me, the god's own fateful prophecy has come to pass!
"Now roll me inside, utterly ill-starred!"[167]
Begone and farewell, my crown; against my will   1250
do I abandon you. "Some other man will take you as his own,
no greater thief, but luckier perhaps."[168]

*Paphlagon tosses the Sausage Seller his crown and swoons
upon the eccyclema.*

SAUSAGE SELLER

Zeus of the Hellenes, yours the prize of victory![169]

First Slave appears at the doorway.

FIRST SLAVE

O hail, fair victor, and bear in mind that you became
a big shot thanks to me. And I'll ask only a small favor,   1255
that you make me your Phanus,[170] your notary for indictments.

THE DEMOS

And now tell me what your name is.

SAUSAGE SELLER

                    Agoracritus,
because I made my way by haggling in the marketplace.[171]

THE DEMOS

Then to Agoracritus' stewardship I commit myself,
and to his custody I commit this Paphlagon here.   1260

SAUSAGE SELLER

And you can count on me, Demos, for fine service,
so you'll agree you've never seen anyone better
than me for the city of Suckerthenians!

The eccyclema is withdrawn as Demos and Sausage Seller go inside.

CHORUS

strophe
What finer way
for drivers of swift horses   1265
to begin or end a song than by singing
nothing against Lysistratus,
nor bringing the homeless Thumantis[172]
further grief
light-heartedly?
Because he's always hungry, dear Apollo,   1270
and weeping hot tears
he clutches your quiver in holy Pytho,
begging relief from his cursed poverty.

CHORUS LEADER

There's nothing invidious about calling bad people names;
it's a way to honor good people, if you stop to think about it.   1275
Thus, if the man who's about to be called a lot of bad names
were well known, I wouldn't mention a gentleman who's
        a friend of mine.
But it's a fact that there's no one who doesn't know Arignotus,[173]
if they can tell the light tune from the Orthian.
Well, Arignotus has a brother of unkindred character,   1280

Ariphrades the vile.[174] Yes, that's how he likes to be.
But he's not merely vile, or I wouldn't even have noticed him,
nor even utterly vile. No, he's added new meaning to the term.
He pollutes his own tongue with disgraceful gratifications,
licking the detestable dew in bawdyhouses,   1285
besmirching his beard, churning the ladies' hotpots,
acting like Polymnestus and on intimate terms with Oeonichus.[175]
Anyone who doesn't loathe such a man
will never drink from the same cup with me.

CHORUS

antistrophe
Oft in the dark of night   1290
have I communed with my thoughts
and wondered where on earth Cleonymus[176]
gets off eating so happy-go-luckily.
For they do say that he used to pig out
on the substance of rich men   1295
and wouldn't leave the trough,
though they would all beg him,
"By your knees we implore you, sir,
have mercy on the table and leave!"

CHORUS LEADER

They say that the triremes got together for a conference,   1300
and one of them, who was a senior ship, said,
"Young ladies, don't you even ask about this business in the city?
They're saying that somebody's requisitioning a hundred of us for
        Carthage,
a lowlife male citizen, that brackish Hyperbolus."[177]
They all agreed that this was awful and intolerable,   1305
and one of them spoke up, who'd never been boarded by men:
"God forbid he should ever be my commander! If need be,
I'd sooner grow dilapidated right here and be rotted by woodworms!"
"Nor will he command Nauphante, daughter of Nauson,[178] heavens no,
or I wasn't built of pine and sturdy timbers either!   1310
If that's what appeals to the Athenians, then I suggest we sail
to the Theseum[179] or the shrine of the Furies[180] and sit in asylum there.
Never shall he make a fool of the city by being our commander.
If he wants to go sailing, let him sail all by himself to hell,
launching those trays where he used to display his lamps for sale!"   1315

Enter Sausage Seller.

SAUSAGE SELLER

Keep your language pure, everyone, shut mouths, call no more witnesses,
shutter the lawcourts that this city's so fond of,
and to celebrate our revolutionary good luck, let the theater raise a paeon!

CHORUS LEADER

Light of holy Athens and protector of the islands,
what glad tidings do you bring, that we should throng the streets?   1320

SAUSAGE SELLER

I've recast Demos for you, from ugly to handsome.

CHORUS LEADER

And where is he now, you inventor of wondrous conceptions?

SAUSAGE SELLER

He lives in the violet-crowned Athens of old.

CHORUS LEADER

How can we see him? What is he wearing? What has he become?

SAUSAGE SELLER

He's as he was when his messmates were Aristides and Miltiades.[181]   1325
You'll see for yourselves: that's the sound of the Propylaea
    being opened.
Now raise a cheer for the reappearance of the Athens of old,
wonderful and celebrated in so many songs, home of the
    renowned Demos!

A facade is revealed, transforming the scene building into the Athens of Old.

CHORUS

O Athens the gleaming, the violet-crowned, the envy of all,
show us the monarch of Greece and of this land!   1330

Demos emerges from the gates, now young and handsome.

SAUSAGE SELLER

Here he is for all to see, wearing a golden cricket, resplendent
    in old-time dress,
smelling not of ballot shells but peace accords, and anointed with myrrh.

CHORUS

Hail, king of the Greeks! We too share your joy,
for your condition is worthy of the city and the trophy at Marathon.

THE DEMOS

Agoracritus, dearest of men, come over here.   1335
Your recasting has done wonders for me!

SAUSAGE SELLER

                    Me?
My dear fellow, if you only knew what you were like before
and how you used to act, you'd worship me like a god!

DEMOS

Tell me, how did I used to act, and what was I like?

SAUSAGE SELLER

First of all, whenever somebody said in the Assembly,   1340
"Demos, I'm your lover and I cherish you,
and I alone care for you and think for you,"
whenever anybody started a speech with that stuff,
you'd flap your wings and toss your horns.

THE DEMOS

                    I did?

SAUSAGE SELLER

And then in return he got away with cheating you.   1345

DEMOS

You don't say! They did that to me, and I didn't catch on?

SAUSAGE SELLER

They certainly did, because your ears would open up
like a parasol and then flap shut again.

DEMOS

Had I become that mindless and senile?

SAUSAGE SELLER

You certainly were, and if two politicians were making proposals,   1350
one to build long ships and the other
to spend the same sum on state pay,
the pay man would walk all over the trireme man.
Here, why are you hanging your head? Won't you stand firm?

DEMOS

It's that I'm ashamed of my former mistakes.   1355

SAUSAGE SELLER

But you aren't to blame for them, never think it!
The blame's with those who deceived you this way. Tell me now:
if some tomfool advocate declares,
"There won't be any grain for you jurymen
unless you vote to convict in this lawsuit,"   1360
what will you do to that advocate, eh?

DEMOS

I'll hoist him in the air and toss him into the death pit,
with Hyperbolus hung around his throat!

SAUSAGE SELLER

That's the way; now you're talking correctly and sensibly.
As for the rest of your policies, give me an idea how you'll behave.   1365

DEMOS

In the first place, to all the men who row long ships,
as soon as they make port, I'll pay in full what they're owed.

SAUSAGE SELLER

You're making a lot of half-flattened rear ends happy!

DEMOS

Furthermore, no infantryman once entered on a muster roll
shall be transferred to a different list through private influence   1370
but will stay on the list where he was originally enrolled.

SAUSAGE SELLER

That bites Cleonymus right in the shield handle!

DEMOS

And no one without a beard will rendezvous in the marketplace.

SAUSAGE SELLER

Then where will Cleisthenes and Strato do their rendezvousing?[182]

DEMOS

I mean these teenagers in the scent shops,   1375
who sit around chattering like this:
"Phaeax is a sharp one! So resourcefully beat that capital charge![183]
Yes, he's intimidative and penetrative,
a phrase-coiner, and clear, and hard-hitting,
and superlatively terminative of the obstreperative."[184]   1380

SAUSAGE SELLER

To the talkative you're not flippative of the finger, are you?

DEMOS

God no, I intend to force them all to go hunting
after putting a stop to their decree mongering!

Enter a Slave Boy with a chair at Sausage Seller's signal.

SAUSAGE SELLER

On that understanding, please accept this split bottom chair
and a well hung boy to carry it for you.   1385
And if you get the urge, make the boy your split bottom too.

DEMOS

Happy me, I'm really starting to relive the good old days!

SAUSAGE SELLER

You'll certainly say so when I present you with the thirty-year
peace treaties. Come out here on the double, you Treaties!

Enter two Treaties, costumed as girls.

DEMOS

Glory to Zeus, they're pretty! God love me,   1390
is it OK if I lay them down and ratify them?
Where did you ever get hold of them?

SAUSAGE SELLER

           Why, wasn't Paphlagon
hiding these Treaties inside all along, so you couldn't get at them?
Now I'm presenting them to you to take
back home to your farms.

DEMOS

           And Paphlagon,   1395
who behaved this way, tell me how you'll punish him.

SAUSAGE SELLER

Nothing severe; he's merely going to take my old job.
He'll have his own sausage stand at the city gates,
hashing up dog and ass meat instead of politics,
getting drunk and trading insults with the whores,   1400
and drinking the runoff from the public baths.

DEMOS

Well done! You've come up with just what he deserves,
to have shouting matches with whores and bathmen.
And as your reward, I invite you to the Prytaneum,
to sit in the seat where that pariah used to be.   1405
Put on this emerald robe and follow me.
And somebody escort that one to his new place of business,
so the foreigners he used to strongarm can see him now!

Demos, Sausage Seller, Slave Boy, and Treaties lead the Chorus off; Paphlagon, costumed and equipped as a sausage seller, is prodded out of the house by two slaves and marched off in the other direction.

Notes

1 Perhaps including personal or parochial elements; see Lind 1990.
2 For what is known of Cleon's life, see General Introduction, Section VI.3.
3 Paphlagon is never "unmasked" in the play, but not even the dullest spectator would have failed to recognize the allegory, so we must trust the poet's assurance that the audience would recognize him anyway (230–33).
4 For a similar narrative of decline, see Thucydides 2.65. For popular superstition regarding divination during the war, see Thucydides 2.8.2, 8.1.1. Private collections of oracles were also associated with the sixth-century Athenian tyrant, Peisistratus.
5 A modern equivalent would be a street vendor selling hot dogs.
6 For the chorus in the "demagogue" comedies, see Henderson 2013a; for Cleon's feud with the Knights, see *Acharnians* 6 n.
7 See General Introduction VI.4, and the selection in Appendix.
8 For the name and nationality see Introduction. The slave's newly bought status (in contrast with the familiar home-bred slaves) parallels the politician's rise from nowhere; that he suddenly holds such power in the household reflects poorly on the master's judgment.
9 The reputed founder of Greek *aulos* music, of music without words, and of the Phrygian and Lydian modes, which conservative Athenians considered slavish and barbaric.
10 A line from Euripides' *Hippolytus* 345 (produced in 428): Phaedra has a dangerous secret (lust for her stepson) that she is reluctant to reveal explicitly to her nurse.
11 For the reference to Euripides' mother see *Acharnians* 475–478.
12 Not a real demotic – the Pnyx was the meeting place of the Athenian Assembly, inside the city walls to the west of the Acropolis – but a comic toponymic designating Demos' characteristic place, and making it clear that he is a collective personification of the citizenry and not an actual individual.
13 The juryman's daily payment, recently raised from two to three obols on Cleon's motion.
14 For Cleon's recent victory at Pylos, for which his detractors claimed that he did not deserve the credit, see Introduction.
15 Parodying Sophocles' *Return of Helen*, where the heroine says, "For me it's best to drink bull's blood and no longer tolerate these people's slanders" (fr. 178). For this legend about Themistocles – the Athenian hero of the Persian Wars and architect of Athens' naval supremacy – see Plutarch *Themistocles* 31, Diodorus 11.58.
16 A drinking party typically ended with a toast to the *agathos daimon* ("good spirit") with undiluted wine.
17 In a normal household, slaves were not allowed to help themselves to food or wine.
18 Property confiscated from monied malefactors was a source of public (= Demos') revenue (see *Wasps* 659), some of which is "embezzled" by Paphlagon.
19 Pramnian wine was a fine, strong red.
20 The legendary author of oracles that were compiled into books and enjoyed great popular esteem. This oracle, however, will prove to have divine authority.
21 That is, Eucrates of Melite, who had been a general in 432/1 and went on to have a long political career.
22 That is, Lysicles, who lived with Aspasia (see *Acharnians* 527 n.) after Pericles' death and was killed in a battle in Caria in 428 (Thucydides 3.19.2).
23 Suggesting that this oracle, unlike those by Bacis that were invoked or invented by Paphlagon/Cleon, has divine authority and will come true, cf. 153, 193, 220, 229, 1229.
24 The audience, and also the people of Athens.
25 That is, the Assembly (see 42 n.).
26 See *Acharnians* 125 n. For his success at Pylos the people had awarded Cleon privileges there for life. Cock-sucking listed as a perk (instead of dining at state expense) suggests depravity, and also plays on the popular belief that politicians prostitute themselves for advancement, cf. 428, 1242, and similarly *Acharnians* 79.

27 That is, the islands of the Athenian empire, whose annual tribute was a major source of revenue.
28 Neither Caria (a Greek-dominated area of western Anatolia, in modern Turkey) to the east nor Carthage (a city-state in north Africa, in modern Tunisia) to the west belonged to the Athenian empire, but ambitious populists seem to have had designs on them, e.g. Lysicles (132 n.) and Hyperbolus (1304 n.) respectively.
29 Garlic is associated with fierceness (cf. 946) and garlic brine (a relish) was perhaps associated with Paphlagonia (Lucian, *Alexander* 39), cf. 1090–95.
30 See 280 n.
31 Apollo's oracle at Delphi was the most prestigious in Greece and was often consulted on issues of national and international scope; see 123 n.
32 Both the play's chorus and the Knights as a class. For their hatred of Cleon, see Introduction.
33 Aristophanes frequently derides demagogic accusations of conspiracy against the democracy, including aspiration to tyranny (e.g. 257, 452, 476–79, 628, 862, *Wasps* 345, 464–65, 482–83, 487–88, 507, 953, cf. Cleon in Thucydides 3.37.2); in general, see Roisman 2006, Henderson 2003.
34 The spectators will perhaps think of the Calchidian silverware in Athena's treasury on the Acropolis.
35 Calchis was located on a channel strategically and commercially important to Athens; compare Nicarchus' similarly far-fetched accusation in *Acharnians* 915–25.
36 Though the name was not unusual, this is probably the Simon who wrote a treatise on horsemanship (cf. Xenophon, *On Horsemanship* 1.1) and/or the leader of a guild of Heracles in Aristophanes' and Cleon's deme (see Introduction), and so blurs the distinction between comic and actual Knights; see further 268 n. and *Acharnians* 220 n.
37 Probably the Panaetius (or one of two men by that name) denounced in the scandals of 415; see Andocides 1.13.
38 The name of the fabulous whirlpool that threatened Odysseus in *Odyssey*, book 12.
39 See 130 n.
40 Many spectators will have served as jurors, whom Aristophanes consistently portrays as penurious old men dependent on their jury-pay (51 n.) and eager to support the demagogues' attacks on upper-class defendants: see *Wasps*, Introduction and *passim*.
41 When normal public officers embezzle.
42 The Gallipoli Peninsula, where many Athenian settlers and grain merchants resided.
43 Evidently referring to the Knights' success in the expedition against Corinth the prior year, of which they boast at 599–604; that Simon and Panaetius are the leaders of our comic chorus (see 242–43) suggests that they had been commanders (*hipparchs*) on that occasion (cf. Thucydides 4.44.1).
44 Punning on *zomeumata* (stew) and *hypozomata* (hull-braces).
45 See 168 n.
46 The high-born and distinguished Pericles, whose death in 429 after 30 years of political ascendancy opened the way for populists like Cleon, was the epitome of statesmanship.
47 Hermes Agoraios, the patron god of commerce who also represented deceit and theft, had a bronze statue in the Athenian agora.
48 If the Prytaneis (the executive committee of the Council, who enjoyed special seating at the theater) were shown sufficient evidence, they would refer the case to the entire Council for trial; the informer would receive half of any fine levied.
49 Upper and Lower Pergase were two small demes about eight miles north of Athens.
50 The son of Hippodamus, the renowned city-planner from Miletus, was Archeptolemus, who was granted Athenian citizenship and in 425 worked for a negotiated settlement of the war (see 794–796); in 411 he joined the oligarchic regime and was executed after it fell.
51 Compare Cleon's remarks as reported by Thucydides 3.38.2 (on any speaker who advocates a reassessment of the punishment of the Mytilenaeans): "It is plain that such a man

must either have such trust in his rhetoric as to contend that a firm decision remains undetermined, or has been bribed to try to mislead us by working up sophistic arguments."

52 Demosthenes, Eurymedon, and Nicias were in charge before Cleon assumed command (Thucydides 4.2–5).

53 For Cleon's attack on Nicias as the Assembly deliberated about Pylos, see Thucydides 3.27–28.

54 Perhaps Cleon had (or was claimed to have) reneged on a bribe from a political faction on Miletus, a rich and loyal ally of Athens (cf. 927–40); or "big fish" may allude to oligarchs.

55 A very lucrative business, and the main source of Nicias' wealth.

56 As an animal before slaughter is inspected for signs of tapeworm.

57 That is, by taking credit for the victory at Pylos.

58 That is, using the Spartan prisoners to bargain for favorable terms; cf. Thucydides 4.41.

59 Referring to Cratinus' alleged incontinence, cf. 526 ff.

60 Son of the tragic poet Philocles and great-nephew of Aeschylus.

61 The title of a victory ode by Simonides (*PMG* 512).

62 One of the sons of the traditionalist statesman Cimon, Ulius was evidently a grain-inspector and had some sort of legal or political trouble with Cleon; perhaps he was blamed for price increases.

63 Divine patron of the agora, and an appropriate deity for Paphlagon/Cleon to invoke; Sausage Seller matches him at 498–500.

64 In Eupolis' comedy *Maricas* (fr. 194: see Appendix), produced in 421, the titular slave representing the demagogue Hyperbolus says, "And I learned a lot in the barbershops, sitting there inconspicuously and pretending not to be listening" (presumably for information useful politically, or for slander or blackmail).

65 Athens took this strategically important city in 429, but only after a costly two-year siege (Thucydides 2.70).

66 The seventh-century aristocratic faction that killed the followers of Cylon in Athena's sanctuary and whose descendants were accursed (Herodotus 5.71, Thucydides 1.126).

67 Hippias was a tyrant of Athens from 527 until his expulsion in 510; his wife's name was Myrsine, here "Byrsine," punning on *byrsa* "hide."

68 In 424 Argos, a Peloponnesian power, was neutral in the war, but its treaty with Sparta was due to expire in 421 and the Athenians hoped to win the Argives to their side. Presumably Cleon had participated in negotiations there, and is accused here of private dealings with the Spartans in hopes of profiting from the hostages taken at Pylos, cf. 393–94.

69 Athens was still negotiating with the Persians (Thucydides 4.50.3); the term "Medes," recalling the Persian invasions, was used to evoke popular prejudice.

70 Recent diplomatic contacts with democratic factions in Boeotia, hoping to undermine its ruling oligarchy, had included the general Demosthenes; see Thucydides 4.76.

71 As a wrestler is oiled before a match.

72 As were fighting cocks.

73 See 410 n.

74 The meter typical of the Chorus Leader's parabasis-address to the spectators on behalf of the poet: see General Introduction.

75 Maintaining the Chorus' identity as Knights, real-life antagonists of Cleon. In the following lines, the Chorus Leader shifts attention to Aristophanes' hoped-for success as a young comic poet, paralleling Sausage Seller's hoped-for victory.

76 Magnes won a record 11 victories; the only one datable was in 472, but his career may have lasted into the 430s if this booing was something audience members were expected to recall.

77 Placing Cratinus, one of Aristophanes' active rivals (in the present competition his play *Satyrs* would win second prize), between Magnes and Crates implies that Cratinus, too, was a poet of the past. But in fact he would win first prize over Aristophanes' *Clouds* the following year with his *Wine-Flask*, in which he seems to have responded to Aristophanes' caricature of him in *Knights* (see Biles 2011: 97–154).

78 Cratinus won nine victories overall, the last in the following year over Aristophanes' *Clouds*.

79 Like a worn-out lyre.

80 A derogatory nickname for Connus, the renowned musician and teacher of Socrates, who had become a byword for washed-up celebrity; he was the title character in a comedy by Ameipsias that competed against *Clouds* and perhaps also in a comedy by Phrynichus.

81 See 168 n.

82 Crates flourished ca. 450–430 and won three victories. On his preference for "plots and stories" over invective, and on his homespun style, cf. Aristotle, *Poetics* 1449b.

83 The meaning of this phrase is unknown; Lech 2009 reviews interpretations and suggests a reference to the naval victory of Phormio (mentioned in the following song, 562–64) with 11 triremes in 429, which relied (like the poetic success claimed by Aristophanes) on superior skill (Thucydides 2.90.5–91.1).

84 A reference to Aristophanes' early baldness.

85 This god, worshipped jointly with Athena as *Hippios* (Lord of Horses), was lord also of the sea: this prayer deftly links land forces (particularly the cavalry) and naval forces, to prepare for the recollection of the Knights' valor at Solygeia in 595–610.

86 A promontory in southeastern Attica where Poseidon was honored with trireme races.

87 A port in Euboea where Poseidon had an ancient sanctuary.

88 This successful and respected admiral (featured, in character, as a tough commander in Eupolis' comedy *Taxiarchs*) was probably dead by the time of the play.

89 The robe presented to Athena at the festival of the Great Panathenaea every four years.

90 Cleon's father.

91 Long hair was in fashion among wealthy young men and could be taken as snobbish and even unpatriotic, since Spartans also wore their hair long.

92 The title of Athena as guardian of Athens.

93 In Nicias' recent victory at Solygeia, where 200 cavalrymen were transported on ships (Thucydides 4.42–4).

94   Identity unknown; the homonymous crony of Cleon mentioned, for example, in *Acharnians* 134 is out of place in this company.

95 The name (a common one) can be rendered "Victor Forecouncil."

96 "Farting" is a surprise for "sneezing" in a common superstition.

97 That is, to Athena, as was done at the Panathenaea.

98 That is, to Artemis Agrotera, for whom 500 goats were sacrificed each year in fulfillment of a vow made before the battle of Marathon in 490.

99 See *Acharnians* 144 n.

100 A jibe at Hyperbolus (see *Acharnians* 846–847).

101 That is, Demosthenes (his colleague Nicias remained in Athens during Cleon's command).

102 Lumps of iron or lead that were dropped on the enemy's decks.

103 See 132 n.

104 Two notorious courtesans.

105 The date of Cleon's term of service is unknown but likely is 428/7, when war-taxes on the wealthy were increased.

106 See *Acharnians* 182 n.

107 The great Athenian victory over the Persian fleet in 480.

108 Cleon seems to have claimed descent from Harmodius, who with his friend Aristogeiton assassinated Hipparchus, brother of the tyrant Hippias (449 n.). The pair were revered as liberators who opened the way for democracy at Athens and, like Cleon (167 n.), their descendants enjoyed free meals in the Prytaneion; Cleon may in fact have been related by marriage to the sister-in-law of one of them, Harmodius of Aphidna.

109 On these conditions see Thucydides 2.14–17, 52.

110 See 327 n.

111 See 51 n.

112 For such Athenian ambitions in the Peloponnese, see Thucydides 5.29, 47.

113 Thucydides 5.16.1 similarly accounts for Cleon's aggressive pursuit of the war.

114 See 84 n.

115 A quote from Euripides' tragedy, *Telephus* (F 713), whose beggar-king hero is impersonated by Dicaeopolis in *Acharnians* and might remind spectators of Themistocles' period of exile in Argos (Thucydides 1.135).

116 For Themistocles' rebuilding of the Piraeus port and long walls and enlargement of the city, see Thucydides 1.93.

117 As a traitor who died in exile, Themistocles' remains were forbidden interment in the city until his rehabilitation in the following century.

118 The luxurious "Achilles cakes" served in the Prytaneum; see 168 n.

119 In the debate about Mytilene in 427 (Thucydides 3.1–50: see General Introduction), Cleon charged his opponent with having been bribed (38.2); 40 minas equaled 4,000 drachmas, a huge sum.

120 See 55 n.

121 Shards of broken pottery used both in children's games and as ballots for nominating candidates for "ostracism," a special election whose purpose was to break an impasse in political leadership, in which the people could vote to exile any citizen for a period of ten years.

122 In *Clouds* Aristophanes would complain that another comic poet stole this eel-simile and applied it to Hyperbolus, Cleon's successor as leading demagogue.

123 "Hook Nose," identity unknown. Male citizens could lose civic privileges if they were successfully denounced for having ever been sexually penetrated.

124 See 168 n.

125 See 815 n.

126 Literally "a contrivance of Pyrrhander," probably a proverbial phrase used here for the sake of the pun; but a contemporary with this name is attested.

127 See 774 n.

128 Perhaps a reference to the recent doubling of that state's annual tribute.

129 See *Acharnians* 88 n.

130 A slangy version of a famous oracle given to the mythic hero Theseus, predicting that Athens would be storm-tossed but like a wine skin would never be submerged.

131 That is, circumcised; see *Acharnians* 158 n.

132 Probably a dig at a man named Smicythus (not an uncommon name) for effeminacy, but possibly the phrase is a legal tag, since Smicythe was also a common female name.

133 This song, composed in a popular rhythm, would be suitable for performance at private parties (cf. 529–30). Cleon is identified by name only here in the play, appropriately by the Knights, his real-life enemies, and not equated with the character Paphlagon.

134 The adverb *dorodokisti* puns on "Dorian" (a musical mode appropriate for serious and manly themes) and "bribe taking" (*dorodokein*). The statement in the scholia to our play that Cleon had once belonged to the Knights but had been treated badly by them might be connected with the tradition that Cleon renounced his friendships in order to avoid the temptation of favoritism (see Plutarch, *Precepts of Statecraft* 13.1 [806f-807a]).

135 See 123 n.

136 Fictitious (that is, even more bogus than Bacis): *glanis* is a kind of shad.

137 The actual oracle, quoted by the scholiast, went "Blessed polis of Athens, driver of the spoils, having seen and suffered and toiled greatly, you shall become an eagle midst the clouds forever."

138 Like Cecrops (1055) and Aegeus (1067), an early king of Attica.

139 For ridicule of Cleon's claim to be the people's watchdog, see more fully *Wasps* 894 ff.

140 Phoebus, Loxias, and Son of Leto are epithets of Apollo.

141 The mythical Hound of Hell; here the epithet was perhaps intended to remind spectators of the harsh punishment of the rebellious Mytileneans championed by Cleon: "to
kill all the grown males and enslave the women and children" (Thucydides 3.36.1).

142 For the "wooden wall" oracle of 480 that justified the Athenians' confidence in their
navy, see Herodotus 7.141.

143 Punning on *leon* "lion": literally, "how did you turn into Antileon (an early tyrant of
Chalcis) behind my back?" In *Wasps* (1232–35) Cleon is compared to another early
tyrant.

144 1024 n.

145 See 394–95.

146 Thucydides reports (4.27–8) that Cleon's vow to kill or capture the Spartans at Pylos
within 20 days initially drew laughter and its success astonished many.

147 See 1015 n.

148 See 1015 n.

149 A pimp who used that nickname, cf. *Lysistrata* 957.

150 Soldiers on campaign often helped themselves to the locals' land.

151 See 1054 n.

152 An expert on oracles and a prosecutor of atheists and intellectuals; his hand seems to
have been crippled.

153 See *Acharnians* 64 n.

154 That is, Athena.

155 A line from Sophocles' tragedy, *Peleus* (F 487.2).

156 Apparently a crony of Cleon's.

157 See 42 n.

158 For Athens (and by extension, the Athenian demos) as a collective "tyranny" at
home and abroad, note Pericles' speech in Thucydides 2.63.2, with Henderson 2003:
160–61.

159 Essential to Athenian democratic theory was confidence that the people may be
fooled by self-serving leaders but will eventually recover their good sense (see Ostwald 1986: 226–27); here Demos reassures the aristocratic Knights much as in actual
life a committed democrat might do.

160 In Athenian courts a wicker funnel atop the voting urns allowed jurors to cast their
votes unseen.

161 *Pylaimachos* was an actual epithet of Athena, which Paphlagon uses to allude to
Pylos once again.

162 Misremembering a famous verse of Solon's (fr. 4.4 West), substituting "pot" for
"hands."

163 See 566 n.

164 This ancient epithet, of uncertain etymology, was explained in antiquity as deriving
from Lake Tritonis in Libya; here the Sausage Seller puns on tri- (three).

165 In Doric (Spartan) dialect and, according to the scholiast, quoted from Eupolis' comedy *Helots* (fr. 147).

166 From Euripides' tragedy *Telephus*, F 700, in which the titular hero sought refuge at
this Apollo's temple; at Athens the cult of Apollo of Lycia was associated with the
cavalry and infantry.

167 From Euripides' tragedy *Bellerophon*, fr. 310, substituting "roll" for "take."

168 Parodying the dying heroine's farewell in Euripides' tragedy *Alcestis* 177–82.

169 Suggesting that Paphlagon's defeat is a victory not only for Athenians but for all
Greeks.

170 Punning on *sycophantes* (malicious informer) and presumably a crony of Cleon's; he
is among the guests at a party including Cleon in *Wasps* 1220.

171 Sausage Seller comically etymologizes the name, which properly means "chosen by the assembly" (*agora* in its archaic sense), to suit his marketplace origins. It is unlikely that Aristophanes intends an allusion to the famous Parian sculptor of that name who worked with Phidias.

172 Ridiculed for emaciation in Hermippus' comedy *Kerkopes*, F 36.

173 Son of Automenes, a very popular lyre-player; cf. *Wasps* 1277–78.

174 Probably the character in a Socratic dialogue by Aeschines of Sphettus who claimed to be a pupil of Anaxagoras (Athenaeus 5.220b-c); less likely the "ridiculer" of tragic diction criticized in Aristotle *Poetics* 1458b31. Aristophanes attacks him again in *Wasps* 1280–83 and *Peace* 883–85, and perhaps *Merchant Ships* (fr. 425: see Appendix).

175 Polymnestus was a seventh-century musician and poet from Colophon; Oeonichus is mentioned in connection with music in an anonymous comic fragment (*adesp.* 396). Why either of them would be associated with the activity derided here is unknown.

176 See *Acharnians* 88 n.

177 See 174 n.

178 Appropriately nautical names; Nauphante is otherwise unattested in Attica.

179 The shrine of Theseus at Athens served as a refuge for the oppressed poor and fugitive slaves.

180 A prominent sanctuary for suppliants.

181 Athenian leaders regarded as symbolizing the "greatest generation" who won the Persian Wars, and for conservatives like Aristophanes typifying the Athenian good old days before populist leaders became ascendant.

182 See *Acharnians* 118–22.

183 See [Andocides] 4.36–37. Phaeax would later make an important expedition to Sicily (Thucydides 5.4–5) and received votes in the ostracism of Hyperbolus ca. 416.

184 By contrast, Eupolis in his comedy *Demes* calls Phaeax a mere chatterer and an ineffective orator (fr. 116).

4. *Wasps*

Introduction

Wasps was produced at the Lenaea of 422 and placed second; a play entitled *The Preview* (*Proagon*) placed first, and Leucon placed third with *Ambassadors*. The ancient Hypothesis credits Philonides as the producer of both *Wasps* and *Proagon*, but it is very unlikely that one producer could openly compete with two plays at the same festival. The autobiographical comments in *Wasps* confirm Aristophanes as its author and probable producer, but he probably authored *The Preview* as well: ancient citations from it are ascribed to Aristophanes, never to Philonides, who produced at least two other plays for Aristophanes (*Amphiaraus* in 414 and *Frogs* in 405). Perhaps Aristophanes' failure with *Clouds* at the previous year's Dionysia inclined him against producing there in 422,[1] so that he entered two plays at the Lenaea; there may even have been a rule preventing last-place contestants at the Dionysia from producing there in the following year.[2]

Wasps follows the pattern of *Acharnians* and *Knights* in criticizing the demos for its uncritical and self-defeating allegiance to demagogues, which allows them to corrupt and co-opt democratic institutions for their own selfish purposes. This time the focus is not on their militarism or manipulation of Council and Assembly but on jurors – not the jury-system per se – who are criticized for their staunch but misguided devotion to demagogic politicians, who misuse the courts to attack their enemies, to shake down the wealthy, and to enrich themselves at the people's expense. As in *Knights*, the chief demagogue is Cleon, and he is again harshly caricatured on stage, this time as a malevolent watchdog who steals food for himself while denouncing the household's good and loyal dogs.[3] New to the series is a domestic dimension: the antagonists are father and son, so that their political disagreement juxtaposes household (private) and polis (public)[4] and is framed in terms of the generation gap that perturbed Athens in the 420s (and was reflected in two of Aristophanes' previous plays, *Banqueters* and *Clouds*), pitting an uncouth "greatest generation," which had toiled and sacrificed to make Athens great, against the younger generation, which was sophisticated, affluent, spoiled, ambitious, and resentful of populist attacks.

As for Cleon, he had recently recovered from a political eclipse that befell him not long after the production of *Knights*: after the Athenian defeat at Delium in late 424 and the subsequent loss of strategically important Amphipolis, public

DOI: 10.4324/9781003159407-4

opinion turned against his aggressive war policies, so that he was not re-elected to the board of generals, and in spring 423 the Athenians voted, against his advice, in favor of a one-year truce with Sparta. But then his luck turned again: Athens' subject ally Scione defected to the Spartan side, provoking a resurgence of public paranoia and anti-Spartan sentiment that stalled ratification of the truce and revived Cleon's political fortunes. In *Wasps* he is portrayed as seeking judicial revenge against Laches, one of the proposers of the truce. But unlike *Knights*, *Wasps* focuses not so much on Cleon and the demagogues personally but instead on the psychology and motivations of their supporters who served on juries.

In democratic Athens, popular sovereignty was rooted in the jury system: laws enacted by the demos were to be impartially and fairly administered by disinterested peers representing the demos as a whole. Disputes and prosecutions were brought to court by individuals and litigated personally by the parties involved: there were no official prosecutors, advocates, or judges. Each litigant was allowed the same amount of time to make his case and call his witnesses, and trials could last no longer than one day. The cases were heard by large juries composed of any citizen aged 30 or older who wished to serve, and their verdict was final and unappealable. In order to enable poorer men to participate, there was a per diem stipend that was raised from two to three obols on a motion by Cleon. This was not quite a pittance but less than most able-bodied citizens could earn in a day, so that jury service tended to attract old or disabled men and the urban poor: the populists' natural constituents. This arrangement produced friction between the generations and the social classes: the young, wealthy, or powerful could well resent being at the mercy of a "mob" of penurious old men who had been primed by Cleon to distrust them and to view fines as assuring the supply of jury-pay, and they could reasonably regard that jury-pay as an entitlement designed to facilitate populist manipulation of the courts.[5]

Lovecleon (*Philocleon*) is a member of the "greatest generation" that defeated the Persians and built the Athenian empire; he is at least 80 years old, since he recalls military action at least as far back as 478. Lovecleon has surrendered control of his prosperous estate[6] to his elegant, well-to-do son, Loathecleon (*Bdelycleon*), and has now become "addicted" to jury service, spending all his time in the courts. The Chorus, fellow jurors who are costumed as wasps with stingers, symbolizing their irascible and dangerous nature, are poor and must rely solely on their jury pay to support themselves and their families. They are members of the same generation and fought the same battles, implying solidarity and common purpose in the past. They regard Lovecleon as their leader, for he is the fiercest and most dedicated of them all, always ready at daybreak when they come to fetch him. Loathecleon regards his father's passion for the hard life of a juror as sheer madness. After fruitlessly trying several psychiatric and medicinal cures, Loathecleon and his slaves barricade Lovecleon in the house. But attempts to confine the old man prove exhausting in the face of determined escape attempts, and the Wasps are riled. After a battle with the Wasps, who regard Loathecleon as an enemy of the people and would-be tyrant, Loathecleon offers to debate his father on the virtues and rewards of jury service, winner take all. The Wasps agree to referee the debate.

In his (quite rational) defense of jury service, Lovecleon stresses the juror's power and independence, the importance of the juror's pay to the older generation and their families, and the pleasure taken by poor, elderly jurors in lording it over, and especially in convicting, rich young defendants, who would otherwise ignore them, as would everyone else. In his rebuttal, Loathecleon demonstrates that the jurors are actually slaves of men like Cleon, that the defendants they convict are the real benefactors of Athens, and that the real money and power belong to self-dealing politicians; Lovecleon and his friends, whose toil made Athens unprecedentedly prosperous, deserve to live a life of luxury, but as it is, the politicians, who contribute nothing to Athens, reap all the rewards save for the jurors' meager pay. The Wasps are won over to Loathecleon's point of view and can only wish that they had sons like Loathecleon to supply their needs. Loathecleon offers to provide a life of luxury and leisure for his father, if he will abandon the courts and stay at home; when he demurs, Loathecleon suggests that he set up his own lawcourt in the courtyard. Lovecleon has no choice but to obey his son.

Aristophanes now exploits the parallelism between Lovecleon's position in the city (enthrallment by the vulgar Cleon) and his status in own household (dependence on his cultivated son) in order to consider what might happen if men like Loathecleon were to win the allegiance of men like his father, turn them away from participation in public life, and introduce them to the finer things of life – rather like Dicaeopolis in *Acharnians*, who finds a way to set up his own happy polis apart from the war and corruption that afflicts everyone else. At first, the plan goes well. Lovecleon is allowed to judge a case involving two household dogs: Screamon (Cleon) prosecutes Snatches (Laches) for the theft of some Sicilian cheese. Thanks to Loathecleon's benign intervention, Snatches is acquitted on the grounds that he is a good dog who works hard for the people and stole only for their good, while Screamon is well fed for doing nothing.

Then, in the parabasis, Aristophanes claims, much like Loathecleon, that his efforts to expose Cleon and his ilk have always aimed to help the people; and the Chorus recapitulates the contributions of the older generation and vows from now on not to reward today's "drones" but only those who make contributions similar to their own. The Wasps' conversion to the right way of thinking is not unlike the conversion of Demos in the finale of *Knights*. There, Demos was restored by rejuvenation to his and Athens' youthful glory days; in their song at 1450–72 the Wasps similarly express happiness at Lovecleon's change of direction and praise his son's benevolence. But this is not the play's finale: Lovecleon will no longer be going to court, and by the end of the play he is behaving as he did in his youth, carousing and dancing to the songs that were popular then, but he remains his old self and, unlike the Wasps, he has not really changed.

The trouble begins when Loathecleon invites his father to an elegant banquet, makes him put on a new suit of clothes, and coaches him in the etiquette appropriate to an evening with fine gentlemen (Cleon is listed among the guests, implying that his populism is merely a pose). But the banquet is a disaster: Lovecleon becomes drunk and disorderly, insulting the guests, abducting the girl piper, and assaulting every ordinary citizen he meets on his way home. To make matters worse, he rudely rejects every attempt by his victims and his son to settle out of court. Loathecleon can only look on helplessly. Clearly the vulgarity, selfishness, and aggression that Lovecleon displayed as a juror have not been lost but only let loose on society at large. If so, Loathecleon's suggestion – that the ordinary folk who fight for Athens should be allowed to enjoy the fruits of their valor, but leave the details of government to wiser heads – perhaps works better in theory than in practice, at least in the case of the incorrigible Lovecleon.

In *Wasps*, Aristophanes may have tempered the optimism, albeit somewhat cloaked in wishful thinking, that animated Demos' transformation in *Knights*. Perhaps we should consider Lovecleon an anomaly or special case and look instead to the Wasps as illustrating a more optimistic outcome. Or is the problem Lovecleon's personal attitudes and behavior rather than his allegiance to populists, which he seems to abandon? In any case, there is much in the snobbish, sybaritic, and self-centered Loathecleon and his disdain for public life that reminds us of Aristophanes and his own efforts to talk sense to the demos, so that it is not impossible that Loathecleon's character contains a degree of self-parody if not self-criticism, which the Wasps' enthusiasm and admiration would ironically counterpoint.

Characters

SOSIAS, slave of Loathecleon
XANTHIAS, slave of Loathecleon
LOATHECLEON, a wealthy young man
LOVECLEON, his father
BOY, the Chorus Leader's son
SCREAMON, watchdog of Cydathenaeum
VICTIM of Lovecleon
MYRTIA, a breadwoman
ACCUSER of Lovecleon

Mute Characters

DONKEY of Loathecleon
BOYS, sons of the Chorus members
SLAVES of Loathecleon (Midas, Phrygian, and Jaws)
SNATCHES, a dog of Aexone
KITCHEN UTENSILS
PUPPIES of Grabes
DARDANIS, a pipe-girl
VICTIMS of Lovecleon
CHAEREPHON, witness for Mytria
WITNESS for the Accuser
SONS OF CARCINUS, three dancers
CARCINUS
CHORUS of old jurymen, imagined as wasps

The scene building represents the house of Lovecleon and Loathecleon, who is asleep on the roof. Netting covers the entire house, and the slaves Sosias and Xanthias guard the door.

SOSIAS

Hey Xanthias, you damned jinx, what's the matter with you?

XANTHIAS

(*waking up*)
I'm learning how to relieve the night watch.

SOSIAS

Then your ribs will have a serious grudge against you.
Don't you realize what a monster we've got in our custody?

XANTHIAS

Certainly; that's why I want to absent me from solicitude awhile.   5

SOSIAS

Take your own chances then. Why should I care?
Something pleasant is beginning to wash over my eyeballs too.

XANTHIAS

Whoa there, you losing your mind? Or having a corybantic fit?[7]

SOSIAS

No, Sabazius[8] has put me under a sleepy spell.

XANTHIAS

So you're bowing your head to Sabazius just like me.   10
A moment ago a snoozy slumber invaded my eyelids too,
like a platoon of Persians. And I just had an amazing dream.

SOSIAS

Me too – no lie – like none I've ever had.
But you tell yours first.

XANTHIAS

I saw an eagle,   15
a great big one, swoop down into the marketplace,
snatch up a bronzed shield in its talons, and take it to the sky,
and then it became Cleonymus and lost its shield![9]

SOSIAS

Cleonymus does make a fine riddle at that.   20

XANTHIAS

How so?

SOSIAS

A man could challenge his fellow drinkers by asking,
"what beast loses its shield on land, in the air, and at sea?"

XANTHIAS

Uh oh, what sort of bad luck is coming my way,
having a dream like that?

SOSIAS

Don't worry yourself,   25
nothing awful's going to happen, god forbid.

XANTHIAS

Still, there's something awful about a man losing his gear.
But tell me your dream now.

SOSIAS

Oh, it's momentous,
it's about the whole ship of state.

XANTHIAS

Hurry up then and tell me the hull story!   30

SOSIAS

Just as I was nodding off, I dreamed
that sheep were meeting in Assembly on the Pnyx,[10]
wearing cheap jackets and carrying walking sticks;
then I saw a ravening dragon start to harangue   35
these sheep with a voice like a hog on fire.

XANTHIAS

Yuk!

SOSIAS

                What is it?

XANTHIAS

                        Stop talking, stop!
Your dream reeks horribly of rotten hides.[11]

SOSIAS

Then this sickening dragon was holding a pair of scales
and weighing pea pulse.

XANTHIAS

                        Good heavens,   40
he means to divide our people!

SOSIAS

And I dreamed that Theorus[12] was squatting beside the dragon,
on the ground, with the head of a plover.
Then Alcibiades said to me in his baby lisp,
"Wookit! Theowus has the head of a gwoveller!"[13]   45

XANTHIAS

Alcibiades was wight about that!

SOSIAS

Well, isn't it eerie, Theorus turning into
a plover?

XANTHIAS

Not at all; it's a very good sign.

SOSIAS

How so?

XANTHIAS

Look:
first a man, then suddenly he became a plover;
isn't it plain as day and easy to figure out   50
that Theorus is up and leaving us and going to the birds?

SOSIAS

Say, why don't I put you on a two obol salary,
since you interpret dreams so cleverly?

XANTHIAS

All right then, it's time I let the audience in on the plot.
But first I'll give them the following short preface.   55
Don't expect anything terribly grand from us,
or conversely, any jokes swiped from Megara.[14]
We've got no pair of slaves broadcasting
baskets-full of nuts to the spectators,
no Heracles cheated of his dinner,   60
no Euripides once again taking outrageous abuse,[15]
and even if Cleon had the pure luck to shine,[16]
we won't make mincemeat out of the same man twice.[17]
No, ours is a simple plot that has a point,
no brainier than you all are yourselves,   65
but more artistic than lowbrow comedy.
Very well then: we have a master, there he is
sleeping up above, the big man, the one on the roof.
He's put his father under house arrest and posted us
as sentries to prevent him from escaping.   70
His father, you see, suffers from a bizarre sickness,
which no one here will be able to recognize or diagnose
unless we tell you. Go ahead then, take a guess.[18]
Pronapes' son Amynias[19] over here says
he's addicted to gambling at dice.

SOSIAS

                                    That's incorrect.   75
He's using his own symptoms to guess the disease.

XANTHIAS

Right, but the affliction does begin with "addicted to."
Now Sosias here is telling Dercylus[20]
that he's addicted to drink.

SOSIAS

                                    Not even close:
that disease afflicts only gentlemen.   80

XANTHIAS

Nicostratus of Scambonidae[21] has a different guess,
that he's addicted to holding sacrifices or entertaining.

SOSIAS

Doggonnit no, Nicostratus, he's not a philoxenist:
Philoxenus, you know, is a candy-ass.[22]

XANTHIAS

You're getting nowhere; you'll never find the answer.   85
If you really want to know, then quiet down.
I'm going to tell you what the master's sickness is:
addiction to jury service, and the world's worst case!
That's his passion, judging, and he groans
if he can't sit on the very front bench.   90
At night he gets no sleep, not even a wink,
and even if he does nod off for an instant, his mind's
still over there fluttering around the water clock all night.[23]
He's so used to holding a voting pebble
that he wakes up with his first three fingers pressed together,   95
like somebody offering incense at the new moon.
By heaven, if he sees written on a doorway
"Pyrilampes' son Demos sure is hot"
he goes and writes next to it "the ballot box is hot."[24]
When the cock started crowing just after bedtime,   100
he claimed it had been bribed to wake him up late

by the magistrates undergoing audit in his court.
Right after dinner he calls out for his sandals
and goes out to stand watch before the courthouse,
clinging to the post like a barnacle.   105
From nastiness he scratches the long penalty line
for all convicts, and comes home with his nails caked
with wax like a honeybee or a bumblebee.
He was so scared he'd run out of voting pebbles
that he keeps a whole beach in the house.   110
That's how crazy he is, and the more you reason
with him, the more cases he hears. So we've shut him in
behind bars, and we watch so he doesn't escape.
That's because his son's taking the sickness very hard.
At first with soothing words he tried to persuade him   115
not to leave the house in a cheap cloak, but he wouldn't listen.
Next he tried immersion and exorcism, to no avail.
Then he joined him up with the Corybants,[25] but he burst
into Common Court, tom-tom and all, and started hearing cases.   120
Well, the son was getting nowhere with these rituals,
so he sailed his father to Aegina and bedded him down
to spend a night in Asclepius' temple there.[26]
But before daybreak, there he was at the courtroom gate.
After that, we stopped letting him out altogether.   125
But he kept escaping through the gutters and also
through the chinks. So every single gap
we stuffed with plugs and sealed them up.
But then he hammered pegs into the wall
and hopped up and away like a pet crow.   130
We countered by draping the whole courtyard with netting
and standing guard all around the house.
The old man has a name: Lovecleon – I swear! –
and his son is named Loathecleon,
a chap with some high-horsical traits.   135

LOATHECLEON

Hey Xanthias! Hey Sosias! Are you asleep?

XANTHIAS

Uh oh.

SOSIAS

　　　What?

XANTHIAS

Loathecleon's getting up.

LOATHECLEON

One or the other of you two, run around here on the double!
Father's got out and into the kitchen.
He's on all fours, scurrying around like a mouse. Keep an eye   140
on the sink-drain so he doesn't slip out that way.
And you cover the door!

Exit Sosias behind the house.

XANTHIAS

Right, sir.

LOATHECLEON

God almighty, what's all that racket in the chimney?
You in there! Who are you?

LOVECLEON

Me? I'm smoke coming out.

LOATHECLEON

Smoke? All right then, from what kind of wood?

LOVECLEON

Impeach-wood.[27]   145

LOATHECLEON

Of course! That's the most irritating kind of smoke.
But no more evaporation for you. Where's the chimney cover?
Get back in there! Here, let me put a log on top for good measure.
There now, think up some other stratagem.
Really, no one else has the trouble I have!   150
I'm all set to be called the son of Old Smoky!

LOVECLEON

Open up, boy!

XANTHIAS

       He's pushing on the door!

LOATHECLEON

       Then lean into it hard,
good and manly! I'm coming down there too.
And keep an eye on the lock and the bar;
make sure he doesn't munch the nut right off the bolt!   155

LOVECLEON

What are you doing? Let me out, you utter scum,
I've a case to hear! Or Dracontides will beat the rap![28]

XANTHIAS

That would upset you?

LOVECLEON

       Yes! I once consulted
the Delphic oracle,[29] and the god foretold:
if ever I acquitted anyone, I'd dry up and blow away!   160

XANTHIAS

Apollo save us all, what a prophecy!

LOVECLEON

Come on, I beg you, let me out, or I'll explode!

XANTHIAS

By god, Lovecleon, you will never get out!

LOVECLEON

Then I'll gnaw through this netting with my teeth!

XANTHIAS

You haven't any teeth!

LOVECLEON

     O heaven save me,   165
how can I kill you? How? Give me a sword
quick as you can, or better yet, a penalty tablet!

LOATHECLEON

This person is set to commit some awful crime!

LOVECLEON

Not at all, I swear to god! I just want to take
the donkey and its panniers out and sell them.   170
It's market day.

LOATHECLEON

     Surely I myself could sell
him, couldn't I?

LOVECLEON

    Not the way I would.

LOATHECLEON

That's right, I'd do it better.

LOVECLEON

     All right, let the donkey out.

XANTHIAS

What an excuse he tried to hook you with
to let him out. Pretty sly.

LOATHECLEON

     But he didn't catch me   175
with that one; yes, I'm on to his machinations.
But I think I'll go in and get the donkey myself.

I don't want the old man so much as peeping out again.
Loathecleon goes in and fetches the donkey.
Why all the braying, Jack? Don't want to be sold today?
Get along there. Why are you fussing? Unless you're carrying   180
Odysseus or somebody.[30]

XANTHIAS

Wait a minute. Good lord,
he does have somebody curled up under here, look!

LOATHECLEON

What? Let me have a look.

XANTHIAS

There he is.

LOATHECLEON

What's this?
Who might you be, my good man? Well?

LOVECLEON

Noman. Honestly.

LOATHECLEON

You're Noman? From where?

LOVECLEON

Ithaca. Son of Escapides.   185

LOATHECLEON

Well, you're a Noman who'll enjoy no manner of success.
Quick, drag him out from under there. The skunk,
look what he's crawled under! If you ask me,
he's looks just like a gofer for a burro-crat!

LOVECLEON

Leave me alone or we'll soon be in a fight.

LOATHECLEON

A fight about what?

LOVECLEON

                    About the donkey's shadow![31]

LOATHECLEON

You're a master villain and totally out of control.

LOVECLEON

Me a villain? Certainly not! I'll have you know
I'm perfectly fine. But maybe you'll find that out
when you sink your teeth into a cut of tough old juryman.   195

LOATHECLEON

You and the donkey giddyap into the house.

LOVECLEON

Fellow jurors! Cleon! I need assistance here!

LOATHECLEON

Do your yelling inside; the door is locked.
You there, stack a pile of stones against the door,
and shoot that bolt right back into its slot,   200
and reinforce it with that plank, and roll the big
millstone against it, and make it snappy!

XANTHIAS

                    Dammit,
where did that dirtball fall down on me from?

LOATHECLEON

Maybe a mouse up there knocked it down on you.

XANTHIAS

A mouse? Certainly not. What's scuttling around up there   205
beneath the tiles is a roof juror!

LOATHECLEON

Oh my god, the man's turning into a sparrow!
He's going to fly his way out! Where's my net? Where is it?
Shoo! Shoo! Go back, shoo! I swear, I'd be better off
blockading Scione than this father of mine.[32]   210

XANTHIAS

Well now, we've shooed him back inside
and there's no way he can sneak past us anymore,
so why don't we break for a teeny bit of shuteye?

LOATHECLEON

You sorry fool, his fellow jurors will soon
be coming here to pick my father up,   215
any minute now!

XANTHIAS

                    What do you mean? It's hardly dawn.

LOATHECLEON

Then they must have got up late today, by god.
Just after midnight's when they usually pick him up,
toting torches and warbling sweet old songs,
those old Sidon Songs by Phrynichus;[33]   220
that's how they call him out.

XANTHIAS

                    Well, if need be
we'll pelt them with stones without any further ado.

LOATHECLEON

You sorry fool, if anyone riles that tribe
of oldsters, it's like riling a nest of wasps.
They've even got stingers, extremely sharp,   225
sticking out from their rumps, that they stab with,
and they leap and attack, crackling like sparks.

XANTHIAS

Don't you worry, if I've got hold of stones
I can scatter a nest-full of numerous jurymen.

Xanthias and Loathecleon sit down and are soon asleep.
The CHORUS, accompanied by BOYS, enters the orchestra and
makes its way toward Lovecleon's house.

CHORUS LEADER

Get along, press on hardy. Comias, you're lagging.[34]   230
By god, you didn't used to; you were sturdy as a dog-leash,
but nowadays Charinades can outwalk you.
You there, Strymodorus of Conthyle, my excellent brother juror,
do you see Euergides anywhere, or Chabes of Phlya?
I'm afraid what's here is – oh my! – all that's left   235
of that youthful time, when we shared guard duty at Byzantium,[35]
you and I. Remember how we two went rambling at night
and got away with pinching the bread-woman's kneading bowl,
and split it up for firewood, and boiled some pimpernel porridge?
Anyway, let's get a move on, lads; Laches is going to get it today![36]   240
Everybody says he's stuffed his hive with money.
That's why yesterday our patron Cleon ordered us
to report for duty in good time, with three days' rations
of evil rage against that bloke, to punish him for his crimes.
Anyway, let's hurry up, old colleagues, before it gets to be daybreak.   245
Let's move out, and take care to search in all directions with our lamps,
in case there's a stone underfoot somewhere waiting to hurt someone.

BOY

Whoa!
Father, father, mind the mud over there!

CHORUS LEADER

Then pick up a twig from the ground and trim the lamp.

BOY

(*holding up a finger*)
No, I think I'll use *this* to trim the lamp!   250

CHORUS LEADER

Who taught you to shove the wick around with your finger,
especially when oil's in short supply, you idiot?
Of course it's not *you* that feels the bite when prices rise!

BOY

Use your fists to teach me that lesson one more time,
and I promise you we'll douse the lamps and go home by ourselves!　　255
Maybe without this lamp you'll stumble around in the dark,
churning up the mud like a marsh snipe!

CHORUS LEADER

I warn you, I dish out punishment to people bigger than you!
Hold on, this looks like mud I'm stepping in.
No question that within four days at the outside　　260
the god will of necessity start making water.
Anyway, look at the mold here on these lamps:
when that's present, he's most fond of making rain.
Well, the crops that aren't up yet could certainly use
a rainfall, and then the breath of the north wind on them.　　265

CHORUS LEADER[37]

Move along, boy, move along.　　290

BOY

strophe
Will you give me something then,
father, if I ask you for it?

CHORUS LEADER

Of course, my lad. Just tell me
what nice thing you want me to buy.
I'm pretty sure you're going to say　　295
knucklebone dice, my boy.

BOY

God no. Figs, daddy!
It's nicer –

CHORUS LEADER

　　　　Absolutely not,
not even if you hang yourselves!

BOY

Then I'll stop guiding you altogether.

CHORUS LEADER

Look, out of this tiny pittance   300
I've got to get barley-meal,
firewood and dinner for the three of us,
and you ask me for figs!

BOY

antistrophe
Tell me then, father,
if the archon doesn't call the court
into session today, how   305
can we buy lunch?
Do you have any firm hope for us,
any "holy way to Helle"?[38]

CHORUS LEADER

Alas and sigh.
I surely don't know   310
where our dinner's coming from.

BOY

Why then, miserable mother, did you bear me?

CHORUS LEADER

So that I'd have the problem of feeding you!

BOY

Ah shopping bag, it seems you've been
a useless ornament to carry!
Boo hoo.   315
All we can do is bawl.

CHORUS LEADER

What's the matter with our brother juror from this house,   266
That he doesn't show up here ready join the crew?
He's never been tardy before. In fact he always
leads us on our way with something from Phrynichus; the man's
an avid singer. Well, gentlemen, I think we should pause here   270
and sing him out of the house. Maybe when he hears
my song he'll be happy to hobble outside.

CHORUS

strophe
Why ever does the old man not appear to us
at his door or answer our call?
Maybe he couldn't find his shoes?   275
Or stubbed his toe on something in the dark
and got a swollen ankle, an oldster like him,
and maybe even a lump in his groin?
I tell you, he was by far the fiercest of us all,
and the only one who couldn't be sweet-talked;
no, when anyone begged for mercy
he'd put his head down like this and say,
"you're trying to cook a stone."   280

antistrophe
Maybe it was yesterday's case,
the guy who somehow slipped through our fingers
by fooling us into believing
that he's a friend to Athens
and the first to tell us what was going on at Samos;[39]
maybe he got sore about that
and took to his bed with a fever.
That's the sort of man he is!   285
But do get up, dear fellow! Don't
eat your heart out and feed your vexation.
There's a plump one on the docket today,
one of those who betrayed the Thracian front.[40]
See that you pot him!

LOVECLEON

(*from a window*)
Friends, I've been pining   317
all this time, listening to you
through this chink.
But since I can't sing,
what am I to do?
These men are watching me because
I'm ever ready to go with you   320
to the voting urns and cause some pain.
Ah, great thundering Zeus,
turn me right now into hot air,
like Proxenides[41] or the son of Bluster[42] here,   325
that climbing vine.
Deign, Lord, to do me a favor,

in pity at my plight: either bake me
with a boiling thunderbolt,
then hoist me aloft, blow off the ashes   330
and toss me into hot salsa;
or else turn me to stone,
the one they count the votes on!

CHORUS

strophe
Just who is it that shuts you in this way
behind locked doors?
You can tell us: we're on your side.   335

LOVECLEON

My son. No, don't shout: that's him down there,
sleeping in front of the house. So tone it down.

CHORUS

On what pretext does he want to treat you this way, silly man?
What's his excuse?

LOVECLEON

Gentlemen, he won't let me hear cases or do any harm.   340
Instead, he wants to wine and dine me, though that's not what I want.

CHORUS

Has the slimy fellow the gall,
this Demagogocleon, to mouth off that way,
because you voiced an awkward truth
about the fleet?[43] This man
would never have dared
to say that unless
he were some sort of conspirator!   345

CHORUS LEADER

Well, under the circumstances it's time you come up with a
    fresh idea
for getting down here behind this fellow's back.

LOVECLEON

What could it be? You come up with one; I'm ready to do anything,
so much do I crave to stroll among the dockets with my voting shell.

CHORUS LEADER

OK, is there a chink that you could excavate from inside   350
and then slip out disguised in rags, like wily Odysseus?[44]

LOVECLEON

Everything's sealed up; not even a gnat could slip through a chink.
You've got to think of something else; I can't turn myself into
     runny whey.

CHORUS LEADER

OK, do you remember when on campaign you stole the skewers
and shot yourself right down from the battlement, when Naxos
     was taken?[45]   355

LOVECLEON

I know; but so what? This is entirely different.
I was young then, I could get away with things, count on my strength,
and nobody was watching me, so I could
escape carefree. But now soldiers in arms are drawn up   360
and patrol the passes,
two of them at the door
holding skewers and watching me
like a cat who stole some meat.

CHORUS

antistrophe
Well, you'd better come up
with a plan this time too, as quick as you can;   365
it's daybreak, little honeybee.

LOVECLEON

Then my best course is to gnaw through the netting,
and may Dictynna of the Nets forgive me if I've nettled her![46]

CHORUS

Now you're talking like a man headed for salvation!
Get that jaw working!   370

LOVECLEON

There, it's cut through. But absolutely no cheering;
let's watch out that we don't alert Loathecleon.

CHORUS

Never fear, old boy, never fear:
if he makes a peep I'll have him
eating his heart out
and running for dear life,   375
so he'll know better
than to wipe his feet
on the Two Goddesses' legislation![47]

CHORUS LEADER

Now lash that cord to the window frame, tie it around you
and let yourself down, and fill your spirit with Diopeithes!   380

LOVECLEON

Say, what if these two catch on and try to get me reeled up
and hauled in, then what will you do? Tell me right now.

CHORUS LEADER

We'll all summon up our hardwood spirit and defend you.
The things we'll do, there will be no containing you!

LOVECLEON

All right, then I'll do it, on your say-so. And listen, if anything
    happens to me,   385
gather me up, give me a funeral, and bury me under the court railings.

CHORUS LEADER

Never fear, nothing will happen to you. Now let yourself down intrepidly,
with a prayer to your ancestral gods, there's a good fellow.

LOVECLEON

Lord Lycus,[48] my next-door hero – for you enjoy the same things I do,
the tears and the wailings of each day's defendants,   390
and of course chose to live where you could best hear them,
the only hero eager to seat himself next to a weeper –
now take pity and rescue your very own neighbor,
and I vow never to piss or fart on your fence!

LOATHECLEON

Hey! Wake up!

XANTHIAS

        What's going on?

LOATHECLEON

        A sound of voices seems to surround me.   395
The old man isn't trying to give us the slip again, is he?

XANTHIAS

        No indeed,
but he's letting himself down on a rope!

LOATHECLEON

What are you doing, you scum of the earth?
    Don't you come down here!
(*to Xanthias*)
Go up the other way, quick, and hit him with those branches.
Maybe he'll back water if he's swatted with the harvest wreath.[49]

LOVECLEON

All you prosecutors out there with cases coming up this year,   400
won't you lend me a hand? Smicythion! Teisiades! Chremon!
    Pheredeipnus![50]
Help me out, it's now or never, before I'm dragged inside instead!

CHORUS

strophe
Tell me, why are we waiting to launch the wrath

we feel when anyone vexes our nest?
Out now, out now   405
with that sharp-tempered stinger that we use to punish,
and brace it for battle.
Now grab your cloaks as quick as you can, lads,
and run and shout, report this to Cleon,
and tell him to come   410
and confront a man who hates his country
and who'll be destroyed
for proposing the idea
that lawsuits be abolished![51]

LOATHECLEON

Gentlemen, consider the facts, but stop your screaming!   415

CHORUS LEADER

I'll scream, by god, and to high heaven!

LOATHECLEON

I assure you I won't release him.

CHORUS

Isn't this terrible? Isn't this bare-faced dictatorship?
Oh my country, oh my god-forsaken Theorus,[52]
oh any other bootlicker who stands up for us!

XANTHIAS

Holy Heracles, they've really got stingers! Look, master!   420

LOATHECLEON

The ones they used to destroy Gorgias' son Philippus,[53] and rightly.

CHORUS LEADER

And we'll destroy you along with them! Now every man wheel
this way, draw stingers and charge him,
with ranks closed, in good order, full of rage and spirit,
so he'll never forget what a swarm he's angered.   425

XANTHIAS

My god, this is really terrible, if we're in for a fight.
I'm scared just looking at their stingers.

CHORUS LEADER

Now let the man go. If you don't, I do declare
that you'll be envying turtles for their shells!

LOVECLEON

At'em then, fellow jurors, sharp-hearted wasps!   430
Division One get riled up and dive bomb his ass!
Division Two stab all around his eyes, and his fingers too!

LOATHECLEON

(*calling into the house*)
Midas! Phrygian! Help me here! You too, Jaws!
Enter SLAVES.
Hold onto him and don't turn him over to anybody.
Otherwise, it's thick leg irons for you and no lunch.   435
I recognize the sound of hot air when I hear it.
Loathecleon and Xanthias enter the house.

CHORUS LEADER

Let him go, or you'll get something stuck into you!

LOVECLEON

Lord Hero Cecrops, Dracontides below the waist,[54]
will you simply watch when I'm being manhandled this way
        by barbarians,
the very ones I myself taught how to cry at four tears to the quart?   440

CHORUS LEADER

So doesn't old age truly hold evils in abundance?
Obviously it does: these two manhandle their former master
assaultively, completely forgetting about
all the jackets and tunics he used to buy them,
and the caps, and how in wintertime he saw to their feet   445
so they wouldn't always be frozen. But in their eyes
there's no respect at all for their former footwear.

LOVECLEON

You still won't let me go, you vile animal?
Even when you recall the time I caught you stealing grapes,
marched you to the olive tree, and did a right manly job
   flaying you raw,   450
so that everyone envied you? But you were apparently ungrateful.
Come on you two, let me go, before my son darts out.

CHORUS LEADER

Ah, but this will soon cost you both very dearly.
It won't be long now before you know the character of men
who are sharp-spirited, righteous, and look mustard at you.   455

*The Chorus attacks. Enter Loathecleon with a smokepot and
Xanthias with a stick.*

LOATHECLEON

Xanthias, beat the wasps, beat them away from the house!

XANTHIAS

That's what I'm doing! But you help too: blow lots of smoke on them!

LOATHECLEON

Shoo! Get the hell away! Go! Lay on with your stick!

XANTHIAS

And you, suffocate them with a billow of Aeschines, son of Hotair![55]

The Chorus retreats.

LOATHECLEON

I knew we'd eventually shoo you all away.   460

LOVECLEON

But you wouldn't have escaped them so very easily
if they'd been munching on songs by Philocles.[56]

CHORUS

antistrophe
Don't the poor folk see it plainly,
how dictatorship has sneaked up on me
from behind and tried to jump me,   465
now that you, you troublesome troublemaker, you long-haired
        Amynias,[57]
debar us from our country's established legal rights,
without making any excuse
or dextrous argument,
but autocratically?   470

LOATHECLEON

Is there any possibility that we might enter into discussion
and compromise without this fighting and shrill screaming?

CHORUS

Discussion with you, you enemy of the people, you lover of monarchy,
you buddy of Brasidas,[58] with the woollen fringes on your clothes   475
and the untrimmed beard on your face?

LOATHECLEON

I swear I'd do better to write my father off altogether,
instead of battling day after day in such a sea of troubles.

CHORUS LEADER

Hah! You haven't even got past the soup course yet, or the
        salad either –   480
we'll toss that in from our stock of ten-gallon metaphors.
No, your present pain is nothing. Just wait until a prosecutor
dumps these very charges over your head and calls you a conspirator!

LOATHECLEON

Heavens above, I do wish you'd get off my back!
Or is it decided that we'll spend the day skinning each other alive?   485

CHORUS

No, never, not while there's any breath left in my body –
for a man who plans to be our dictator!

LOATHECLEON

How you see dictatorship and conspirators everywhere,
as soon as anyone voices a criticism large or small!
I hadn't even heard of the word being used for at least fifty years,[59]   490
but nowadays it's much cheaper than sardines.
Look how it's bandied about in the marketplace.
If someone buys perch but doesn't want sprats,
the sprat seller next door pipes right up and says,
"This guy buys fish like a would-be dictator."   495
And if he asks for a free onion to spice his sardines a bit,
the vegetable lady gives him the fish eye and says,
"Say, are you asking for an onion because you want to be dictator?
Or maybe you think Athens grows spices as her tribute to you?"

XANTHIAS

My slut too, when I went to her crib yesterday noon.   500
I told her to ride me, and she got mad and asked
if I was jockeying for a dictatorship à la Hippias![60]

LOATHECLEON

These people do enjoy hearing talk like that, if I'm any indication.
Just because I want my father to abandon all of these
dawn-wandering, nuisance-suing, jury-serving, trouble-seeking habits   505
and live a genteel life like Morychus,[61] for my efforts
I get called a conspirator with dictatorship in mind.

LOVECLEON

Yes, and rightly so! Not even for pigeons' milk[62] would I
trade the living you'd take away from me now.
Skate and eels don't tempt me either. I'd much rather   510
sit down to a nice little lawsuit baked en casserole.

LOATHECLEON

Sure, because you're addicted to that kind of gratification.
But if you'll hold your tongue and open your mind to what I say,
I think I'll enlighten you about the total error of your ways.

LOVECLEON

Jurying is an error?

LOATHECLEON

        What's more, you don't realize   515
that you're the laughingstock of men you all but grovel to.
You're unaware that you've been enslaved.

LOVECLEON

        Stop talking about slavery.
I'm master of everyone!

LOATHECLEON

        Not you. You're just a slave
who thinks he's a master. No? Then describe for us, father,
what profit you get from reaping the fruits of Greece.   520

LOVECLEON

By all means, and I want these men to be our arbitrators.

LOATHECLEON

        So do I.
Let him go, everyone.
The Slaves go back into the house.

LOVECLEON

        And give me a sword.
If I lose the debate to you, I'm going to fall on it!

LOATHECLEON

Tell me, what if you fail to – what's the term? – abide by the arbitration?

LOVECLEON

Then never again will I toast the Good Genie[63] with unmixed jury pay!   525

CHORUS

strophe
Now the chap from our school
must argue a novel case.
See that you turn out –

LOATHECLEON

Someone bring me out my writing case right away.
Now then, what sort will he show himself to be, if that's
what you're urging?   530

CHORUS

– to top this youngster in debate!
For you can see that you face a great contest now,
where everything's at stake.   535
Because if, god forbid,
this man does beat you in debate –

LOATHECLEON

That I shall, and I'm going to jot down every single point he makes.

LOVECLEON

What were you saying will happen if he beats me in debate?

CHORUS

– then the elderly crowd   540
are no damn good anymore.
They'll mock us
all over town
and call us olive-bearers,[64]
mere shells of affidavits!   545

CHORUS LEADER

So I call on you, who are to make the case for our whole monarchy,
to take courage now and throw your whole tongue into the task!

LOVECLEON

I will indeed, and right out of the gate I'll demonstrate
that our sovereignty is no weaker than any monarchy.
What living thing is there today more fortunate and felicitated
    than a juror,   550
more coddled or commanding, oldster though he is?
To begin with, I crawl out of bed to find at the court railings
big men, six-footers, watching for me.[65] As soon as I approach,
one of them gives me his soft hand, fresh from stealing public money.
They beg and grovel, pitifully pouring out their pleas: 555
"Pity me, father, I beg you! Maybe one time you too pocketed something

when holding office or procuring field rations for your messmates."
He wouldn't even have known I exist if I hadn't gone easy on him
last time.

LOATHECLEON

Let me make a note of that: *the supplicants*.

LOVECLEON

Then after I've been supplicated and had my anger wiped away,   560
I go inside and act on none of those promises I made.
I just listen to them spouting every sort of alibi.
Tell me, is there any brand of wheedling I don't hear in court?
Some of them bewail their poverty and go on exaggerating
their troubles until they somehow seem as bad as my own.   565
Others tell us stories, others something amusing from Aesop.[66]
Others crack jokes to make me laugh and put away my anger.
And if none of this persuades us, he starts dragging his kids
up there by the hand, daughters and sons, and I listen
while they cringe and bleat in chorus, and then for their sake   570
the father implores me, trembling as if I were a god, to let him
      off in his audit:
"If you enjoy the bleat of the lamb, please pity the cry of the kid!"
And if I enjoy a bit of pork, I'm supposed to heed the cry
      of his daughter.[67]
And then we wind down the pitch of our anger a little.
Isn't this high authority, then, and derision of wealth?   575

LOATHECLEON

I'll make a note of that too: *derision of wealth*.
Now please mention the benefits you get from your alleged rule
      over Greece.

LOVECLEON

Well, when boys are being examined for citizenship, we get
      to look at their privates.
And if Oeagrus[68] comes to court as a defendant, he won't get off
until he chooses the best speech from *Niobe* and recites it for us.[69] 580
And if a piper wins his case, the price he pays the jurors
is to put on his harness and pipe us an exit tune as we leave.
And if a dying father bequeaths his heiress daughter to someone,
we tell that last will and testament to go soak its head,
and the same to the clasp sitting so pretty over its seals,   585
and we award that girl to whoever talks us into it.[70]
And we do all this with impunity, which no other office holders
      can claim.

LOATHECLEON

Yes, that's the only thing you've said that I congratulate you on.
But it's wrong of you to unclasp the heiress' endowments.

LOVECLEON

Furthermore, when the Council and People can't decide a big case,   590
they vote to hand over the wrongdoers to the jurymen.
Then Euathlus[71] and Toadyonymus[72] here, the weighty shield-shedder,
swear that they'll never betray us, that they'll fight for the masses.
And no one ever carries a motion before the People unless
he's proposed to adjourn the courts after the very first case tried.   595
And even Cleon, the scream champion, takes no bites out of us!
No, he puts his arm around us and swats away the flies.[73]
You've never done anything of the kind, for your own father!
But Theorus[74] – and he's every bit the big-shot Euphemius[75] is –
takes the sponge right from his pail and starts shining my shoes.   600
Look what advantages you're locking me out of and holding
        me back from,
the ones you said you'd demonstrate were really slavery and drudgery!

LOATHECLEON

Have your fill of talking; you're bound to stop eventually and
        stand revealed
as an asshole that can't be washed clean, for all that grand authority
        of yours.

LOVECLEON

But the nicest part of all, which had slipped my mind,   605
is when I come home with my pay. That's when everyone
gives me a warm welcome because of the money. First my daughter[76]
washes me and oils my feet and bends down to kiss me,
calling me "daddy" and fishing out the three-obol piece with her tongue.[77]
And the little woman fusses over me and brings me a puff pastry,   610
and then sits next to me and coaxes me, "Eat this,
eat this up!" I love all that, and I don't have to look to you
and your steward to see when he'll get around to serving my lunch
with his usual curses and grumbles. And if he's tardy with my pastry,
I've got this pay to shield me from troubles, a "bulwark
against missiles."   615
And if you won't pour me a drink of wine, I carry this
        donkey-eared flask
full of wine, tip it up, and pour myself a drink. It opens wide
        and brays a great big soldierly fart at that goblet of yours.
So don't I wield a great authority, no less great than Zeus?

I'm even spoken of in the same way as Zeus.   620
For instance, if we're in an uproar,
Everyone who passes says,
"Zeus Almighty,
the jury's really thundering!"
And if I look lightning, the fat cats   625
and the VIPs
say a prayer and shit their pants.
And you're very much afraid of me yourself.
Oh yes, by Demeter, you're afraid. But
I'll be damned if I'm afraid of you!   630

CHORUS

antistrophe
Never have we heard anyone
speak with such clarity
and intelligence!

LOVECLEON

Right; he thought this would be easy, just picking unwatched vines.
He knew very well that I'm the boss in this business!   635

CHORUS

And how he's explored every avenue,
and left nothing out! I for one
swelled with pride as I listened,
and I saw myself judging
in the Isles of the Blessed,[78]   640
basking in the sound of his voice.

LOVECLEON

Yes, he's fidgeting now! Now he's off his stride!
Yes indeed, I'll have you looking whipped today!

CHORUS

You'll have to weave
every wile in the book   645
to win acquittal,
because it's hard <for a youth>
to soften my anger
if I don't like what I hear.

CHORUS LEADER

So unless you've got something sensible to say, it's time you
    went looking
for a good millstone with new treads, hard enough to grind down
    my temper.

LOATHECLEON

It's a hard, and needs formidable intellect beyond the scope
    of comedians,   650
to heal an inveterate sickness endemic to the city.
But here goes. Our father, son of Cronus —[79]

LOVECLEON

Stop that; don't be "fathering" me!
The topic was how I'm a slave, and if you don't explain that to me
    right now,
you'll surely meet your death, even if I'd be barred from
    sacrificial meat![80]

LOATHECLEON

Then listen, pop, and relax your frown a bit.   655
First of all, calculate roughly, not with counters but on your fingers,
how much tribute we receive altogether from the allied cities.[81]
Then make a separate count of the taxes and the many one percents,
court dues, mines, markets, harbors, rents, proceeds from confiscations.[82]
Our total income from all this comes to nearly 2000 talents.   660
Now set aside the annual payment to the jurors, all six thousand of them,
"for never yet have more dwelt in this land." Left, I reckon, is 150 talents.

LOVECLEON

So our pay doesn't even amount to one tenth of the revenue!

LOATHECLEON

It certainly doesn't.

LOVECLEON

    In that case, where is the rest of the money routed?   665

LOATHECLEON

To this I-won't-betray-the-Athenian-rabble bunch,
and I'll-always-fight-for-the-masses! You choose them to rule
    you, father,

because you've been buttered up by these slogans.
And then they extort bribes at fifty talents a pop
from the allied cities by terrifying them with threats like this: 670
"You'll hand over the tribute, or I'll upend your city with
    my thundering!"[83]
while you're content to gnaw the rinds of your own empire.[84]
The allies have caught on that you and the rest of the riff-raff
are starving on what you get from the ballot funnel and splurging on
    nothing,
so they figure you for the Simple Simon vote, while they
    bring presents   675
for these guys: jugged fish, wine, coverlets, cheese, honey, sesame,
lounge pillows, chalices, capes, crowns, necklaces, tumblers,
    healthy wealthiness!
And for you? You rule them, having "tirelessly tramped the land
    and rowed the waves,"
but not one of them gives you a head of garlic for your chowder.

LOVECLEON

They certainly don't! I've ordered three cloves from Eucharides'[85]
    grocery myself.   680
But you're rubbing me the wrong way by not spelling out
    my alleged slavery.

LOATHECLEON

How's this for sheer slavery? All these guys hold office
and draw salaries, themselves and their flunkies too,
while you're content if someone gives you those three obols,
    the ones you earned
by your own hard work, rowing and soldiering and laying siege.   685
What's more, you march to their tune. It really lifts my gorge
when in comes some young candy-ass, Chaereas' son,[86]
spreading his legs like this, all dandied up and waggling his ass,
and he tells you to show up bright and early for jury duty and don't be late,
"because any of you who misses the signal won't get his
    three obols."   690
But he gets his prosecutor's pay, six obols, even if he does come late.
And he splits with a fellow office-holder any bribe a defendant
    might offer,
the two of them teaming up on the case and keeping a straight face,
then going to work like a couple of sawyers, one pulling while
    the other pushes.
But you're so busy panting after the paymaster that you don't
    see what's going on.   695

LOVECLEON

Is that how they treat me? Heavens me, what are you saying?
    You're shaking me to
my very depths, pulling me closer to your viewpoint, doing
    I don't know what to me!

LOATHECLEON

Then consider this: you could be rich, and everyone else too,
but somehow or other these populists have got you boxed in.
You, master of a multitude of cities from the Black Sea to Sardinia,   700
enjoy absolutely no reward, except for this jury pay, and that
they drip into you like droplets of oil from a tuft of wool,
always a little at a time, just enough to keep you alive.
Because they want to keep you poor, and I'll tell you the reason:
so you'll recognize your trainer, and whenever he whistles at you
to attack one of his enemies, you'll leap on that man with
    savage growls.   705
If they wanted to provide a living for the people, it would be easy.
A thousand cities there are that now pay us tribute.
If someone ordered each one to support twenty men,
then twenty thousand[87] loyal proles would be rolling in hare meat,
all kinds of garlands, beestings and eggnog,   710
living it up as befits their country and their trophy at Marathon.[88]
As it is, you traipse around for your employer like olive pickers!

LOVECLEON

Heavens me, what can it be that's creeping over my hand like a paralysis?
I can't even hold my sword; I've gone limp.

LOATHECLEON

But whenever they're scared themselves, they promise you Euboea[89]   715
and get set to supply you with fifty bushel rations of grain.
But they never give it to you, not counting five bushels yesterday,
    only after
proving your citizenship, and then it was barley in one-quart installments.
Which is why I kept you locked up:
I wanted to feed you and I didn't want these   720
blowhards to make a chump of you.
And now I want to provide you
with absolutely anything you want,
except paymaster's milk to drink.

CHORUS LEADER

"Don't judge till you've heard both sides of the story": 725
whoever said that was wise, for in this case you've won my
    vote hands down.
I've slackened my anger and now throw in the towel.
Wherefore, brother of our same age and order,

CHORUS

strophe
listen, listen to his words, and don't be irrational,
or too unyielding and tough a man. 730
I wish I had some kinsman or relative
to give me that kind of good advice.
Now some god
has shown up before your very eyes
to help with your problem, and he's clearly doing you good.
You show up too, and accept his help. 735

LOATHECLEON

That's right, and I'll support him by providing
whatever a senior citizen needs: gruel to lick up,
a cozy cloak, an overcoat,
a whore to massage his cock
and his tailbone. 740
But I can't help being disturbed
that he's silent and won't so much as grunt.

CHORUS

antistrophe
He's been criticizing himself for the activities
he was crazy about before. For he's just now seen the light,
and understands that he was wrong 745
not to listen to your past warnings.
Maybe now he's listening
to your arguments
and really being sensible, changing his ways from now on,
and listening to you.

LOVECLEON

What misery!

LOATHECLEON

Here, why are you bellowing?   750

LOVECLEON

Don't promise me any of your promises!
What I yearn for is over there. There is where I want to be,
where the herald says,
"Whoever hasn't voted please stand!"
Yes, I long to stand at the ballot box,
the last of the vote casters!   755
Onward, my soul! Where are you, soul?
Let me pass, thou shadowy – ![90]
Great Heracles,
if you're telling the truth, I'd better not be on a jury
that convicts Cleon of theft!

LOATHECLEON

Please, father, for gods' sake listen to me.   760

LOVECLEON

What would you have me do? Just name it, except for one thing.

LOATHECLEON

What thing, tell me?

LOVECLEON

To stop being a juror. Before I do that
for you, Hades will decide between us!

LOATHECLEON

All right, since that's what you so enjoy doing,
just stop going to court. Stay here instead,   765
and sit in judgment of the household slaves.

LOVECLEON

On what charge? What's this nonsense?

LOATHECLEON

Exactly what's done at court.
Say the maid opens up the door without permission.
For that offense vote her only a single stiff penalty –
anyway, it's what you used to do regularly at court.[91]   770
And now you'll do your judging in a reasonable way,
outside in the sun if the day dawns warm;
if it's snowing, then sitting by the fire;
if it's raining, you'll go indoors. And if you sleep till noon,
no magistrate will close the gate on you.   775

LOVECLEON

That I like.

LOATHECLEON

And that's not all. If someone's
making a long speech, you needn't sit there hungry,
gnashing your teeth and the defendant too.

LOVECLEON

Then how will I be able to decide cases as competently
as before, if I'm still chewing on my food?   780

LOATHECLEON

A lot more competently! People do say
that when witnesses lie, the jurors get to
the meat of the matter by chewing it over.

LOVECLEON

You know, you're winning me over. But one thing you've yet
    to address:
where will I get my pay?

LOATHECLEON

                    From me.

LOVECLEON

                    Good!   785

Then I'll be getting paid individually and not with a partner.
You know, Lysistratus[92] played a very dirty trick on me,
that joker. We got our drachma the other day[93]
and he went to get it changed in the fish market.
Then he handed me three mullet scales,   790
which I popped into my mouth, thinking they were obols.
Then I smelled them and retched and spat them out.
Then I grabbed hold of him.

LOATHECLEON

    And what did he have to say for himself?

LOVECLEON

                                          Get this:
he said I had the intestines of a rooster.
"Anyway," says he, "you decoct your money pretty fast!"   795

LOATHECLEON

You see what a great advantage you'll have there, too.

LOVECLEON

Not too bad! Very well, proceed with your plan.

LOATHECLEON

Then wait here. I'll be right back with the things we need.
Loathecleon goes inside.

LOVECLEON

Lo and behold, the prophecies come true.
I'd heard that someday the Athenians   800
would judge cases in their very own houses,
and that in his courtyard every man would build
himself an itty bitty court of law;
they'd be on doorsteps everywhere, like Hecate[94] shrines.
Loathecleon and Slaves enter with courtroom paraphernalia.

LOATHECLEON

Just look! Now what have you got to say? I've brought   805

everything I said I would, and a lot besides.
For one thing, in case you need to piss, this chamberpot here
will be hanging by that peg, right beside you.

LOVECLEON

That's quite ingenious of you; you've really thought
of the perfect antidote to an old man's incontinence.   810

LOATHECLEON

And here's some fire, and right next to it lentil
soup to slurp, anytime you want some.

LOVECLEON

                       That's handy too.
Even if I have a cold, still I'll get my pay,
because I'll stay right here and slurp the soup.
But why have you brought the rooster out to me?   815

LOATHECLEON

Why, if you fall asleep while a defendant is speaking,
this rooster up here will crow you wide awake.

LOVECLEON

Everything's to my liking, except I need one thing.

LOATHECLEON

                          Namely?

LOVECLEON

Is there any way you could supply the shrine of Lycus?[95]

LOATHECLEON

(*looking at the stage altar, then motioning one of the Slaves onto it*)
There's this. And here's the hero himself!   820

LOVECLEON

Lord Hero, it was hard to see you there.

LOATHECLEON

He's about as hard to see as Cleonymus![96]

LOVECLEON

True, he's a hero but he's got no equipment either.[97]

LOATHECLEON

The sooner you take your seat, the sooner I
can call a case.

LOVECLEON

        Call away; I've been sitting here patiently.   825

LOATHECLEON

Let me see now, what case will I bring him first?
Has any of the household staff misbehaved?
The Thracian girl, who scorched the pot yesterday –

LOVECLEON

Hold on there, you just about did me in!
Do you mean to call the case without court railings,   830
the first of the holy objects to meet our eyes?

LOATHECLEON

Oh god, there aren't any!

LOVECLEON

        Well, I'll run
into the house myself and get something that'll serve.
Lovecleon goes into the house.

LOATHECLEON

Whatever's the problem? How powerful is love of place!
Xanthias runs out of the house, shouting over his shoulder.

XANTHIAS

To hell with him! Imagine keeping a dog like that!   835

LOATHECLEON

What's the matter here?

XANTHIAS

As if that dog Snatches[98]
didn't just now dart into the kitchen and snatch
a wheel of Sicilian cheese and gobble it down!

LOATHECLEON

All right then! This should be the first crime brought
before my father. You stay and prosecute.   840

XANTHIAS

No sir, not me. The other dog says he'll be
the prosecutor if any case is brought.

LOATHECLEON

Very well, go bring the two of them out here.

XANTHIAS

Consider it done.
Xanthias goes inside as Lovecleon comes out with part of a fence.

LOATHECLEON

What's that?

LOVECLEON

It's Hestia's pigpen.[99]

LOATHECLEON

So you've committed sacrilege to get that?

LOVECLEON

Not at all.   845
I'm beginning with Hestia, since I'm about to slaughter someone.
So hurry up and call the case: I'm in a punitive mood.

LOATHECLEON

All right then, let me fetch the dockets and indictments.

LOVECLEON

Good grief, you'll kill me, doddling and wasting the whole day!
(*holding up a penalty tablet*)
I've been itching to plow up this plot here.[100]   850

LOATHECLEON

Here you are.

LOVECLEON

                    Then call the case!

LOATHECLEON

                              All right.

LOVECLEON

                              Who's
this first one here?

LOATHECLEON

                    Oh hell! How annoying
that I've forgotten to bring out the voting urns.

LOVECLEON

Hey you, where are you running off?

LOATHECLEON

                              To get the urns.

LOVECLEON

                              Don't bother,
I've already got these soup ladles.   855

LOATHECLEON

They'll do just fine. So now we've got everything
we need – everything except a water clock!

LOVECLEON

(*points to the chamberpot*)
And what's this here if it isn't a water clock?

LOATHECLEON

You've truly got our native resourcefulness.
On the double now, somebody fetch fire   860
and myrtle wreaths and the incense from the house,
so that we can begin by praying to the gods.

CHORUS

And to celebrate your truce
and your prayers
we shall sing you a propitious song,   865
because like gentlemen
you've settled your warfare and strife.

LOATHECLEON

First let there be respectful silence now.

CHORUS LEADER

Pythian Phoebus Apollo, bless with fair fortune

CHORUS

strophe
the experiment this man has devised   870
right on his doorstep,
and may it work for us too,
when our roving is over.
Hail, Paean!

LOATHECLEON

Sidewalk Apollo,[101] Lord, Master, and Neighbor, Forefront of
My Forecourt,   875

accept a new rite, Lord, which we're launching for my father.
Purge him of this excessively harsh and hardhearted disposition,
infusing his dear little heart with a bit of honey, like syrup.
Let him now treat people
gently, and have more pity   880
for the defendants than the prosecutors,
and shed a tear when people beseech him,
and put away his bad temper,
from his anger
drawing the sting.

CHORUS LEADER

We join you in these prayers and chime in with a song   885
for your new regime, on the strength of your pronouncements.

CHORUS

antistrophe
Yes, we have been on your side
since we sensed that you cherish the people
more than anyone else,
at least among the younger generation.   890

LOATHECLEON

If any juror is at the door, let him enter.
We'll admit no one once speeches have begun.

LOVECLEON

So who's this defendant? He's really going to get it!

LOATHECLEON

Now all hear the charge: bringing the charge is Screamon,[102]
the watchdog of Cydathenaeum,[103] against Snatches of Aexone,   895
for criminally devouring a Sicilian cheese all by himself.
The proposed penalty: a collar of impeach-wood.[104]

LOVECLEON

No, he'll get death, a dog's death, if he takes this fall!

LOATHECLEON

The aforesaid defendant is here present.

LOVECLEON

The dirty scum! He's got thief written all over him, too!   900
Look at him grin, thinking he'll fox me.
But where's the prosecutor, Screamon of Cydathenaeum?

SCREAMON

Bow wow wow!

LOATHECLEON

       He's present.

XANTHIAS

             This one's just another Snatches,
good at barking and licking clean the bowls!

LOATHECLEON

Sit down and be quiet. You, take the stand and prosecute.   905

LOVECLEON

Well now, while that's going on I'll pour myself some soup to slurp.

SCREAMON

Men of the jury, you have heard the indictment that I have filed
against this defendant. He has indeed perpetrated
the most shocking deeds against me and the whole yo-ho-ho.[105]
Sneaked off to a corner he did, and sicilized   910
a big cheese, and bolted it down under cover of darkness.

LOVECLEON

By god, he obviously did it! There, just now
he blew a horrible cheesy belch at me,
the disgusting cur!

SCREAMON

And he didn't share any with me

when I asked. So tell me, who will be able to give you   915
a square deal unless a scrap gets thrown to me, your watchdog?

LOVECLEON

He didn't even share it with the public, that's me!
Yes, the guy's as hot as this soup of mine.

LOATHECLEON

Good heavens, father, don't prejudge his guilt
before you hear both sides.

LOVECLEON

But dear boy,   920

it's an open and shut case. The facts bark for themselves!

SCREAMON

Just don't you let him off, because of all dogs
he's far and away the most selfish hog of a man.
Sailed round and round the platter he did,
and nibbled the rind clean off the cities!   925

LOVECLEON

And me without enough plaster to patch my water pot!

SCREAMON

Under the circumstances you must punish him –
as they say, one copse cannot support two robbers –
so all my barking won't have been for nothing.
Otherwise, I won't be barking next time.   930

LOVECLEON

Wowee!
What a mass of misdeeds he's denounced!
What a thieving piece of work the man is! Don't
you agree, Mr. Rooster? By god he does, to judge by his wink.
Mr. Chairman? Where is he? Give me my chamber pot please!   935

LOATHECLEON

Get it yourself, I'm summoning the witnesses.
Witnesses for Snatches please be present: Bowl,
Pestle, Cheesegrater, Brazier, Cooking Pot,
and all other utensils summoned to testi-fry.
Enter Utensils from the house.
Are you still pissing? Haven't you sat down yet?   940

LOVECLEON

No, but I think that *he'll* be shitting himself today!

LOATHECLEON

Won't you stop being so hardhearted and ill tempered,
and toward defendants to boot? Must you chew on them?
(*to Snatches*)
Come forward, present your defense. Why are you silent? Speak up!

LOVECLEON

This one seems to have nothing to say for himself.   945

LOATHECLEON

No, I think the same thing's happened to him
that once happened even to Thucydides
when he was on trial: his jaws suddenly froze.[106]
Move over for me; I'll present your defense.
It is difficult, gentlemen of the jury, to speak on behalf   950
of a slandered dog, but speak I nevertheless shall.
For he's a good dog, and he chases away the wolves.

LOVECLEON

No, he's a thief and a conspirator!

LOATHECLEON

On the contrary, he's top dog of his generation,
able to control a multitude of sheep.[107]   955

LOVECLEON

What good is that, if he gulps down the cheese?

LOATHECLEON

Why, he fights for you and stands watch at your door,
and he's an all-around top dog. If he did steal,
pardon him. You see, he never learned how to play the lyre.[108]

LOVECLEON

I wish he'd never learned reading and writing either;   960
then he couldn't have submitted dishonest accounts to us.

LOATHECLEON

My dear sir, please listen to my witnesses.
Take the stand, Cheesegrater, and speak up loud and clear.
Your position was Steward? Answer intelligibly.
Didn't you grate your consignment for the troops?   965
He says he did.

LOVECLEON

              Sure he does, but he's lying.

LOATHECLEON

My dear sir, have some pity for the careworn.
Snatches here lives on a diet of giblets and bones,
and he's never in the same place for long.
And the other one – look what *he* is: a mere watchdog.   970
He stays right here, and whatever's brought home
he demands a cut, and if he doesn't get it, he bites.

LOVECLEON

Oh no! What can it be that's softening me?
Something bad is closing in and changing my mind!

LOATHECLEON

Come on, father, I beg you, be merciful to him,   975
and don't destroy him! Where are his puppies?
Enter Snatches' Puppies.
Take the stand, poor things. Whimper, beg, grovel, and weep!

LOVECLEON

Step down, step down, step down, step down!

LOATHECLEON

I'll step down,
even though that outcry "step down" has fooled   980
a great many people. Still, I'll step on down.

LOVECLEON

Damn it to hell! It's no good, all this slurping.
Now I've cried away my better judgment,
and all because I filled up on hot soup!

LOATHECLEON

He's not getting off, then?

LOVECLEON

It's hard to say.   985

LOATHECLEON

Come on, daddy, turn over a new leaf now.
Take this pebble, shut your eyes, rush over
to the second urn, and vote to acquit him, father.

LOVECLEON

Absolutely not! I never learned to play the lyre either.

LOATHECLEON

Very well, I'll usher you around this way, it's quickest.   990

LOVECLEON

This is the first urn?

LOATHECLEON

It is.

LOVECLEON

There she goes!

LOATHECLEON

(*to the audience*)
He's fooled; he voted for acquittal unawares.
(*to Lovecleon*)
Let's do the count.

LOVECLEON

So what's our verdict then?

LOATHECLEON

I think it will soon be clear. Snatches, you're acquitted!
The courtroom parties depart.
Father, father, what's the matter? Dear me! Water!   995
Raise yourself up!

LOVECLEON

Just tell me one thing:
did he really get off?

LOATHECLEON

He did indeed.

LOVECLEON

Then I'm done for!

LOATHECLEON

My dear father, don't even think about it. Just stand up.

LOVECLEON

How am I going to live with this on my conscience,
now that I've let a defendant off? What will become of me?   1000
O gods so deeply venerated, please forgive me.
I did it unintentionally, it was unlike me!

LOATHECLEON

Don't take it so hard. I'm going to take care of you
in fine fashion, father, and take you with me everywhere,

to dinner, to drinking parties, to spectacles,   1005
so that you'll spend the rest of your days pleasantly;
and no longer will Hyperbolus make a fool of you with his lies.[109]
Now let's go on inside.

LOVECLEON

              All right then, if you like.
Lovecleon takes Loathecleon into the house.

CHORUS

Bon voyage, wherever you're going.
And you meanwhile,
you countless thousands,   1010
take care that the good words to follow
don't simply fall to the ground;
that's what happens to stupid spectators,
and is hardly expected from you.

CHORUS LEADER

Now then, people, give me your attention, if you like frank talk.   1015
Our poet wishes to chastise the audience today.
He claims they've wronged him, though he's treated them
        abundantly well,
at first not openly but secretly, by helping other poets,
taking his cue from the prophetic intelligence of Eurycles:[110]
slipping into other men's bellies and emitting lots of comic material.   1020
After that, he took his chances openly on his own,
holding the reins not of someone else's team of muses, but his own.[111]
When raised to greatness and honored among you as no one
        has ever been,
he says he didn't end up getting above himself, his head didn't swell,
and he didn't cruise the wrestling schools looking for a pickup.[112]
        And if a man in love   1025
pressed him to satirize a favorite of his, with whom he was angry,
he says he never went along with any such request, on
        the high-minded principle
that he shouldn't turn the muses he employs into pimps.[113]
And when he first began to produce,[114] he says, he didn't attack
        ordinary people,
but in the very spirit of Heracles he came to grips with the greatest
        monsters,[115]   1030
boldly standing up from the very start to old Jagged Teeth himself,
whose eyes like the bitch Cynna's flashed terrible beams,[116]

and there licked a hundred heads of damned flatterers
all around his pate; and he had the voice of a death-dealing torrent,
the smell of a seal, the unwashed balls of a Lamia,[117] and the
    asshole of a camel.   1035
On seeing such an apparition, he says, he didn't tremble and take
    bribes,[118]
but fought then as he fights now on your behalf. And he says
    that after him
he came to grips last year[119] with the shivers and the fevers
that by night throttled fathers and strangled grandfathers,
that climbed into the very beds of the peaceable citizens among you,   1040
pasting together affidavits, summonses, and depositions,
so that many people jumped up in terror and ran to the polemarch.[120]
Such a bulwark against evil, such a purifier of the land had you found,
when last year you double-crossed him, when he sowed a
    crop of brand-new ideas
that you made fruitless by your failure to understand them clearly.[121] 1045
And yet over and over again he swears solemnly by Dionysus
that no one ever heard any comic poetry better than that.
So you're all disgraced for failing to appreciate it right away,
though our poet is no worse off in the eyes of the sagacious
if while overtaking his rivals with a novel conception he took a spill.   1050
But from now on, dear people,
cherish and foster more
the poets who seek to find something fresh to say;
save up their ideas   1055
and put them in your hampers
with the potpourri.
If you do that, next year
your clothes will be fragrant
with the sweet scent of wit.

CHORUS

strophe
Ah, once upon a time we were valiant in choruses,
and valiant in battle,   1060
and above all most valiant where *this* is concerned.[122]
But that's long, long ago,
all gone now, and these locks of mine
bloom whiter than a swan.   1065
But even from these ruins we must
summon up youthful strength,
for I think that my old age outdoes
any number of young men with their
ringlets, their getups, and their candy-assedness.   1070

CHORUS LEADER

Spectators, if any of you has noticed our appearance
and wonders, when he sees our waspish waists,
what's the idea behind these stingers of ours,
I can easily edify him, "be he ever so unversed before."[123]
We who sport this on our rumps   1075
are the only truly indigenous, native Athenians,
a most virile breed and one that very substantially
aided this city in battle,[124] that time the barbarian arrived
spewing smoke over all the city and incinerating it,
intent upon forcibly eradicating our hives.   1080
Right away we charged forth "with spear, with shield,"
and we fought them, steeped in bitter spirits,
each man standing beside the next, biting his lip with fury.
We couldn't see the sky for all the arrows overhead,[125]
but still, with the gods' help, towards evening we pushed them back;   1085
for before the battle an owl had flown over our troops.[126]
Then we pursued them, harpooning their baggy pants,
and they kept running, stung in the jaws and the eyebrows.
That's why to this day barbarians everywhere insist
that there's nothing manlier than an Attic wasp.   1090

CHORUS

antistrophe
Yes, I was awesome then, so everybody feared me,
and I upended
my opponents when I sailed against them on my triremes.
No, in those days we didn't care
about getting ready to make a good speech
or to trump up a charge against someone,   1095
but only about who would be
the best oarsman. That's why
we took many cities from the Medes[127]
and are chiefly responsible
for the tribute's being brought to Athens,
for the younger generation to steal.   1100

CHORUS LEADER

All things considered, you'll find that generally,
in character and lifestyle, we most resemble wasps.
First, no creature is more sharp-tempered than us
when irritated, or more cantankerous.   1105
Then again, we engineer everything else just like wasps:
we gather together in swarms as if into nests,

some of us judging in the archon's court, some before the Eleven,
and some in the Odeum, packed in tight against the walls
like this, hunched toward the ground and hardly moving,   1110
just like grubs within their cells.
We're very resourceful at making a living, too:
we sting everybody and so provide our daily bread.[128]
But the problem is, there are drones sitting among us
who have no stingers, who stay at home and feed   1115
off the fruit of the tribute without toiling for it.
And we're very nettled if some draft dodger
gulps down our pay, when in defense of this country
he's never raised an oar, a lance, or a blister.
No, I think that from now on any citizen, bar none,   1120
who doesn't have a stinger should not be paid three obols.[129]

Enter Lovecleon, Loathecleon, and a Slave, who carries a
fine cloak and boots.

LOVECLEON

No, I'll never take this off, not while I'm alive!
It was my sole salvation when I was in the ranks,
when the great north wind made war on us.[130]

LOATHECLEON

You don't seem to want anything nice done for you.   1125

LOVECLEON

God no! That has never done me any good.
Once before, when I'd gorged on sprats,
I had to pay the cleaner three obols.

LOATHECLEON

Anyway, at least try it on. After all, you have
put yourself in my hands for good treatment.   1130

LOVECLEON

So, what do you want me to do?

LOATHECLEON

Take off that ratty jacket
and try on this natty cloak.

LOVECLEON

Why should we bear and rear children anyway,
when now this one wants to smother me?

LOATHECLEON

Here, pick that up and put it on, and stop your chatter.   1135

LOVECLEON

What the hell is this, for heaven's sake?

LOATHECLEON

Some call it a Persian cloak, others a tasseled astrakhan.

LOVECLEON

I thought it was an overcoat from Thymaetidae.[131]

LOATHECLEON

No wonder; you've never done the trip to Sardis.[132]
Otherwise you'd have recognized it; as it is, you don't.   1140

LOVECLEON

I admit I certainly don't. But it looks to me
exactly like Morychus' knapsack.[133]

LOATHECLEON

No it doesn't; these are woven in Ecbatana.[134]

LOVECLEON

In Ecbatana they make woollen sausages?

LOATHECLEON

Where do you get that notion, good sir? No, the natives   1145
weave these, at great expense. You know, this one
easily sucked down a talent's worth of wool.

LOVECLEON

Then instead of an astrakhan, wouldn't it be better
to call it a woolpool?

LOATHECLEON

                  Wear it, good sir.
And stand still while getting a change of clothes.

LOVECLEON

                          Good grief,   1150
what a hot belch the rotten thing blew at me!

LOATHECLEON

Please put it on.

LOVECLEON

           I absolutely refuse.

LOATHECLEON

                    But good sir –

LOVECLEON

If this is compulsory, dress me in an oven instead.

LOATHECLEON

Very well, I'll dress you myself.
(*to Slave*)
                  You may go.

LOVECLEON

But at least put a meat-hook nearby.

LOATHECLEON

Why is that?

1155

LOVECLEON

So you can pull me out before I fall apart.

LOATHECLEON

All right, please take off those accursed sandals.
Hurry up and get into these Spartans.[135]

LOVECLEON

How in the world could I ever have the nerve
to put on "hateful leathers from enemy lands"?[136]

1160

LOATHECLEON

Put it in here any time now, sir. Push down firmly
into that Spartan, and hurry up.

LOVECLEON

It's a crime
to make me set my foot upon enemy sole!

LOATHECLEON

There. Now the other.

LOVECLEON

Please, not this foot:
one of its toes is very anti-Spartan!

1165

LOATHECLEON

You have no choice.

LOVECLEON

Then I am godforsaken,
with not a single corn to look forward to in my old age!

LOATHECLEON

At least hurry up with the boots. Now step out like this,
as the wealthy do, with a sort of voluptuous swagger.

LOVECLEON

All right, then. Watch my gait, and tell me which   1170
man among the wealthy walks most like it.

LOATHECLEON

Which one? Someone who's dressed a boil with garlic.

LOVECLEON

I'm actually trying to do the hoochie koochie.

LOATHECLEON

Now then, will you know how to recount impressive stories
in the presence of educated and intelligent gentlemen?   1175

LOVECLEON

Sure I will.

LOATHECLEON

               What story would you tell, then?

LOVECLEON

                              I've got lots.
First of all, how Lamia farted when captured.[137]
Then how Cardopion[138] got hold of his mother and –

LOATHECLEON

I don't want fairytales, I want stories with human interest,
the sort we most often tell, at-home stories.   1180

LOVECLEON

Well, I know one that's very much about home,
the one that goes, "Once there was a mouse and a cat" –

LOATHECLEON

You ignorant oaf – as Theogenes said
to the dung collector, and only while quarrelling.[139]
Do you intend to talk about mice and cats among gentlemen?   1185

LOVECLEON

What sort of stories *should* I tell?

LOATHECLEON

                    Impressive ones,
such as how you went on an embassy with Androcles[140] and
     Cleisthenes.[141]

LOVECLEON

I've never been on an embassy anywhere,
except to Paros, and then I was paid only two obols.[142]

LOATHECLEON

Well, in that case, you should at least recount Ephudion's   1190
fine battle with Ascondas in the pancration,[143]
when he was old and grey but still he had
that deep chest, those hands and flanks, and
those magnificent arms.

LOVECLEON

                    Hold on now, that's nonsense!
How could he have fought in a pancration armed?   1195

LOATHECLEON

That's how sophisticated people typically tell stories.
Now tell me something else: if you were drinking
with unfamiliar people, what do you think
you'd recount as the bravest exploit of your youth?

LOVECLEON

I know, I know! The bravest of my exploits: 1200
the time I swiped Ergasion's vine poles.[144]

LOATHECLEON

You'll be the death of me! Vine poles? No, tell how
you once hunted boar or hare, or ran a torch race.
Come up with something extraordinarily lusty.

LOVECLEON

Well, I know what was the very lustiest: 1205
when I was still a young bull and went after Phaÿllus[145]
and beat him – in a lawsuit for defamation, by two votes.

LOATHECLEON

Stop! But now come over here and recline, and learn
how to be symposiastic and convivialistic.

LOVECLEON

How do I recline, then? Hurry up and tell me.

LOATHECLEON

                                              Gracefully.   1210

LOVECLEON

You're telling me to recline like this?

LOATHECLEON

                                    Not at all.

LOVECLEON

                                        Then how?

LOATHECLEON

Extend your legs and pour yourself out
on the coverlets in a fluid, athletic way.
Then sing the praises of one of the bronzes,
gaze at the ceiling, admire the room's curtains.   1215
Water for our hands; the tables are being served;
we're dining; now we've cleaned up; now libations.

LOVECLEON

Good heavens, are we dining on dream food?

LOATHECLEON

The piper girl has started to play. Your drinking companions
are Theorus,[146] Aeschines,[147] Phanus,[148] Cleon,   1220
and a second foreigner next to Acestor.[149]
Among men like these, now, relay the songs in fine fashion.

LOVECLEON

Oh really? I'll do it better than any Diacrian.[150]

LOATHECLEON

OK, let's find out. Suppose I'm Cleon, then,
and I start up the Harmodius Song,[151] and you're next up.   1225
"Never was a man in Athens born . . ."

LOVECLEON

  . . . so great a scoundrel, and such a thief!

LOATHECLEON

Is that what you're going to do? You'll be shouted to death!
He'll vow to destroy you and annihilate you
and hound you out of the country.

LOVECLEON

                              If he threatens me,   1230
by god I'll sing another one:
"You there, the fellow who seeks the high authority,
you shall upend the city yet; it's poised to tilt."[152]   1235

LOATHECLEON

But what happens when Theorus, reclining at your feet,
grasps Cleon by the right hand and sings:
"Remember, friend, the story of Admetus,
and cherish the good people."[153]
What song will you cap that with?

LOVECLEON

I'll be lyrical: 1240
"You cannot be foxy
or befriend both sides."[154]

LOATHECLEON

After him, Aeschines the son of Hotair will take it up,[155]
a sophisticated and cultured gentleman, and he'll sing:
"Money and substance   1245
for Clitagora and me
midst the Thessalians . . ."[156]

LOVECLEON

. . . Yes, we did a lot of boasting, you and I!

LOATHECLEON

This part you seem to understand reasonably well.
It's time we were off to Philoctemon's[157] house   1250
for dinner. Boy, boy! Pack dinner for the two of us, Chrysus,[158]
so we can have a real booze-up at long last!

LOVECLEON

Oh no! Drinking's bad. What happens with wine is
doors broken in, assault and battery,
then with a hangover paying fines for the damage.   1255

LOATHECLEON

No, not if you're in the company of fine gentlemen.
They'll beg the victim off, you see, or else
you yourself can tell him some witty story,
something funny by Aesop[159] or about Sybaris,[160]
something you learned at the party, and then you've turned it   1260
into a joke, so he lets you off and goes on his merry way.

LOVECLEON

Sure, I'd better learn lots of those stories,
if I'm to owe no damages when I do something bad.
Enter a Slave with two dinner baskets.

Come on now, let's go; let nothing stop us now!
Exit Lovecleon, Loathecleon and Slave.

CHORUS

strophe
I've very often thought that I
am naturally intelligent   1265
and never ever stupid,
but Amynias son of Hotair,
he of the Hairbun family,[161] is even more so.
He's the one I once saw
dining with Leogoras[162]
instead of eating apple and pomegranate,
for he's as hungry as Antiphon.[163]   1270
And he even went along on an embassy to Pharsalus,[164]
then spent his time there one on one
with the Thessalian Paupers,[165]
being himself a pauper
second to none.

CHORUS LEADER

Lucky Automenes,[166] we think you are so lucky!   1275
You've begotten children as virtuosic as can be.
First there's a man universally loved and very talented,
the outstanding lyre player,[167] whom Charm herself attends.
Then there's another, the actor,[168] so awfully talented.
And then there's Ariphrades,[169] by far the most intrinsically talented,   1280
who, his father once swore, needed no teacher to learn
how to use his tongue creatively when visiting a whorehouse.

<CHORUS>[170]

CHORUS LEADER

There are some[171] who said that I'd made peace, that time
when Cleon laid into me and tried to shake me up some,   1285
and did sting me with abuse. Then while I was being skinned alive,
the crowd outside kept laughing as they watched him shouting hard,
with no concern at all for me, save only to see
if I would toss up some little joke when squeezed.
I saw all this and pulled a little monkey business;   1290
and today the stake's played the vine for a fool.[172]
Xanthias runs in.

XANTHIAS

Ah tortoises, I envy you your shells!
It was good and brainy of you to put a roof over
your backs with tile and so cover up your sides.   1295
Me, I've been bruised to perdition by a walking stick!

CHORUS LEADER

What is it, boy? Yes, it's fair to call anyone "boy"
who takes a beating, even if he is an old man.

XANTHIAS

Yes, hasn't the old man turned out to be an utter calamity,
and by far the most drunk and disorderly man at the party,   1300
even though Hippyllus[173] was there, and Antiphon,[174] Lycon,[175]
Lysistratus,[176] Thuphrastus,[177] and Phrynichus' crowd.[178]
He was far and away the most outrageous of them all.
As soon as he'd sated himself with lots of good food,
he jumped up, pranced about, farted, and ridiculed people,   1305
like a little donkey living it up on barley.
And he beat me lustily, all the while yelling "boy, boy."
Then Lysistratus took a look at him and made a comparison:
"Old fellow, you're like a nouveau riche teenager,
or an ass that's slipped away to a bran pile!"   1310
But he bellowed back with his own comparison of Lysistratus
to a locust missing the wrappers off his cloak,
and to Sthenelus shorn clean of his stage props.[179]
Everyone applauded, with the sole exception of Thuphrastus,
who pursed his lips, as being intelligent.   1315
Then the old man asked Thuphrastus, "Tell me now,
why do you act the bigwig and pretend to be stylish,
when you're a clown sucking up to anyone who's doing well?"
That's the way he insulted them, one after the other,
mocking them like a yokel and also telling stories   1320
that were completely inappropriate to the situation.
And after he gets drunk, he starts for home,
hitting everyone who happens to encounter him.
Look, here he comes now, staggering along.
I'm taking off before I start catching punches!   1325

*Xanthias runs into the house. Lovecleon staggers in, one hand
holding a torch and the other the piper-girl Dardanis. Following
are Lovecleon's VICTIMS.*

LOVECLEON

Give way! Make way!
Some of those people back there following me
are going to be very sorry!
You scoundrels, if you don't scatter off,   1330
oh how I'll make fried fish of you
with this torch!

VICTIM

You'll certainly have to answer for this tomorrow,
to all of us, even if you *are* a young blade.
We'll all be here together, with summonses.

LOVECLEON

Goodness me! Summonses!   1335
How old-fashioned of you. Don't you know
that I can't even stand to hear
about lawsuits? Yuk, yuk!
This is what I like! Down with voting urns!
Get along! Where's   1340
a juryman, eh? Get out of here!
VICTIMS run away.
Come up this way, my little blonde cockchafer.
Grab hold of this cable here with your hand.
Hang on, but be careful, the cable's worn out;
all the same, it doesn't mind being tugged.
Did you see how handily I sneaked you away   1345
just when you were supposed to start sucking the guests?
For that you owe this cock of mine a favor.
But you won't pay up, you won't come through, I know it.
You'll trick me and stick your tongue way out at it;
you've done the same to lots of other men.   1350
But if you don't act like a mean woman to me now,
I promise that, as soon as my son passes away,
I'll free you and keep you as a concubine, my little pussy.
As it is, I don't control my own property.
I'm young, you see, and I'm very carefully guarded: 1355
my little son watches me, and he's a grouchy one,
and on top of that he's a cress- and cumin-peeling skinflint.
You see, he's worried that I'll end up spoiled;
for he's got no other father except for me.
But here he comes! He seems to be chasing you and me.   1360

Quick now, take this torch and stand very still,
so I can play some teenage tricks on him,
the same tricks he played on me before my initiation.[180]
Enter Loathecleon.

LOATHECLEON

You there! Yes you, you psychotic pussy groper!
You seem to be fondly infatuated with a fresh – coffin!   1365
You won't get away with this behavior, by Apollo you won't.

LOVECLEON

I can see you'd enjoy the taste of a good sour lawsuit!

LOATHECLEON

How dare you pull my leg, after stealing the piper
from the partiers!

LOVECLEON

                    What piper's that? What's this
you're raving about, like a man who's taken leave of his – tomb?   1370

LOATHECLEON

By god, that's got to be Dardanis[181] you've got here!

LOVECLEON

No, it's a torch in the marketplace burning for the gods.

LOATHECLEON

This is a torch?

LOVECLEON

                    Yes, a torch. Don't you see its cleavage?

LOATHECLEON

And what's this dark patch in the middle here?

LOVECLEON

That's easy: the pitch is coming out because it's hot.   1375

LOATHECLEON

And behind here, isn't this an asshole?

LOVECLEON

No, that's a knothole sticking out of the torch.

LOATHECLEON

What do you mean? Knothole!
(*to Dardanis*)

You get over here!

LOVECLEON

Hey, hey, what do you think you're doing?

LOATHECLEON

Grabbing her
and taking her away from you, because I'm convinced   1380
that you're worn out and utterly unable to perform.

LOVECLEON

Listen to me now. When I was at Olympia on an embassy,
Ephudion put up a fine fight against Ascondas,[182]
even as an old man. Then the older man   1385
hit the younger with his fist and knocked him down.
Lovecleon knocks Loathecleon down.
The moral: you should beware of getting a pair of black eyes.
Dardanis runs off.

LOATHECLEON

Good god, you've certainly learned the lesson about Olympia!

Enter MYRTIA with an empty tray, and Chaerephon.

MYRTIA

(*to Chaerephon*)
Come here and stand by me, I beg you in the name of the gods.
That's the one, the man who did me in,
hitting me with his torch and knocking ten obols' worth   1390
of bread off here, plus four loaves more.

LOATHECLEON

See what you've done? We're sure to have trouble and lawsuits,
because of your drinking.

LOVECLEON

                    Not at all! Because
some adroit story-telling will settle the matter.
I know just how to I'll reconcile myself with this woman.   1395

MYRTIA

No, by the Twin Gods,[183] you'll not sweet-talk Myrtia,
daughter of Ancylion and Sostrate,[184]
after you have ruined my stock like this!

LOVECLEON

Listen, madam; I'd like to tell you a charming
story.

MYRTIA

     Not to me you won't, good sir.   1400

LOVECLEON

When Aesop[185] was walking home from dinner one evening,
a bold and tipsy bitch started barking at him.
And he said, "Bitch, bitch, if you'd trade that nasty tongue of yours
for some flour, I think you'd be showing better sense."   1405

MYRTIA

Laughing at me too? I'm summonsing you, whoever you are,
to appear before the commissioners of the marketplace
for ruining my stock, with Chaerephon[186] here as my witness.

LOVECLEON

No! Just listen and see if you think I'm making sense.
Once Lasus[187] and Simonides[188] trained rival choruses,   1410
and then old Lasus said, "I couldn't care less."

MYRTIA

So that's your attitude?
Myrtia and Chaerephon walk off.

LOVECLEON

Tell me, Chaerephon,
are you really acting as a summons witness for a woman?
You look like a sallow Ino clutching the feet of Euripides![189]

LOATHECLEON

Here's someone else on his way to summons you;   1415
and look, he's got a witness with him too.
Enter ACCUSER with Witness.
Oh, what a calamity! I summon you, old man,
for assault!

LOATHECLEON

    Assault? No, don't summons him for that! Good heavens!
I'll compensate you on his behalf, whatever amount
you propose, and you will also have my gratitude.   1420

LOVECLEON

No, I will volunteer to settle with him,
for I admit I punched him out and pelted him.
(*to Accuser*)
Come over here. Will you permit me to decide how much
I'll compensate you in this matter, and then we'll be friends
from now on, or will you make a proposal to me?   1425

ACCUSER

You say. I don't need any lawsuits and trouble.

LOVECLEON

A man from Sybaris[190] fell out of a chariot,
and somehow he got his head very seriously injured.
It happens he wasn't an experienced driver of horses.
And then a friend of his stood over him and said,   1430
"Let each one practice the craft that he knows best."
So do the same and run off to Pittalus' place![191]

LOATHECLEON

You know, this is just like the rest of your behavior.

ACCUSER

In that case, see that you remember his reply.

LOVECLEON

Listen, don't run away! Once upon a time in Sybaris,   1435
a woman broke her pot.

ACCUSER

Witness, take note!

LOVECLEON

So this pot told its companion to be a witness.
Then the Sybarite woman said, "By Kore,
if you'd let this witness business go and bought a bandage
right away, you'd have shown much greater sense!"   1440

ACCUSER

Go on, be outrageous – until the magistrate calls your case!

LOATHECLEON

By Demeter, you'll not stay out here any longer;
I'm going to pick you up and carry you –

LOVECLEON

What are you doing?

LOATHECLEON

Doing?
I'm carrying you into the house. If I don't,
the people who want to summons you will run out of witnesses!

LOVECLEON

One time the Delphians accused Aesop[192] –

LOATHECLEON

I'm not interested!   1445

LOVECLEON

– of stealing a bowl from the god.
He told them how once upon a time the beetle –

LOATHECLEON

Damn it, you'll be the death of me with these beetles of yours!
Loathecleon muscles his father into the house.

CHORUS

strophe
I do envy the old man
his luck; what a turn-around
from his arid habits and lifestyle!   1450
Now he's learned different ways,
and he'll make a really great change
to a life of delicate luxury.
But maybe he'll not want that;   1455
it's hard for anyone to depart
from his normal and natural character.
Yet many have had this experience;
when exposed to others' ideas,
they have changed their habits.   1460

antistrophe
With high praise from me
and from others with good sense,
he'll go his way, thanks to
filial love and understanding,   1465
this son of Lovecleon.
So kind a man I've never
met, nor with anyone's behavior
have I been so ecstatic and melted away.
For where in his rebuttals   1470
was he not superior, in his wish
to adorn his begetter
with more dignified pursuits?
Xanthias comes out of the house.

XANTHIAS

By Dionysus, some god has set our house
awhirl with some truly baffling business!   1475
Since the old man hadn't had a drink for so long
or heard the pipes, he's overjoyed with this business,
and all night long he hasn't stopped his dancing
to those old routines that Thespis[193] used in his competitions.
And he says that pretty soon he'll take on the modern   1480
tragic dancers and show them up as old Cronuses.[194]
Lovecleon appears at the door.

LOVECLEON

Who couches at the outer gates?

XANTHIAS

There he is, here comes the trouble!

LOVECLEON

Let these gates be unbolted! Look here,
the opening steps –   1485

XANTHIAS

Maybe more like the onset of madness!

LOVECLEON

– where you bend the torso vigorously.
How the snout snorts, and
the spine cracks!

XANTHIAS

Drink hellebore![195]

LOVECLEON

Phrynichus crouches like a rooster[196] –   1490

XANTHIAS

Soon you'll be pelted![197]

LOVECLEON

– kicking his legs sky high!
The asshole gapes –

XANTHIAS

Watch yourself there!

LOVECLEON

– because now my hip joints
roll smoothly in their sockets!   1495
Wasn't that good?

XANTHIAS

It certainly was not; it's crazy business!

LOVECLEON

Come now, I'm making a statement and challenging all comers!
Any tragic performer who claims to be a good dancer,
come right up here and dance against me!
Anyone? No one?

XANTHIAS

　　　　　　　Only that one over there.   1500
A Son of Carcinus, costumed as a crab, enters the orchestra.

LOVECLEON

Who is this unfortunate person?

XANTHIAS

A son of Carcinus,[198]
the midmost one.[199]

LOVECLEON

Who, him? He'll be eaten alive!
I'll demolish him with a *pas de fist*!
Rhythmically, he's nothing.

XANTHIAS

You sorry fool,
here's another Carcinite tragedian coming,   1505
this one's brother![200]
Enter a second Son of Carcinus.

LOVECLEON

Then by god, I've got a tasty meal!

XANTHIAS

No you haven't; you've got nothing but three crabs,
because here comes yet another son of Carcinus!
Enter a third Son of Carcinus.

LOVECLEON

What's this thing crawling towards us? A scorpion or a spider?

XANTHIAS

This one's the pea-crab of the family,   1510
the tiniest, the one who composes tragedy.[201]

LOVECLEON

Ah Carcinus, congratulations on your fine offspring!
What a flock of wagtails has alighted here!
Well, I must go down to compete with them; you
be stirring up the broth for them, in case I prevail.   1515
Lovecleon descends into the orchestra; Xanthias goes into the house.

CHORUS LEADER

Come then, let's all give them a bit of room, so that
they can spin themselves before us without interference.

CHORUS

Up, you renowned children
of Sir Salty,[202]
jump along the sand   1520
and the shore of the barren sea,
brethren of shrimps;

whirl a swift foot all around,
and someone kick out
the Phrynichus caper,   1525
so that seeing the foot in the air
the audience will cry ooh!
Whirl! Sidle around and slap your belly;
throw a leg sky high; pirouettes included please!   1530
Carcinus enters the orchestra.
Because the Lord and Master of the Deep scuttles hither himself,
delighted with his very own children, the triple duckers!
Now lead us out of here dancing, if you please,   1535
and quickly; for no one has ever done this before,
to take a comic chorus off in dance.

Notes

1 In the revised parabasis of *Clouds* (520–23) Aristophanes notes that he might have produced that play elsewhere had he known that the audience would not appreciate its excellence. If one of the plays produced in 422 had been intended for the Dionysia, it was probably *The Preview*, which had a theatrical and thus more broadly appealing theme, while the topical satire *Wasps* would be better suited to the Lenaea.

2 A plausible interpretation of a statement by the ancient scholar Eratosthenes about Plato Comicus (T 7): "when he first produced his own play, *Staff-Bearers*, he placed fourth and was shunted back to the Lenaean contest."

3 For the caricature, see see 894 n.

4 For this justaposition in Aristophanic comedy generally, see Hutchinson 2011.

5 For the system and its operation, see Gagarin 2021.

6 This is clear at once from his house and its numerous slaves, as well as his son's wealth and sophistication.

7 The Corybants were Asiatic divinities whose worship featured frantic dancing.

8 A Phrygian god associated with Dionysus and popular with women and slaves.

9 See *Acharnians* 89 n.

10 See *Knights* 42 n.

11 Identifying the dragon as Cleon, portrayed as a tanner in Knights.

12 This crony of Cleon's had appeared as a character in *Acharnians* (134–66).

13 See *Acharnians* 716 n.

14 See *Acharnians* 738 n. Athenian contempt of Megarian humor as crude and trite (as in the following examples) responds to the Megarians' counter claim to be the inventors of comedy, which is in fact attested early there; see Aristotle *Poetics* 1448a28–38, cf. 1449a38-b9.

15 As in *Acharnians*, though there, ridicule co-exists with emulation.

16 Perhaps referring to the recent revolt of Scione, which occurred only days after the Athenians, on the advice of Laches (240 n.), had made a truce with Sparta against Cleon's advice; Cleon then passed a motion to besiege and punish Scione (Thucydides 4.118–22).

17 A reference to Aristophanes' attack on Cleon in *Knights*.

18 The individuals recognized in this bit of "audience participation" would have been expected to be sitting up front and thus must have held an important office this year (e.g. councilor, general, priest) or, like Cleon, enjoyed honorific front-row seating (see *Acharnians* 125 n., *Knights* 167 n.).

19 Identity uncertain but evidently wealthy and a pro-Spartan sympathizer, cf. 466, 1264–74.

20 Neither man is identifiable.

21 A perennially successful commander and an associate of Nicias.

22 Identity uncertain: the name was not uncommon.

23 A device used to time litigants' speeches in court.

24 The standard formula for pederastic graffiti (see *Acharnians* 144 n.). Pyrilampes, son of Antiphon, was a descendant of Solon, an associate of Pericles, and the stepfather of Plato, and his son Demos, who would also enjoy a distinguished career (the name signals enthusiasm for democracy), is represented by Plato as being the object of a crush on the part of Callicles (*Gorgias* 481d).

25 See 8 n.

26 Asclepius was a healing god, and incubation in his temples was a popular form of therapy.

27 "Figwood" (*sykinos*) puns on "malicious prosecutor" or blackmailer (*sykophantes*), a type much maligned in comedy (as was Cleon) for preying on the wealthy.

28 Several contemporaries with this name ("Serpentine") are known.

29 Like a (tragic) king or head of state; see *Knights* 220n.

30 The following routine parodies Odysseus' escape from the cave of the Cyclops in Homer's *Odyssey* 9.424 ff. Like Odysseus, Lovecleon is past his prime but compensates by his determination, wiliness, and resourcefulness. Later in the play (350 ff.), Lovecleon's escape attempts will recall another of Odysseus' exploits.

31 Proverbial for something not worth fighting about.

32 Hard duty, since this siege took place mainly during winter; cf. 62 n.

33 A tragedian of the Persian War period famous for his lyrics; the "Sidon Songs" were from his *Phoenician Women*, produced some 50 years earlier (between 478 and 473).

34 The names given to several members of the chorus (for this feature, see *Acharnians* 220 n.) may be generic, but the rare "Euergides" is attested in a casualty-list from 411 and the equally rare "Strymodorus" may reflect a personal link to Aristophanes: see *Acharnians* 273 n.

35 Modern Istanbul, re-captured from the Persians 56 years earlier.

36 Laches of Aexone was a successful general and political ally of Nicias (and the title character of a dialogue of Plato), who the previous year had sponsored a one-year treaty with Sparta. Later in this play (835–43, 891–1002) there is a mock prosecution of Laches by Cleon for misconduct in Laches' Sicilian campaign of 427–5: this may reprise an actual trial or deposition from the generalship (which would have occurred in 425), or else Aristophanes may be imagining a trial in response to recent threats by Cleon against Laches, in which the Sicilian business would have been brought up.

37 I follow Olson and Biles 2015 in adopting Srebrny's suggested transposition of lines 266–289 to follow lines 290–316, which makes better sense of the action; presumably a page of the manuscripts' exemplar was inserted in the wrong place.

38 Pindar fr. 189.

39 The Samians had revolted from the Athenian empire in 440 (see General Introduction VI.2 and 3); the scholia here identify the informant as one Carystion, who was rewarded with citizenship.

40 Perhaps Laches: see 240 n.

41 Ridiculed as a boaster also in Aristophanes' *Birds* 1126.

42 Both Aeschines (cf. 459, 1243) and Amynias (cf. 74–6, 1267) are thus called.

43 Literally "ships": a mysterious comment. Perhaps Lovecleon and his fellow jurors had (at the urging of Cleon?) criticized the wealthy citizens who were responsible (as trierarchs) for maintenance of the ships in their charge. Alternatively, we could read "about the younger generation": the difference depends on the word's accentuation, which was not specified in the earliest copies of the play.

44 During the siege of Troy Odysseus entered the city disguised as a beggar (cf. *Odyssey* 4.242–58); for Lovecleon recalling Odysseus, see 181 n.

45 Around 470 (Thucydides 1.98.4).

46 A goddess of hunting and fishing similar to Artemis.

47 Demeter and Kore, the principal deities of the Eleusinian Mysteries, the most august of Athenian cults. This is the earliest attestation of the populist criticism of the elite as despisers of the Mysteries, an indicator of potential tyranny, which would culminate in the scandal of 415 for profaning the Mysteries, involving Alcibiades and dozens of others: see Henderson 2003: 168–70.

48 An Athenian hero whose shrine was next to a lawcourt.

49 Hung on house doors during the autumn Pyanopsia festival for Apollo and left there during the year.

50 The first two names are unidentifiable; the last two are comic distortions ("Needy" and "Dinner-Getter").

51 Exaggerating Loathecleon's intentions in alarmist fashion.

52 See 42 n.

53 Philippus was probably not literally the son but a disciple of Gorgias, the Sicilian rhetorician who visited Athens in 427 and was reportedly childless; these two are paired again eight years later in Aristophanes' *Birds* as exemplifying self-serving virtuosity in litigating lawsuits.

54 An early (perhaps the first) king of Athens, who had a shrine on the Acropolis and a statue in the agora. He was typically portrayed as serpentine (his name is from *drakon* "snake") because the Athenians regarded themselves as autochthonous: Cecrops thus represents genuine Athenians.

55 Not identifiable (the name is common) but ridiculed elsewhere (for example, 1243–48) for exaggerating his wealth; later in the play he is listed among the guests at a party along with Cleon (1220).

56 Nephew of Aeschylus and a tragic poet himself (he was victorious over Sophocles' *Oedipus the King*); he was nicknamed "son of Briny" for his harsh and bitter style.

57 See 74 n. and for long hair, *Knights* 580 with n.

58 The leading Spartan general of this period, currently active on the Thracian front, cf. 288.

59 Fifty-seven, to be exact, when the Persian king Xerxes attempted to install the family of Peisistratus (Herodotus 7.6, 8.52); for recollections of Athens' tyranny and later politicization of the threat, see *Knights* 450, Henderson 2003.

60 The name is cognate with *hippos* "horse."

61 See *Acharnians* 887 n.

62 Proverbial for a culinary delicacy.

63 See *Knights* 85 n.

64 A function performed by very old men in the great Panathenaic parade.

65 Lobbying of jurors was routine and, given the logistics of handling large volunteer juries, probably unavoidable.

66 The traditional author of animal fables, with their moralizing exempla, dating from the early sixth century. The use of such fables by wealthy miscreants to defuse disputes does not work for Lovecleon himself later in the play.

67 See *Acharnians* 739 n.

68 Evidently a tragic actor, unattested elsewhere.

69 Both Aeschylus and Sophocles wrote plays with this title; Niobe, whose children were killed by Artemis and Apollo after she had compared them favorably to their mother Leto's, was the mythological paradigm of grief.

70 The estate of a father with only a female heir was attached to her, and the right to marry her and thus acquire the estate could be determined by bequest (provided the deceased had adopted the designated groom as his son), or else determined by the deceased's closest male kin or, if a claimant's degree of kinship was contested, by the jury in a legal action.

71 See *Acharnians* 705 n.

72 That is, Cleonymus: see *Acharnians* 88 n.

73 Compare *Knights* 58–60.

74 See 42 n.

75 Unknown, and perhaps corrupted in transmission from Euphemus or Euphemides.

76 Since in classical Athens marriages were essentially property transactions arranged by the families involved, it was not abnormal for a man even as old as Lovecleon to have a young wife and daughter. But we are not invited to speculate about the precise demographics of Lovecleon's household: the vignette here is generic.

77 Greek clothing lacked pockets, so that small coins were normally carried in the mouth (cf. 788–92) when a slave was not in attendance; perhaps Lovecleon's carrying of his own money is part of his lower socio-economic characterization.

78 A paradise inhabited by the souls of individuals whom the gods deemed worthy by virtue of their excellence.

79 That is, Zeus, so invoked for the sake of the following joke.

80 He would be polluted for having committed homicide and therefore barred from sacred altars.

81 This, the largest source of revenue for imperial Athens, was a matter of public record and great public interest.

82 See *Knights* 103 n.

83 The detail of the loud voice points to Cleon.
84 Loathecleon repeatedly stresses that it was Lovecleon's "greatest generation" that repelled the Persian aggressor and won the empire.
85 Unknown.
86 Both father and son are unknown.
87 The male citizen population (excluding women, children, resident aliens, and slaves) was conventionally 30,000, a number consistent with the demographic indicators that survive.
88 This monument, erected in mid-century and commemorating the Athenian-Plataean victory over the Persian invaders in 490, had come to symbolize Athenian power and to justify her sway.
89 This island just off the northeast coast of Attica was an important source of grain during the war but a reluctant member of the Athenian empire.
90 From Euripides' *Bellerophon*; the full line (fr. 308) is, "Let me pass, thou shadowy foliage, let me cross the watery dells; I am eager to see the heaven above."
91 For slave-rape as a punishment compare *Acharnians* 271–75 (trespass and theft); here the slave-girl presumably sneaks off for a tryst.
92 For Lysistratus, see *Acharnians* 854 n.
93 Jury pay was distributed in drachmas (one drachma equaled six obols), which each pair of jurors would have to change into obols on their own.
94 A deity of roads and traveling, whose image, like that of Apollo Agyieus (875), stood before many an Athenian doorway.
95 See 389 n.
96 See *Acharnians* 88 n.
97 I.e., the slave wears no phallus, as Cleonymus had lost his weapons.
98 In Greek "Labes" (from *labein* "snatch") puns on the name of Laches; see 24 n.
99 The goddess of the hearth, to whom domestic sacrifice was offered and with whose name all sacrifices, prayers, and oaths began.
100 I.e., to scratch the long line for conviction.
101 See 804 n.
102 In Greek *Kyon* (Dog) is close in sound to *Kleon*, who had evidently styled himself "the people's watchdog" (cf. *Knights* 1017); the provision of Cleon's deme assured that no member of the audience would fail to recognize the caricature and grasp the political significance.
103 The home deme (political district) of both Aristophanes and Cleon.
104 See 145 n.
105 Sailors, who belonged mainly to the lower classes and were generally as penurious as jurors, were enthusiastic supporters of Cleon.
106 See *Acharnians* 703–12 with notes.
107 Perhaps suggesting an ability to control the gullible among the citizenry, cf. 31–33.
108 As did the male members of well-to-do families.
109 See *Acharnians* 846 n.
110 A familiar spirit whose voice seer-ventriloquists produce, cf. Plato, *Sophist* 252c, Plutarch, *The Obsolescence of Oracles* 9 (414e).
111 The contrast seems to be between an early career phase, when the young poet shared his ideas with established playwrights for their use, and his own career, which began with *Banqueters* in 427; see similarly *Knights* 541–45.
112 It sounds as if Aristophanes had a particular rival in mind, who had boasted that his success made him attractive to young men; that he actually cruised for pickups is probably an exaggeration. The scholia to Aristophanes' *Peace* 762–63 identify the rival as Eupolis, and he is indeed the likeliest candidate.
113 Compare *Knights* 817.
114 Most likely referring to *Knights*, the first of his plays that he produced himself and the first devoted to attacking populist politics generally and Cleon in particular.

115 The following description takes off on Hesiod's iconic description of the monster Typhoeus, whom the young Zeus defeated in combat (*Theogony* 824–30, 853–68); in Euripides' *Heracles* it was the hero who defeated the monster.
116 Cynna (the name puns on *kunos* "dog") was a notorious prostitute.
117 A shape-shifting ogress, evidently hermaphroditic, who fed on children; she was a character in plays by the comic poet Crates and the tragic poet Euripides.
118 That is, to keep quiet about the criminality of Cleon and his associates.
119 Referring to a play produced at the Lenaea of 423: probably *Merchant Ships*, possibly *Farmers*: for these lost plays see Appendix.
120 One of the nine archons, the polemarch dealt with disputes between Athenian citizens and non-Athenians. Ignorance of the play in question leaves the following details mysterious.
121 Referring to the defeat of *Clouds* at the Dionysia of 423, which Aristophanes repeatedly blamed on the spectators' lack of sophistication and failure to appreciate originality.
122 Indicating their virility, possibly their stage-phalli, if individual chorus-members wore them; not their stingers, which, as the following song shows, are still effective.
123 A quotation from Euripides' *Stheneboea* (fr. 663), of Eros inspiring poets.
124 The following reminiscences amalgamate details of the Persian invasions of 490 (especially the battle of Marathon) and 480–79 (especially the burning of Athens and the battles of Salamis and Thermopylae), minus the contributions of other Greek states, notably Sparta, for the sake of the image of wasps' defending their nest from smoke and flame.
125 So also Herodotus 7.226, of the battle of Thermopylae.
126 The owl was Athena's bird and so a good omen, especially for Athenians; Plutarch, *Themistocles* 12.1 assigns this omen to the battle of Salamis.
127 That is, the Greek cities that had been tribute-paying subjects of the Great King; now those cities pay tribute to Athens; for a similar attitude of entitlement toward the imperial tribute, see *Acharnians* 643–45.
128 Thinking of the fines paid by convicted defendants as public revenue that funds their jury-pay.
129 See 684 ff.
130 "North wind" is a surprise for "the great king" (of Persia); Lovecleon has been wearing his cloak for over 50 years.
131 A coastal deme not far north of Piraeus; the point of the joke is unclear.
132 Former capital of Lydia, to which well-connected Athenians might be sent on luxurious embassies or trade missions; cf. *Acharnians* 61–90, 599–617.
133 Morychus was a noted gourmand.
134 See *Acharnians* 64 n.
135 Red boots with straps, worn only by men.
136 The source of the quotation or parodied line is unknown.
137 See 1035 n.
138 Unknown.
139 A common name at this period, and the incident to which the anecdote refers is unknown, but clearly Loathecleon is apologizing for his harsh expression.
140 A demagogic politician who in 415 would be prominent in the prosecution of Alcibiades for impiety and in 411 assassinated by oligarchs.
141 See *Acharnians* 118 n.
142 Paros was a prosperous, tribute-paying ally of Athens, two obols a pittance; the point of the joke is unclear.
143 The Arcadian athlete Ephudion won the Olympic pancration (free-style wrestling) in 464 while in his prime; nothing is known about Ascondas.
144 The name was probably chosen because it means "Workman."
145 See *Acharnians* 213 n.

146 See 42 n.
147 See 459 n.
148 See *Knights* 1256 n.
149 A tragic dramatist ridiculed in comedy as a foreigner and parasite with the slavish nicknames "Mysian" and "Sacas" (implying Asian ancestry); the implication is that Cleon is also a foreigner, as in *Knights*.
150 Diacris was a district in the foothills of Mt. Parnes in northern Attica; the point of the allusion is obscure.
151 See *Acharnians* 980 n.
152 Adapted from Alcaeus' poem warning of the rise of the sixth-century tyrant, Pittacus (fr. 141).
153 The first line of a poem by Praxilla of Sicyon (fr. 3); Admetus' story was dramatized by Euripides in *Alcestis*.
154 Source unknown.
155 See 459 n.
156 *Clitagora* was a popular drinking song, but nothing certain is known about it or its author.
157 An attested name, but probably chosen here because it means "fond of possessions."
158 "Goldy": a slave-name.
159 See 566 n.
160 The destruction of this luxurious south-Italian city by the neighboring Crotonians ca. 510 inspired many tales about the ineptitude of its pampered inhabitants.
161 See 74 n. Hair-buns were popular among affluent men of the prior generation.
162 Father of the orator Andocides and a member of an ancient and wealthy family from Aristophanes' and Cleon's deme.
163 The best candidates are the famous sophist and later oligarch, known for high living (cf. Xenophon, *Memorabilia* 1.6), or (more likely) Antiphon son of Lysonides, a wealthy man ridiculed also in Cratinus' *Wine-Flask* of 423 (fr. 212).
164 An allied city in Thessaly, recently of great strategic importance to the war-effort.
165 The *Penestai,* a subject local population.
166 Unknown, but obviously head of a theatrical family, like Carcinus (1501–13).
167 Arignotus, cf. *Knights* 1278.
168 His name is unknown.
169 Brother of Arignotus; his vice is also mocked in *Knights* (1284–89).
170 A structurally necessary choral song, the *antistrophe* responding to 1265–74 and no doubt containing more personal mockery, had already gone missing from the text in antiquity.
171 Perhaps rival comic poets responding to Aristophanes' claims of courage in standing up to Cleon.
172 The date, circumstances, and terms of such a settlement can only be guessed, but it must have occurred at some point after *Knights* and included a promise by Aristophanes to mitigate his attacks; the "monkey-business" was a trick that allowed Aristophanes in *Wasps* ("today") to ignore the agreement. Demont 1997: 477 suggests that Aristophanes let it be known that the lead character would be named "Love-cleon"! This is the last mention of Cleon in the play.
173 Unknown; the name suggests "equestrian" wealth.
174 See 1270 n.
175 A socially prominent man frequently satirized in comedy for high living, as were his wife and son, the handsome athlete Autolycus, who is portrayed in Xenophon's *Symposium*.
176 See *Acharnians* 854 n.
177 Unknown; the name was common.
178 Among several candidates are (1) the comic poet (cf. *Clouds* 566); (2) the oligarch of 411 (cf. *Frogs* 689, Thucydides 8.25.1); (3) the man implicated in the mutilation

of the herms in 415, called "the ex-dancer" by Andocides (1.47); and, if this is not the same man, (4) a tragic actor or dancer mentioned in the scholia here, at *Clouds* 1091, and (as "son of Chorocles") *Birds* 750. (3) and/or (4) may be the tragic dancer mentioned in 1490, if this is not a reminiscence of the dead tragic poet (see 220 n.).

179 A tragic dramatist whose writing Aristotle considered uninspired, *Poetics* 1458a18–21. The implication here is that for this poet the props were more important than the poetry; compare *Acharnians* 464 (of Euripides).

180 That is, into the Eleusinian Mysteries, which featured ritual mockery of initiates.

181 The name means "Dardanian" from Dardania, a city in the Troad; Loathecleon recognizes her from the banquet, and it is not impossible that she was an actual piper (the name is not attested elsewhere in Athens).

182 See 1190 n.

183 Demeter and Kore: a women's oath.

184 Myrtia stresses her citizen status; whether she and/or the parents named were actual Athenians (the father's name, Ancylion, is rare), and recognizable to the spectators, is unknown.

185 See 566 n.

186 A long-time friend of Socrates, and nicknamed "The Bat" for his spectral appearance, which may explain his availability as a witness at this time of night.

187 Lasus of Hermione was invited to Athens by the tyrant Hipparchus between 527 and 514, where he may have helped to establish the contests in dithyramb, his poetic specialty. Collections of his witty sayings were still read in Roman times (cf. Athenaeus 8.338).

188 Simonides of Ceus, one of the greatest Greek lyric poets, was, like Lasus, invited to Athens by Hipparchus; he boasted 56 first prizes in dithyramb (*Epigrams* 27 Campbell), and his wise sayings were collected.

189 Substituting the tragedian for one of his characters, probably Ino's husband Athamas, whose second wife Ino had tricked into killing her own children instead of Ino's. The point of Lovecleon's allusion is elusive.

190 See 1259 n.

191 See *Acharnians* 1032 n.

192 Alluding to a well-known Aesopic fable (3 Perry, Schol. *Peace* 130) whose moral was that a determined victim, no matter how powerless, can have his revenge; for the legend of Aesop's death at Delphi, see the *Life of Aesop* 124–42 Perry.

193 The earliest known tragic poet, for whom a victory is attested in 534.

194 Zeus' father Cronus, deposed and retired, epitomized the passé.

195 A plant used to make a purgative thought to relieve some mental disorders.

196 See 220 n.

197 That is, with stones by passersby, a common way to treat madmen.

198 Carcinus was a tragic poet, an older contemporary of Aristophanes; the name means "crab." It is unclear whether his actual sons (Xenotimus, Xenarchus and Xenocles) performed in this scene, but in the following year Aristophanes' chorus does warn the spectators never to dance with Carcinus' sons (*Peace* 781–86), perhaps an allusion to trouble with their performance in *Wasps*.

199 Xenarchus.

200 The eldest son, Xenotimus.

201 The youngest son, Xenocles, who would defeat Euripides' *Trojan Women* in 415 and also had a political career (cf. *Women at the Thesmophoria* 440–42).

202 Carcinus had shared command of an Athenian fleet in 431.

Appendix: Selected Fragments of Lost Plays

Here is a selection of fragments from lost comedies composed by Aristophanes and his rivals that attacked populist politicians as such and in a thematic way (as distinct from incidental mockery, which is widespread); the fragments are selected for their political interest and presented in chronological order by date or probable date.

Aside from a few scraps of ancient texts on papyrus, most of the fragments of Aristophanes and other comic poets come from ancient works whose authors quote from comedies now lost to us. Occasionally these authors tell us something about the author, the plot, or the characters of the play they are citing (such bits of information are called testimonia), but for the most part we must infer the original context from the fragment itself or from other fragments cited from the same play; when inferences can be drawn at all, they are usually tentative to some degree, since fifth-century comic poets, like most humorists, prized originality and surprise. Nevertheless, it is worthwhile to be aware, as much as possible, of the dramatic range of fifth-century comedy beyond Aristophanes' eleven extant plays, and to that extent the fragments assist us in forming a more comprehensive picture.

The numbering of the fragments and testimonia (T) follows *PCG*, the current standard edition. Freshly edited editions of all comic fragments, with translation and full commentary, is underway in the series *FrC*. When something is known or can be inferred about a play's date, plot, or characters, a brief synopsis is provided; in the dates, D specifies the City Dionysia festival in the spring, L the Lenaea festival in the winter.

CRATINUS, *Chirons* (436–432)

The chorus identifies themselves with Chiron the wise centaur, tutor of heroes like Achilles and the substitute for Prometheus chained. The play seems to have contrasted a golden age, perhaps exemplified by the sixth-century poet, lawgiver, and sage Solon, who appeared as a character, with a contemporary Athens whose decadence began with Pericles and his mistress Aspasia, assimilated to Zeus and Hera as tyrannical rulers.[1] Fragments 258 and 259 recall the genealogy of the gods in Hesiod's *Theogony*.

258

Political Deadlock (*stasis*) and venerable Time joined in love and bore the greatest of all tyrants; him the immortals called their Head Man.[2]

259

and the goddess of the well-reamed ass bore a Hera to gladden his heart,[3] a bitch-faced concubine

HERMIPPUS

T   Plutarch, *Life of Pericles* 32.1 About this time [at the trial of Phidias] Aspasia faced the charge of impiety, the prosecutor being Hermippus the comic poet, who added the charge that she made her house available to freeborn women for trysts with Pericles.

CRATINUS, *Nemesis* (431)

In the epic tradition, Zeus raped the maiden goddess Nemesis ("Retribution") after both had taken the form of geese, and Helen was born from their egg; her beauty ended up triggering the disastrous Trojan War. Cratinus apparently adapted a local variant of this myth (Nemesis had a major shrine in the Attic deme Rhamnous, grandly renovated at about this time) in which Zeus, with the help of Aphrodite and Hermes, took the form of a swan in order to seduce Nemesis; the resulting egg was taken to Sparta where it was incubated by the princess Leda, who adopted Helen as her child. F 118, where "head god" is a pun alluding to Pericles' misshapen head, suggests that he was assimilated to Zeus; if Aspasia figured in the allegory it was perhaps as Aphrodite. Sexual escapades involving Pericles and Aspasia figure centrally in Dicaeopolis' account of the causes of the Peloponnesian War (*Acharnians.* 515–39). See further Henderson 2012.

114

and so you'll have to become a big bird

118

come, o Zeus, patron of foreigners and head god

123

with his neck in the stocks

CRATINUS, *Dionysalexander* (430)

Much of a *hypothesis* (or summary) of the play survives on papyrus (T) and tells us that Cratinus' play burlesqued the myth of the Judgment of Paris, in which the handsome Trojan shepherd-prince Paris (in the epic tradition also called Alexander) presided over a beauty contest between three important goddesses: when as a bribe Athena offered him martial success, Hera power, and Aphrodite sex, Paris chose Aphrodite, who awarded him Helen in fulfillment of her promise. Cratinus' play, in which the boastful but cowardly god Dionysus disguises himself as Paris, evidently implied parallels with Pericles' leadership at the outset of the war: as in *Nemesis* (above) Helen suggests Pericles' concubine, Aspasia; the Greeks lay waste the territory around Troy, as the Spartans did around Athens (Thucydides 2.18–23); Dionysus hides, as Pericles held no Assembly (2.22.1) and sticks to a defensive strategy; Pericles is called "king of satyrs" in Hermippus' *Moirai* (below), which probably alludes to Cratinus' play, since satyrs only rarely constituted a comic chorus.

T   . . . judgment. Hermes departs and these [the chorus] speak a bit to the spectators about the poets,[4] and when Dionysus appears they ridicule and abuse him. After he is presented with absolute tyranny from Hera, bravery in battle from Athena, and irresistible attractiveness from Aphrodite, he judges her the winner. After this he sails to Sparta, takes Helen away, and returns to Ida. Soon he hears that the Greeks are torching the countryside and looking for Alexander. So as fast as he can he hides Helen in a basket, changes himself into a ram, and awaits what comes next. Alexander arrives, finds each of them in a search, and orders that they be taken to the ships and handed over to the Greeks. When Helen balks, he feels sorry for her and keeps her as his fiancée, but he sends Dionysus off to be handed over. The satyrs follow him, expressing encouragement and promising not to betray him. In the play Pericles is comedized quite skillfully through innuendo for bringing the war upon the Athenians

Moirai ("Fates" or "Allotments") (430)

F 47 may allude to the assimilation of Pericles to Dionysus in Cratinus' *Dionysalexander*, which had a chorus of satyrs, unusually for comedy.

T   Plutarch, *Life of Pericles* 33.6–8 [Pericles] locked up the city, garrisoned all parts of it for safety, and followed his own strategems, paying scant attention to the loudmouths and malcontents. And yet many of his friends beset him with requests, and many of his enemies with threats and accusations, and choruses sang ditties and lampoons, insulting his generalship as cowardly and abandoning everything to the enemy. Cleon, too, was already on his case, exploiting the citizens' anger against him to make his own way toward the leadership of the people (*demagogia*), as these anapestic verses of Hermippus show:

47

King of satyrs, why won't you wield a spear, but come out with impressive speeches about the war, while there lurks within you the spirit of Teles? And if a dagger gets sharpened on a hard whetstone, your teeth chatter, bitten by blazing Cleon

CRATINUS, *Ploutoi* ("Wealth Gods") (429)

The play seems to have taken off on an Aeschylean version of the liberation of Prometheus and the Titans from Zeus' tyrannical oppression, with the Titans (who formed the chorus) out to punish those who had unjustly enriched themselves and perhaps to restore a golden age. If Pericles allegorically parallels Zeus on the human level, then the allusion is to his trial and punishment in 430/29 (Thucydides 2.65.3–4).

171, lines 22–23

(Chorus) now that tyrannical rule <is over> and the people hold the power

ARISTOPHANES, *Babylonians* (426, probably D)

Aristophanes' second play, and his first with a mainly political theme, prompted Cleon to prosecute him; Aristophanes escaped conviction and responded in his own defense in the following year's play, *Acharnians*; both plays were produced by Callistratus. Only a few details about the plot of *Babylonians* are recoverable.[5] The chorus consisted of tattooed Babylonian mill-slaves brought to Athens by Dionysus, who was put on trial but had an opportunity for acquittal by bribing demagogues. Apparently the Babylonians somehow represented Athenian allies, who were characterized as being both oppressed by Athenian imperial maladministration and deceitful in their diplomatic representations to Athens (see *Acharnians* 633–42).

T 1   Scholia on *Acharnians* 378 ("on account of last year's comedy") He means *Babylonians*. For Ar. produced this play before *Acharnians* and abused many people in it. He ridiculed the allotted and elected offices and Cleon in the presence of foreigners, for he entered the play *Babylonians* in the festival of the Dionysia, which is held in the spring and where the allies delivered their tribute. Angry because of this, Cleon brought against him a lawsuit for wronging the citizens, accusing him of writing these things to insult the people and the council, and he charged him with being an alien and took him to trial.

T 2   *Life of Aristophanes* 19 Aristophanes hated Cleon because he had charged him with being an alien and with having in his play *Babylonians* slandered the allotted offices of the Athenians in the presence of foreigners.

68

(A) Two hundred drachmas are needed. (B) So where will they come from? (B) Give this cup

71a

Hesychius σ 150 "the Samian demos": someone says this in Aristophanes upon seeing those from the mill . . . and being shocked and critical at the sight of them. There is also another account, according to which he called the demos many-lettered because, among the Greeks, the Samians were the first to become many-lettered in having used and introduced to the other Greeks the 24-letter system.

71b

Suda σ 77 "The Samian demos how many-lettered": Aristophanes in *Babylonians*, mocking those tattooed. For the Samians, having been oppressed by the tyrants, for want of free citizens granted civic equality to the slaves at the price of five staters, as Aristotle says in *The Samian Constitution* (fr. 575 Rose[3)]. Or because among the Samians the 24 letters were first invented by Callistratus, as Andron says in *Tripod* (fr. 7 *FHG* 2.348) . . . Lysimachus in Book 2 of *Returns* (*FGrH* 382 F 7) says that the Athenians tattooed Samian war-prisoners with an owl and the Samians <tattooed Athenians> with the *samaina*, which is a ship with two banks of oars first built under the Samian tyrant Polycrates, but this is an invention of Douris (*FGrH* 76 F 66).

71c

Plutarch, *Life of Pericles* 26.4 (*on the Samian War, 441–39*): The Samians in requital of an affront tattooed the Athenian prisoners of war on the forehead with an owl, because the Athenians had tattooed them with a *samaina* . . . so called because it first appeared in Samos when Polycrates the tyrant built it. They say it is to these tattoos that Aristophaners alludes in the line, "it's the Samian demos: how many-lettered!"

72

stand in rows all of you, to form three ranks of shields

73

O Zeus, how comely a sight this band of youths

74

a man among us is an agitator

75

Athenaeus 2.494d And in Ar.'s *Babylonians* we hear of the shallow saucer, when Dionysus says of the demagogues at Athens that they asked him for "two shallow saucers" as he made his way to the trial, for we must imagine that they asked him for nothing other than drinking-bowls.

81

I suppose by ranks they [i.e. the chorus] will be screeching something in barbaric fashion

84

Scholia on *Birds* 1556 (of Pisander, on whom see Platon, *Peisander*, below) And Aristophanes in *Babylonians* said he took bribes, as follows: "or else, demanding gifts, with Pisander they (*var.* he) would supply a military office"[6]

89

Zenobius, *Athous* 1.49 (2.22) "Just like Hermion": the proverb is used of those saving their slaves, since at Hermion in the Peloponnese there was a shrine of Kore and Demeter offering asylum to refugees; Aristophanes mentions it in *Babylonians*.

90

Aristophanes in *Babylonians* calls the foreheads of slaves Istrian because they are tattooed, for those living by the Istros tattoo themselves and wear pied clothing.

EUPOLIS, *Golden Race* (before 422)

The title refers to Hesiod's Golden Race (*Works and Days* 109–26), who lived under Cronus "like gods, with carefree hearts" and after an easy death became underworld deities who guard and enrich humanity. Such a race was probably contrasted, or ironically associated, with Cleon's Athens. F 316a, from the parabasis, addresses the spectators; F 316b is not certainly from our play.

300

then the barber will hold his shears under the beard and trim off the property tax[7]

316a

O fairest city of all, however many Cleon oversees![8] How blessed you were in the past, and now you will be more so[9]

316b

First, there should have been equal freedom of speech for everyone. How would anyone not be pleased to associate with a city like that, where it's possible for someone very slight and of bad appearance

ARISTOPHANES, *Farmers* (D 424 – D 422)

Like *Acharnians* and *Merchant Ships*, *Farmers* evidently portrayed the hardships and inconveniences suffered by countrymen forced to live in the city during wartime and looked forward to their return to the countryside. F 102 mocks the general Nicias for surrendering his command at Pylos to Cleon, and F 103 cites a mock-oracle associated with Cleon also in *Knights* (963).

102

(A) I want to be a farmer!
(B) And who's stopping you?
(A) All of you! So I'm contributing a thousand drachmas if you release me from my duties.
(B) We'll take them: with Nicias' contribution, that makes two thousand

103

(A) . . . what you think the state especially needs.
(B) If you ask me, to be a leather bottle: haven't you heard?

ARISTOPHANES, *Merchant Ships* (423–421)

The chorus (which would be female, cf. *Knights* 1300–15 and F 425) impersonated the merchant ships that brought goods to Athens from all over the world. In F 415 an Athenian and a Spartan acknowledge mutual suffering and perhaps have concluded a truce, and there was an attack on malicious prosecutors like Euathlus (F 424, spoken by the chorus-leader). This was likely the "last year's play" to which the chorus of *Wasps* refers in boasting of the poet's courage in attacking such prosecutors (T 2); if so, the play was produced at the Lenaea of 423, since *Clouds* was produced at the Dionysia.

T 1   Hypothesis A3 to Aristophanes' *Peace* This is not the only play that Aristophanes produced in favor of peace, but also *Acharnians* and *Knights* and *Merchant Ships*, and everywhere he pleads this case, ridiculing Cleon, who opposed peace, and constantly attacking Lamachus the war lover.

T2   Aristophanes' *Wasps* 1037–42
And he [the poet] says that after him
he came to grips last year with the shivers and the fevers
that by night throttled fathers and strangled grandfathers,
that climbed into the very beds of the peaceable citizens among you,
pasting together affidavits, summonses, and depositions,
so that many people jumped up in terror and ran to the polemarch.

415

good heavens, Spartan, how greasy and cumbrous
our mutual troubles turn out to have been!

420

Ah, Sparta, what then shalt thou suffer today?

422

the beardless boys, <Cleisthenes and> Strato[10]

424

our generation has an accuser, a certain base archer,
much as you young men have your Euathlus[11]

425

devouring, carving, lapping up
my sea-nettle below[12]

PLATON, *Peisander* (probably L 421)

Peisander was a prominent populist politician at least since 426, when in *Baby-lonians* Aristophanes attributed his support of the war to corrupt motives (F 84, above); in the summer of 411, however, he abruptly switched his allegiance to the oligarchs, upon whose downfall he defected to the Spartan side and was condemned to death *in absentia*. In comedy he was frequently mocked for obesity, gluttony, physical awkwardness, and (especially) cowardice, for which he became proverbial. Platon's *Peisander* (not produced under his own name) was evidently the first to portray its demagogue not allegorically, as a barbarian slave, but in his own person. If *Peisander* is in fact datable to the Lenaea of 421, then it was one of two demagogue-comedies (along with Eupolis' *Maricas*) produced at that festival; the choice of the demagogue theme was perhaps encouraged both by the death of Cleon, the foremost proponent of prosecuting the war, in the Athenian defeat at Amphipolis the previous summer, and by the Peace of Nicias then in prospect. Unfortunately, the fragments of *Peisander* are uninformative politically.

Eupolis, *Maricas* (L 421)

Like *Knights* – indeed too much so, according to Aristophanes: T – Eupolis' *Maricas* portrayed a populist leader, this time Hyperbolus, as a wicked slave with a fictitious name suggesting barbarian origins, this time Persian; upbringing and education in the marketplace; a master who may again have been Demos; a decisive contest including a meeting of the Assembly; and business with seal-rings. Eupolis seems to acknowledge his debt to *Knights* but also stresses his originality: novel are semichoruses of rich and poor; an elite antagonist to Maricas; and an old woman from the same milieu as Aristophanes' Sausage Seller to represent Hyperbolus' mother, an itinerant bread-seller who dances the indecent *kordax*.

T1 Aristophanes, *Clouds* 549-56: I'm the one who hit Cleon in the belly when he was at the height of his power, but I wasn't so brazen as to jump on him again when he was down. Not so these others: from the moment Hyperbolus lowered his guard, they have been stomping the wretch without letup, and his mother too. First of all Eupolis dragged his *Maricas* before you, hacking over our *Knights*, hack that he is, and tacking onto it a drunken crone for the sake of the *kordax*, the same crone that Phrynichus long ago put onstage, the one the sea monster wanted to eat.

193
(MARICAS) So then, how long since you associated with Nicias?
(B) Never saw him, except just now standing in the agora.
(MARICAS) The man admits that he has seen Nicias! And why would he have seen him, unless he was engaged in treason?
(CHORUS OF POOR MEN) Did you hear that, age-mates, Nicias caught in the act?
(CHORUS OF RICH MEN) Really, you numbskulls, how could you ever pin anything wicked on a fine man?

194
And I learned a lot in the barbershops, sitting there inconspicuously and pretending not to be listening

195
(A) Hear now how Psesander is done for!
(B) The cross-eyed one?
(A) No, the large one, the donkey-driver[13]

201
You will hear: for we two, gentlemen, are neither horsemen[14]

203
be that as it may, my own advice is that you (*sg.*) not punish Maricas

204

wearing the/his signet-ring and exuding body cream

207

the city-sacker Maricas has now crossed over[15]

208

Quintilian 1.10.18 Maricas, who is Hyperbolus, admits that he knows nothing of education except the alphabet

209

Scholia to Aristophanes, *Wealth* 1037 (Eupolis in *Maricas*) compares Hyperbolus' mother to a *telia* . . . on which bakers place loaves to dry . . . but if we also turn to the passage in *Maricas* where he says that Hyperbolus' bones (or "dice") have been cast onto a *telia* it will be even more puzzling.

211

Scholia to Aristophanes, *Clouds* 549b there (in *Maricas*) Eupolis mentions Cleon as dead

213

I didn't think there was a Slave City

214

we're turned out like Thessalians[16]

HERMIPPUS, *Breadwomen* (420 or perhaps 419)

Aristophanes (T with scholia) informs us that this play contained an attack on Hyperbolus; no doubt Hermippus included a caricature of Hyperbolus' mother, an element that had recently been introduced to demagogue-comedy by Eupolis in *Maricas*.

T   Aristophanes, *Clouds* 557–58: Then Hermippus again attacked Hyperbolus in a play (*Breadsellers*), and now all the others are launching into Hyperbolus, copying my own similes about the eels.

1

you decrepit common whore and horny sow

7

the large man, Peisander himself, came forward silently, like the one on the poles at the Dionysia[17] . . . olive-tree . . . leaning on a pack-ass

PLATON, *Hyperbolus* (probably 419)

182

(A) Congratulations, master!
(B) For what?

(C) You were selected for a seat on the Council – all but. See, you weren't selected but virtually were, if you think about it.

(A) What do you mean, think about it?

(B) Well, you're an alternate to a vile, foreign, and unfree gentleman.

(A) Get out of here! Let me explain the situation to you [spectators]: gentlemen, I'm an alternate on the Council to – Hyperbolus!

183

Dear Fates, he simply couldn't speak Attic. Whenever he ought to say "I used to live" he would say "I yousta live," and whenever he should have said "a little" he would say "a liddle."

184

and he's so enjoyed the lush life that <now> he's quite destitute

185

Scholia to Lucian, *Timon* 30 Polyzelus in his *Demo-Tyndareus*, calls him (Hyperbolus) a Phrygian, joking about his foreign nature, and Platon the comic poet says in *Hyperbolus* that he is a Lydian of the race of Midas.

EUPOLIS, *Demes* (between 417 and 412)

We know from ancient testimonia that in this play four great Athenian leaders of the past – Solon (ca. 630 – ca. 560), Miltiades (ca. 555–489), Aristides (530–468), and Pericles (ca. 495–429) – are brought back from the Underworld to Athens by a comic hero named Pyronides ("Fiery" or "Purifier"), presumably in order to rescue the Athenians from (one or a combination of) political, legal, military, and social ills, which were present in abundance in 412, the production-date that best suits our evidence: in 413 the great armada against Sicily had been destroyed, key allies had begun to defect, emergency measures had to be taken to stabilize the economy and rebuild the navy, the Spartans had re-occupied the countryside, and political unrest was brewing that would lead to the oligarchic coup of 411. Pyronides' plan was a success: those responsible for the problems were discredited and the statesmen apparently stayed on as tutelary guardians. The chorus represented the demes (the political units of Attica, 139 in total): these included both urban and rural districts but the term could be used in the sense "country villages," and that seems to have been the chorus' identity in this play; like the titular Acharnians in 425, they were cooped up once again in the city, their farms in enemy hands. The demagogue denounced in F 99 could be Hyperbolus if the play is dated to 417, just before his ostracism, but more likely he was Cleophon or Archedemus.

99

(from an address by the Chorus to the spectators)

(lines 23–34) . . . and he's fine with leading the people, even though just the other day he was without citizen kin in our community, nor would he speak Attic Greek were he not embarrassed before his friends . . . of the male whores who shun politics and not of upper-crust men, he should have

ducked his head and gone into the bonking-house, but . . . his friends . . . of
their political club . . . and messing with elections for generalships and . . .
the comic poets. Remember Mantineia, when the god was thundering and
the generals wouldn't let you attack, and he said he would clap them in the
stocks by force?[18] Anyone who votes for such men as leaders, may his flocks
be barren and his crops bear no fruit!
(lines 85–90) (A) What did you do, you scoundrel and dice-shooter? (B)
I ordered the foreigner to give me 100 gold staters: he was rich . . . and he
told me to say that after drinking . . . and then I took the gold . . . let him do
whatever he wants

110

(Pericles) And is my bastard son still alive?

(Pyronides) Yes, and he would long ago have been a real man, if trouble about
your whore didn't make him skittish[19]

PLATON, *Cleophon* (L 405, third prize)

Cleophon, associated with lyre-making and Athens' leading populist during the
last years of the war, was executed by the Thirty in early 404; he was among the
fiercest advocates of fighting to the bitter end, though the story (Aristotle, *Ath.*
34.1) that after the battle of Arginusae he entered the Assembly drunk and wearing
a breastplate probably derives from comedy. He was also harshly attacked in Aristophanes' *Frogs*, which was produced at this festival and won the first prize. As
in the caricatures of Hyperbolus, Platon included Cleophon's mother, evidently
portrayed as a Thracian and a fish-seller.

57

as for you, old lady, he has settled you there, putrid as you are, as food for sea
perch, sharks, and bream

58

so that we may be rid of a most rapacious fellow

59

but on the contrary, you (m. sg.) will take off with other people's property

60

being beardless he would wank himself

61

(scholia to Aristophanes, *Frogs* 618) "Thracian swallow": so that he might
disparage him as a foreigner. He is ridiculed as being the son of a Thracian
woman. This is the man named Cleophon, the lyre-maker. Platon in his play
Cleophon depicts his mother addressing him in a barbarian language. She
was said to be Thracian.

62

(Athenaeus 3.76f) There is a flower called peony, shaped very much like a fig, which women avoid eating because it gives them gas, as Platon the comic poet says in *Cleophon*.

ARCHIPPUS, *Rhinon* (ca. 402)

Rhinon was among the group of Ten who guided the democratic restoration after the fall of the Thirty Tyrants in 403 (Aristotle, *Ath.* 38.3), and he was elected general in 403/2. The play's three brief fragments do not reveal anything about the plot, or whether Rhinon was the play's hero or its target.

THEOPOMPUS, *Teisamenus* (ca. 402)

The play may have featured the democratic politician Teisamenus, who proposed a decree to reinstate Solon's laws after the fall of the Thirty and for the orator Lysias exemplified a general decline in the quality of political leaders. But the name was not uncommon in Athens (indeed it is reportedly the name of Theopompus' father) and nothing is known of the plot.

Unassigned Fragments

Eupolis

331

For you were the first, Cleon, to bid us salutations while doing the city great harm

Unknown Author

297

leather-hat (meaning Cleon)

461

Cleon is a Prometheus – after the fact

701

wielding an awesome thunderbolt on his tongue (of Pericles)

702

(Plutarch, *Life of Pericles* 13.14) When the comic poets got hold of the story, they showered him with indecency, impugning the wife of Menippus, his friend and deputy commander, and the exotic bird-breeding of Pyrilampes, who was an associate of Pericles and accused of using peacocks as bait for women whom Pericles was seducing.

703

(*ibid.*, 16.1) While Thucydides describes Pericles' power in straightforward fashion, the comic poets treat it with malicious insinuation, dubbing his associates "new Pisistratids"[20] and bidding him swear not to aim for tyranny, on the grounds that his supremacy was out of sync with democracy and quite oppressive.

704

(*ibid.*, 24.9) In comedies (Aspasia) is presented as a new Omphale, as Deianeira, and also as Hera.[21]

Notes

1 On Cratinus' treatment of Pericles see Bakola 180–229.
2 A reference to Pericles' oddly shaped head.
3 The adjective is *aspasian*, but this may be an intrusive gloss explaining the allegory.
4 Text uncertain: possibly "about the creation of sons" or "about adopted sons," perhaps alluding to Pericles' illegitimate son with Aspasia.
5 In *FrC* 10.3: 558–80 Orth summarizes 54 past scholarly reconstructions.
6 Or "a *casus belli*"
7 Levied on Athens' subject allies in 428/7, apparently on Cleon's initiative (Thucydides 3.19.1); compare the similar threat in *Knights* 923–26.
8 Compare *Knights* 75.
9 Compare *Knights* 973–76.
10 See *Acharnians* 118–22.
11 See *Acharnians* 705 n.
12 Aimed at Ariphrades? (see *Knights* 1281 n.).
13 In *Breadwomen* F 7, below, Hermippus also associates Peisander with donkeys: perhaps he owned a cartage business and the joke was (as on "Cleon the tanner") that he drove them himself.
14 Probably from the prologue, with two speakers explaining the situation (plot) to the spectators, as in *Knights*; but here the point may be to differentiate *Maricas* from *Knights*.
15 Recalling Aeschylus, *Persians* 65–66, where the chorus of Persian elders express anxiety about what the gods may have in store for King Xerxes' expedition against Greece.
16 That is, wearing the short cloak worn by soldiers and horsemen generally but associated especially with Thessalians.
17 Probably the statue of Dionysus or the processional phallus.
18 Where the Athenians had lost a major battle in 418: here the Chorus-Leader recalls that bad weather sent by Zeus was an omen that should have been heeded.
19 A disparaging reference to his mother, Aspasia.
20 Pisistratus and his sons were tyrants in Athens during the sixth century.
21 Females of myth with unusual power over their men: Omphale, the barbarian queen (of Lydia), purchased and enslaved (but later married) Heracles, who was forced to exchange clothing with her; Deianeira (the name means "man-destroyer") was Heracles' final wife, who killed him with a poisoned robe; and Hera was Zeus' domineering wife.

Bibliography

Abbreviations

CJ *Classical Journal*

CQ *Classical Quarterly*

FOC *Fragments of Old Comedy*, ed. Ian C. Storey. 3 vols. Loeb Classical Library, Harvard University Press: Cambridge, MA.

FrC *Fragmenta Comica*, dir. Bernhard Zimmermann. Verlag Antike: Heidelberg (2012–).

GRBS *Greek, Roman and Byzantine Studies*

JHS *Journal of Hellenic Studies*

PCG *Poetae Comici Graeci*, ed. Rudolph Kassel and Colin Austin. 8 vols. DeGruyter: Berlin/New York, 1983–2001.

PMG *Poetae Melici Graeci*, ed. D. L. Page. Oxford, 1962

TAPA *Transactions of the American Philological Association*

Bakola, Emmanuela. 2010. *Cratinus and the Art of Comedy*. Oxford University Press: Oxford.

Baragwanath, Emily and Foster, Edith, eds. 2017. *Clio and Thalia: Attic Comedy and Historiography*. Histos *Suppl.* 6. Newcastle upon Tyne.

Biles, Zachary P. 2011. *Aristophanes and the Poetics of Competition*. Cambridge University Press: Cambridge.

Boedeker, Deborah and Raaflaub, Kurt, eds. 1998. *Democracy, Empire, and the Arts in Fifth- Century Athens*. Harvard University Press: Cambridge, MA.

Bowie, Angus M. 1993. *Aristophanes. Myth, ritual and comedy*. Cambridge University Press: Cambridge.

Cairns, Douglas L. and Knox, Ronald A., eds. 2004. *Law, Rhetoric, and Comedy in Classical Athens. Essays in Honour of Douglas M. MacDowell*. Classical Press of Wales: Swansea.

Chaniotis, A. 2007. "Theatre Rituals," in Wilson 2007, 48–66.

Collard, Christopher and Cropp, Martin, eds. 2009. *Euripides*. Volume VIII. Loeb Classical Library, Harvard University Press: Cambridge, MA.

Compton-Engle, Gwendolyn. 2015. *Costume in the Comedies of Aristophanes*. Cambridge University Press: Cambridge.

Connor, W. Robert. 1971. *The New Politicians of Fifth-Century Athens*. Princeton University Press: Princeton.

Csapo, Eric. 2010. "The Production and Performance of Comedy in Antiquity," in Dobrov, 103–42.

Csapo, Eric and Slater, William J. 1995. *The Context of Ancient Drama*. University of Michigan Press: Ann Arbor.

Csapo, Eric and Wilson, Peter. (2020) *A Social and Economic History of the Theatre to 300 BC*. Vol. II. *Theatre Beyond Athens: Documents with Translation and Commentary*. Cambridge University Press: Cambridge.

Demont, P. 1997. "Aristophane, le citoyen tranquille et les singeries," in Thiercy and Menu, 457–79.

Dobrov, Gregory, ed. 1997. *The City as Comedy: Society and Representation in Athenian Drama*. University of North Carolina Press: Chapel Hill/London.

———, 2010. *Brill's Companion to the Study of Greek Comedy*. Brill: Leiden.

Dover, Sir Kenneth. 1972. *Aristophanic Comedy*. University of California Press: Berkeley.

———. 1974. *Greek Popular Morality in the Time of Plato and Aristotle*. University of California Press: Berkeley.

———. 1978. *Greek Homosexuality*. Harvard University Press: Cambridge, MA.

Edmunds, Lowell. 1987. *Cleon, Knights and Aristophanes' Politics*. University Press of America: Lanham.

Edwards, A. 1991. "Aristophanes' Comic Poetics," *TAPA* 121:157–79.

———. 1993. "Historicizing the Popular Grotesque: Bakhtin's Rabelais and Attic Old Comedy," in Scodel, 89–117.

Foley, Helene. 1988. "Tragedy and Politics in Aristophanes' *Acharnians*," *JHS* 108:33–47.

Foley, Helene and Rosen, Ralph, eds. 2020. *Aristophanes and Politics*. Columbia Studies in the Classical Tradition, vol. 45. Brill: Leiden.

Fontaine, Michael and Scafuro, Adele C. 2014. *The Oxford Handbook of Greek and Roman Comedy*. Oxford University Press: Oxford.

Foster, E. 2017. "Aristophanes' Cleon and Post-Peloponnesian War Athenians: Denunciations in Thucydides," *Helios* Supplement 6: 129–52.

Gagarin, Michael. 2021. *Democratic Law in Classical Athens*. University of Texas Press: Austin.

Gagné, Renaud and Hopman, Marianne Govers, eds. 2013. *Choral Mediations in Greek Tragedy*. Cambridge University Press: Cambridge.

Hartwig, A. 2015. "Self-Censorship in Ancient Greek Comedy," in *The Art of Veiled Speech: Self-Censorship from Aristophanes to Hobbes*, ed. Hans Baltussen and Peter J. Davis. University of Pennsylvania Press: Philadelphia, 18–41.

Harvey, David and Wilkins, John, eds. 2000. *The Rivals of Aristophanes: Studies in Athenian Old Comedy*. Duckworth: London.

Heath, M. 1997. "Aristophanes and the Discourse of Politics," in Dobrov, 230–49.

Henderson, Jeffrey. 1990. "The Demos and the Comic Competition," in Winkler-Zeitlin, 271–313.

———. 1991. *The Maculate Muse. Obscene Language in Attic Comedy*. Oxford University Press: Oxford.

———. 1998. "Attic Old Comedy, Frank Speech, and Democracy," in Boedeker and Raaflaub, 255–73.

———. 1998–2007. *Aristophanes. Edited and Translated* (5 vols.). Loeb Classical Library, Harvard University Press: Cambridge, MA.

———. 2003. "Demos, Demagogue, Tyrant in Attic Old Comedy," in Morgan, 155–79.

———. 2007. "Drama and Democracy," in Samons, 179–95.

———. 2012. "Pursuing Nemesis: Cratinus and Mythological Comedy," in Marshall and Kovacs, 1–12.

———. 2013a. "A Brief History of Athenian Political Comedy (c. 440-c. 300)," *TAPA* 143:249–62.

———. 2013b. "The Comic Chorus and the Demagogue," in Gagné-Hopman, 278–96.

———. 2017. "Thucydides and Attic Comedy," in *The Oxford Handbook of Thucydides*, ed. Edith Foster, Sara Forsdyke, and Ryan Balot. Oxford University Press: Oxford, 605–20.

———. 2020. "Patterns of Avoidance and Indirection in Athenian Political Satire," in Foley and Rosen, 45–59.

Holzberg, Niklas. 2008. *Aristophanes. Eine Bibliographie*. Munich (available online).

Hubbard, Thomas K. 1991. *The Mask of Comedy: Aristophanes and the Intertextual Parabasis*. Cornell University Press: Ithaca.

Hutchinson, G. O. 2011. "House Politics and City Politics in Aristophanes," *CQ* 61:48–70.

Kyriakidi, Natalia. 2007. *Aristophanes und Eupolis*. Walter de Gruyter: Berlin and New York.

Lateiner, D. 2017. "Insults and Humiliations in Fifth-Century Historiography and Comedy," in Baragwanath and Foster, 31–66.

Lech, M. 2009. "The Knights' Eleven Oars: In Praise of Phormio? Aristophanes' *Knights* 546- 7," *CJ* 105:19–26.

Lind, Hermann. 1990. *Der Gerber Kleon in den 'Rittern' des Ar. Studien zur Demagogenkomödie*. Peter Lang: Frankfurt am Main.

MacDowell, Douglas M. 1995. *Aristophanes and Athens*. Oxford University Press: Oxford.

Marshall, C. W. and Kovacs, G. A. 2012. *No Laughing Matter: New Studies of Old Comedy*, eds. C. W. and G. A. Kovacs. Bristol Classical Press: Duckworth.

Mastromarco, Giuseppe and Totaro, Piero, eds. 1983. *Commedie di Aristofane I*. UTET: Turin.

Morgan, Kathryn A., ed. 2003. *Popular Tyranny: Sovereignty and its Discontents in Ancient Greece*. University of Texas Press: Austin.

Ober, J. and Strauss, B. 1990. "Drama, Political Rhetoric, and the Discourse of Athenian Democracy," in Winkler and Zeitlin, 237–70.

Olson, S. Douglas. 1996. "Politics and Poetry in Aristophanes' *Wasps*," *TAPA* 126:129–50.

———. 2002. *Aristophanes Acharnians*. Oxford University Press: Oxford.

———. 2007. *Broken Laughter: Select Fragments of Greek Comedy*. Oxford University Press: Oxford.

———. 2010. "Comedy, Politics, and Society," in Dobrov, 35–69.

Olson, S. Douglas and Biles, Zachary P. 2015. *Aristophanes Wasps*. Oxford University Press: Oxford.

Osborne, Robin and Hornblower, Simon, eds. 1994. *Ritual, Finance, Politics. Athenian Democratic Accounts Presented to David Lewis*. Oxford University Press: Oxford.

Ostwald, Martin. 1986. *From Popular Sovereignty to the Sovereignty of Law*. University of California Press: Berkeley.

Parker, Laetitia P. E. 1997. *The Songs of Aristophanes*. Oxford University press. Oxford.

Pickard-Cambridge, Sir Arthur. 1988. *The Dramatic Festivals of Athens*, 2nd ed., revised by J. Gould and D. M. Lewis. Oxford University Press: Oxford.

Pütz, Babette. 2007². *The Symposium and Komos in Aristophanes*. Aris and Phillips: Oxford.

Reckford, Kenneth J. 1987. *Aristophanes' Old-and-New Comedy*. University of North Carolina Press: Chapel Hill.

Revermann, Martin. 2006. *Comic Business: Theatricality, Dramatic Technique, and Performance Contexts of Aristophanic Comedy*. Oxford University Press: Oxford.

————, ed. 2014. *The Cambridge Companion to Greek Comedy*. Cambridge University Press: Cambridge.

Rhodes, Peter and Marr, John L., eds. 2008. *The "Old Oligarch": The Constitution of the Athenians Attributed to Xenophon*. Aris & Phillips: Oxford.

Rhodes, P. J. 2003. "Nothing to Do with Democracy: Athenian Drama and the Polis," *JHS* 123:104–19.

Robson, James. 2009. *Aristophanes: An Introduction*. Duckworth: London.

Roisman, J. 2006. *The Rhetoric of Conspiracy in Ancient Athens*. University of California Press: Los Angeles/London.

Roselli, David K. 2011. *Theater of the People. Spectators and Society in Ancient Athens*. University of Texas Press: Austin.

Rosen, Ralph. 2007. *Making Mockery: The Poetics of Ancient Satire*. Oxford University Press: Oxford.

Rosenbloom, D. 2014. "The Politics of Comic Athens," in Fontaine and Scafuro, 297–320.

Rotstein, Andrea. 2010. *The Idea of Iambos*. Oxford University Press: Oxford.

Saldutti, Vittorio. 2014. *Cleone. Un politico Ateniese*. Edipuglia: Bari.

Samons, Loren J. 2007. *The Cambridge Companion to the Age of Pericles*. Cambridge University Press: Cambridge.

————. 2015. *Pericles and the Conquest of History*. Cambridge University Press: Cambridge.

Scholtz, A. "Friends, Lovers, Flatterers: Demophilic Courtship in Aristophanes' *Knights*," *TAPA* 134:263–93.

Scodel, Ruth, ed. 1993. *Theater and Society in the Classical World*. University of Michigan Press: Ann Arbor.

Seidensticker, Bernd. 1982. *Palintonos Harmonia. Studien zu komischen Elementen in der griechischen Tragödie*. Vandenhoeck and Ruprecht: Göttingen.

Shear, Julia L. 2011. *Polis and Revolution: Responding to Oligarchy in Classical Athens*. Cambridge University Press: Cambridge.

Silk, Michael S. 2000. *Aristophanes and the Definition of Comedy*. Oxford University Press: Oxford.

Simonton, Matthew. 2017. *Classical Greek Oligarchy. A Political History*. Princeton University Press. Princeton/Oxford.

Slater, Niall W. 2002. *Spectator Politics: Metatheatre and Performance in Aristophanes*. University of Pennsylvania Press: Philadelphia.

Sommerstein, Alan H. 1980. The Comedies of Aristophanes, vol. 1. *Acharnians*. Aris and Phillips: Warminster.

————. 1981. The Comedies of Aristophanes, vol. 2. *Knights*. Aris and Phillips: Warminster.

————. 1983. The Comedies of Aristophanes, vol. 4. *Wasps*. Aris and Phillips: Warminster.

————. 1996. "How to Avoid Being a *komodoumenos*," *CQ* 46:327–56.

————. 1998. "The Theatre Audience and the Demos," in López Férez, 43–62.

————. 2000. "Platon, Eupolis and the 'Demagogue-Comedy'," in Harvey and Wilkins, 437–51.

————. 2001. "Addenda to Previous Volumes," in The Comedies of Aristophanes, vol. 11. *Wealth*. Aris and Phillips: Warminster, 219–72.

————. 2004a. "Comedy and the Unspeakable," in Cairns and Knox, 205–22.

————. 2004b. "Harassing the Satirist: The Alleged Attempts to Prosecute Aristophanes," in *Free Speech in Classical Antiquity*, ed. Ineke Sluiter and Ralph M. Rosen. Brill: Leiden, 145–74.

————. 2009. *Talking About Laughter and Other Studies in Greek Comedy*. Oxford University Press: Oxford.

——. 2014. "The Politics of Greek Comedy," in Reverman, 291–305.

Sommerstein, Alan H., ed. 2019. *The Encyclopedia of Greek Comedy*. 3 vols. Wiley-Blackwell: Hoboken.

Sommerstein, Alan H. et al., eds. 1993. *Tragedy, Comedy and the Polis*. Levante Editori: Bari.

Spence, I. G. 1993. *The Cavalry of Classical Greece. A Social and Military History*. Oxford University press: Oxford.

Storey, Ian C. 2003. *Eupolis. Poet of Old Comedy*. Oxford University Press. Oxford.

Strauss, Barry S. 1986. *Athens after the Peloponnesian War*. Cornell University Press: Ithaca.

Taplin, O. 1986. "Fifth-Century Tragedy and Comedy: A Synkrisis," *JHS* 106:163–74.

——. 1993. *Comic Angels and Other Approaches to Greek Drama through Vase-Paintings*. Clarendon Press: Oxford.

Thiercy, Pascal and Menu, Michel. 1997. *Aristophane: la langue, la scène, la cite*. Levante Editore: Bari.

Van Steen, Gonda. 2000. *Venom in Verse: Aristophanes in Modern Greece*. Princeton University Press: Princeton.

Wallace, R. W. 1994a. "Private Lives and Public Enemies: Freedom of Thought in Classical Athens," in Boegehold and Scafuro, 127–55.

——. 1994b. "The Athenian Laws Against Slander," in Thür, 109–24.

West, Martin L. 1992. *Ancient Greek Music*. Oxford University Press: Oxford.

Whitehead, David. 1986. *The Demes of Attica 508/7-ca. 250 b.c.* Princeton University Press: Princeton.

Willi, Andreas. 2003. *The Languages of Aristophanes. Aspects of Linguistic Variation in Classical Attic Greek*. Oxford Classical Monographs: Oxford.

Wilson, Nigel G. 2007. *Aristophanis Fabulae I*. Oxford University Press. Oxford.

Wilson, Peter J. 2000. *The Athenian Institution of the Khoregia: The Chorus, the City and the Stage*. Cambridge University Press: Cambridge.

——, ed. 2007. *The Greek Theatre and Festivals*. Oxford University Press: Oxford.

Winkler, J. J. and Zeitlin, F. I., eds. 1990. *Nothing To Do With Dionysos? The Social Meanings of Athenian Drama*. Princeton University Press: Princeton.

Yu, K. W. 2017. "The Divination Contest of Calchas and Mopsus and Aristophanes' *Knights*," *GRBS* 57:910–34.

Zimmermann, Bernhard, ed. 1997. *Griechisch-römische Komödie und Tragödie II = Drama 5*. M&P: Stuttgart.

Zumbrunnen, John. 2012. *Aristophanic Comedy and the Challenge of Democratic Citizenship*. University of Rochester Press: Rochester, NY.

For Product Safety Concerns and Information please contact our EU
representative GPSR@taylorandfrancis.com
Taylor & Francis Verlag GmbH, Kaufingerstraße 24, 80331 München, Germany

www.ingramcontent.com/pod-product-compliance
Lightning Source LLC
Chambersburg PA
CBHW071541110726
47908CB00007B/1958